D0205687

Music in American Life

*A list of books in the series appears
at the end of this volume.*

CARL RUGGLES

CARL RUGGLES

Composer, Painter, and Storyteller

Marilyn J. Ziffrin

UNIVERSITY OF ILLINOIS PRESS
Urbana and Chicago

Publication of this book was supported by grants from the Sonneck Society for American Music, John S. and Patricia N. Lucas, and the Winona Foundation.

Library of Congress Cataloging-in-Publication Data

Ziffrin, Marilyn J., 1926–
    Carl Ruggles : composer, painter, and storyteller / Marilyn J. Ziffrin.
        p.   cm. — (Music in American life)
    Includes bibliographical references and index.
    ISBN 0-252-02042-1 (cloth : acid-free paper)
    1. Ruggles, Carl, 1876–1971. 2. Composers—United States—Biography. I. Title. II. Series.
ML410.R9Z5   1994
780′.92—dc20
    [B]   93-9914
                                                                                 CIP
                                                                                 MN

Dedicated to the memory of my father,
Harry B. Ziffrin,
and to Mr. Edward Barry,
Carl's friend in the nursing home

To Carl Ruggles from Winona
(11 March 1970)

Even now our town
remembers what our country
knows not even now—
the bounty of that fabric
one man's magic can make sound
—John Lucas

Contents

Acknowledgments

I have received much help and encouragement in the course of writing this book, and it is my pleasure to thank all those who aided me, including some who are no longer alive. Surely I must thank Carl himself, who, in spite of his age, charmed me with the force of his personality and saw to it that I met his friends. Thanks, too, to his son and daughter-in-law, Micah and Rosemary Ruggles, who became good friends and offered assistance at every turn.

I cannot name everyone with whom I spoke, either in person or by telephone, about Carl's life and works, but to each of them I extend my heartfelt thanks.

Some must be named, however, and in the Vermont area, these include: Margaret and John Whalen, Dorothy and Orlando Cullinan, Gene Pelham, George Hughes, Lea Ehrich, and Dr. James O'Neill; the faculty of Bennington College including Tom Brockway, Lionel Nowak, Margaret and Julian DeGray, George Finkel, Henry Brant, and Louis Calabro.

To those who knew of Carl's Winona years, I must especially thank Mrs. Anne Schaeffer, Clifford Reckow, Mr. and Mrs. Hillyer, and Earl Wood. Special thanks, too, to Jan Saecker for allowing me to read her master's thesis on those years in Carl's life.

I must also extend my gratitude to Edgard and Louise Varèse, Mimi Salzedo, Charles Seeger, Tomas Bouchard, Virgil Thomson, James Tenney, Carolee Schneemann, Eileen and Joseph Barber, Mrs. Max Atherton Wycoff, Mrs. Reginald Marsh, Merton Brown, Otto Luening, Nicolas Slonimsky, and Frank Wigglesworth. Others who must also be thanked include: Joseph Tarpley, Mrs. Frances Reed, Lawrence Tremblay, Donald Justice, and Dr. Charlton Tebeau.

The Ruggles family letters are deposited at the John Herrick Jackson Music Library of Yale University, and I am most grateful for the kindness of the staff while I worked there and for permission to quote freely from this source, which contained all of the letters quoted in this book with the exception of Henry Schnakenberg's letters to his mother (these are deposited at the National Institute of Arts and Letters). I also wish to express my deep gratitude to the librarians in the following institutions: the George Russell Memorial Library of Arlington; the public libraries of Bennington and Manchester, Vermont; the public libraries of New York; Lawrence, Massachusetts; Winona; and Miami, Florida; the Tamiment Library of New York University; the National Institute of Arts and Letters, the Winona Historical Society, the University of Miami Library, and the Southern Vermont Art Center. Finally, and by no means least, I must acknowledge my gratitude to my friend, Mary Wirth, director of the Raymond H. Danforth Library of New England College. She never failed to find the answers to my Ruggles questions, even if it took extra time and effort.

In addition, I am grateful to the following: Jeffrey D. Marshall, University Archivist and Curator of Manuscripts, University of Vermont, for permission to quote from the letters of Dorothy Canfield Fisher; Ellis J. Freedman for permission to quote from the letters of Charles and Harmony Ives; Shirley Kent Gorton, The Rockwell Kent Legacies, for permission to quote from the letters of Rockwell Kent; Michael Seeger for permission to quote from the letters of Charles Seeger; Johanne R. Coiner for permission to quote from the letters of Boardman Robinson; and Lyman Field, Trustee of the Benton Trusts, for permission to quote from the letters of Thomas Hart Benton.

Grateful thanks is due to the following periodicals for permission to reprint excerpts from these articles: "Angels—Two Views," *The Music Review* 29:3 (Aug. 1968): 184–96; "Interesting Lies and Curious Truths about Carl Ruggles," *College Music Symposium* 19:2 (Fall 1979): 7–18; "Carl Ruggles: Music Critic," *American Music Teacher* (Feb.-Mar. 1983): 42–46; "Carl Ruggles and the University of Miami," *ex tempore* 4:2 (Spring-Summer 1987): 115–35.

The American Council of Learned Societies awarded me a travel grant for my research, and I am indebted to them. I also wish to express appreciation to Mrs. Henry Cowell for permission to quote from the letters of Henry Cowell, and to offer my thanks to Susan Faulkner for permitting me to read her master's thesis on Carl's *Evocations*.

Words of thanks are inadequate to express my gratitude to John Kirkpatrick and his wife, Hope. John gave freely of his time, his Ruggles material, and his advice. He and Hope opened their home to me, and I cherish the memories of our conversations. I am also deeply grateful to the distinguished composer, Lou Harrison, who gave up an entire day to talk with me about Carl, and has continued to encourage me in this project. Both men have graciously permitted me to quote from their letters to Carl and their other writings.

One happy by-product of this book has been the opportunity to make new and close friends. Nedra McNamara, who gave invaluable help on Carl's Florida years, has continued to prod and support. Beatrice L. Breese kindly provided information and encouragement, and continues to provide a superb place in which to work. Betty Madden never failed to offer me insights into the lives of Carl and Charlotte, whom she knew from childhood, and to share with me some of the more intimate stories, which, along with her letters, she has allowed me to use.

And how shall I thank Mr. and Mrs. John Lucas? Jack and Pat first brought me to Winona. They not only gave me their home but opened the doors to many homes in that lovely place, and over the years I have counted on their friendship and support. My thanks, too, for allowing me to use the opening poem, which is quoted from *Leap Year Choice, Selected Poems,* by John Lucas (Carleton College, Northfield, Minnesota, 1976).

Constance Carrier, the distinguished poet, was my critic, teacher, reader, and good friend. Her criticisms were at once telling and gentle, and I doubt I could have finished this book without her help. It is my pleasure to publicly express my debt and my gratitude.

Prologue

I first met Carl Ruggles in late August 1964. He was living alone at the Cut Leaf Maples Motel in Arlington, Vermont. He was eighty-eight years old.

I had never heard of him or his music until a few months before, when a professor at the University of Chicago, where I was studying for an advanced degree, suggested that I look him up when I went on my vacation to New England. He said in effect, "There's an important composer out there named Carl Ruggles, but he's a character. He won't answer letters and he swears all the time and maybe he'll see you and maybe he won't." I was intrigued, and though forewarned, I wrote to Mr. Ruggles anyway asking if I could pay him a visit. There was no reply.

Undaunted but somewhat nervous, I put a tape recorder in the car, and early on a very hot summer afternoon I drove over to Arlington from New Hampshire, where I was visiting. Shortly after passing the road sign identifying the village, I came to the white clapboard Cut Leaf Maples Motel. It looked deserted except for one car that I now know belonged to the owner, Dorothy Cullinan. When I walked into the lounge, carrying my tape recorder, there was no one around. I stood uncertainly for a few minutes, and then out from the swinging door to the kitchen came a pleasant, dark-haired woman wiping her hands on her apron.

When I asked for Carl Ruggles, she motioned with her hand to the dining room off the little hall. "He's in there. Go on in. But he's pretty deaf. I don't know if he'll be able to hear you." Then she turned and went back into the kitchen. I turned to my left and walked into the large dining room filled with tables, each covered with a checkered oilcloth and unoccupied, except for one. Beside the far window sat the sole occupant with his profile to me. It was Carl.

He was wearing a navy sport jacket over a white shirt open at the collar. I could tell he was a short man even though he was seated, and his head was completely bald. In that profile view his long pointed nose stood out like a beak. Both hands were on the table, and they seemed extra large for the size of his body. He was eating and spilling crumbs over his jacket as he lifted the food to his mouth.

He had not heard me enter the room so I walked over to his table and in a very loud voice, shouting really, introduced myself and said that I had come to see him, to interview him, and maybe to write a book about him. He heard me then, and turned to look directly at me, a quizzical look in his very blue eyes. There was a moment of silence, and then he said, "All right. You sit right down there," motioning to another chair at his table, "and we'll talk—as long as you're not one of those goddamned musicologists!"

I breathed a sigh of relief and assured him that I was not. Thus began a conversation that was to last for the rest of his life, though I certainly did not know it then. When he finished lunch we moved to the lounge, and by that time I felt brave enough to ask if I could tape our interview. His answer came quickly. "Throw that goddamned thing away!" he snarled. That was the only time I tried to get his voice on tape. For all the rest of our times together, and there were many, I took copious notes, writing out direct quotations. He didn't mind that at all.

On that first visit we talked about his music, which I soon learned was his favorite subject. Before going East I had been able to see some of his scores, those published by New Music Quarterly, so we could discuss them a little. But I still had not heard a performance. That was to come later. Nor did I stay long that afternoon. I did not want to tire him, and I had the feeling that I needed to think more about what I was doing.

When I left I told him I would not see him again for a whole year since I had to return to Chicago both to teach and to study. I promised, however, to come back the next summer, and we both expected him to be there. I also told him that I was planning for a sabbatical leave from my teaching post and when that happened I would return East to spend more time with him. He said that would be just fine, and we parted.

I did return, I did spend my sabbatical with him, and I continued to see him regularly until he died. Even at his advanced age, there was an engaging vitality about him, and gradually I found myself committed to him and to telling his story. Not necessarily the one he would want me to tell, but the more honest one, as far as I could determine it. I never did get that degree, but here is Carl's story.

1

Family and Early Years in Marion
1876–90

Charles Sprague Ruggles, or Carl as he came to be known, tried very hard to invent his own family background. He insisted that his grandfather was a great sea captain, which he was not. He vowed that *all* the Ruggles men, himself included, were Harvard men. Not true. On occasion he swore that he himself had no brothers or sisters or living relatives. Also not true. He told these and other stories with such vehemence and so eloquently that when any truth was finally uncovered, friends and acquaintances often preferred to believe the fable rather than the fact.

It is true that he came from a long and distinguished family line. The earliest account of a direct ancestor is in Shaw's *Antiquities of Staffordshire,* where one Robert de Ruggele lived in 1220. The name is said to be of Anglo-Saxon origin and to be derived from two words meaning Rugged Land. In 1637, Thomas Ruggles, with his wife and eight year old son, Samuel, sailed from Nazing, Essex to Roxbury, Massachusetts, founding the branch of the family that provided the direct line to Carl. Thomas's son Samuel became a captain in the militia, a selectman of Roxbury, and a representative to the General Court. His son, also Samuel, continued in the same offices.

The Harvard tradition began with Timothy Ruggles, who graduated in 1707 and was ordained in 1710. He became minister of the First Christ Church in Rochester, Massachusetts—thus beginning a family association with the Rochester area that has continued to this day. Timothy's youngest son, Nathaniel, became a captain in the First Plymouth Regiment, and Nathaniel's son, Elisha, fought in the Revolutionary War. After the war he returned to Rochester, married Polly Clapp, and raised a family of five sons. The first, Nathaniel Sprague, was the ancestor after whom Carl's father was named. The second, Micah Haskell, was Carl's great-grandfather for whom Carl's only son was named.

Micah Haskell fought in the War of 1812 and lived in Rochester until 1826. His first wife died in 1821, after having six children. Two years later, over the angry objections of members of his family, he married Lydia Rodman of New Bedford, Massachusetts, the thirty-three-year-old daughter of Elizabeth and Samuel Rodman, who were Quakers. His new father-in-law was president of the Pocasset Manufacturing Company in Fall River, and in 1826 he brought Micah Haskell into the business. By 1837, Micah was both the agent and the treasurer of the concern. He quickly became one of the leaders of the community, and when the Fall River Savings Bank was organized in 1828, he was made president, continuing in that office until his death in 1857.

He is important to Carl's story in two very special ways. For one thing, he bought the property in East Marion, Massachusetts, where Carl was born. It was a large tract at the tip of Great Neck, known as Butler's Point. He may have purchased it as an investment, for he seems never to have lived there himself. In the 1844 tax listing for Marion, his name is listed in the nonresidence section. In addition he left a sizable estate that enabled the family to live comfortably until Nathaniel, Carl's father, took charge of it.

Micah Haskell was survived by his widow, Lydia, and three children: two sons from his first marriage, Charles Henry and Edward, and a daughter from his second. Charles Henry was Carl's grandfather, and he figured prominently in Carl's youth and continued as a major figure in his imagination and memory throughout his life. Charles Henry was born in Rochester in 1814, the oldest of six children, four of whom had died by the time he was seven years old. In that year he also lost his mother. After his father remarried he saw two more step-brothers die.

At the age of fifteen, in 1829, Charles Henry was sent to the Maine Wesleyan Seminary in Readfield, a new institution that opened in 1824. Today it is known as Kents Hill School, and its records indicate that Charles Henry studied there from the fall term of 1829 to the fall term of 1832. He studied languages, mathematics, history, geography, surveying, mechanical labors, and agricultural labors.[1] When he completed the training, Charles Henry obtained employment on the riverboats that worked the inland waterways of the Ohio, Illinois, and Mississippi rivers. He made his home in Saint Louis. Carl always wished that his grandfather had been a captain of one of the great whaling ships that went out from his boyhood home in Marion, but he was only a riverboat captain.

On one of his trips up the Illinois River to Peoria, he met Violetta Johnson, a nineteen-year-old girl who had moved from Marietta, Ohio, where she was born. They were married in Peoria on Wednesday, August 29, 1838. The couple settled in Peoria, and eventually Charles Henry gave up river life to run a succession of hotels. He was known as Captain Ruggles by this time, and the Peoria newspapers speak of him as "the politest captain on the river" and a "whole-souled jovial" host.[2]

Charles Henry and Violetta had two children, both born in Peoria: Nathaniel Sprague, Carl's father, presumably born on March 25, 1847, and Sophia, born in 1854. Then Micah Haskell died. His estate was left to his wife, Lydia, and the three surviving children. Charles Henry's share included the land and house in East Marion, and by the end of 1859 he and his family had moved there. It was a large working farm that Charles Henry managed for the rest of his days.

The property in East Marion juts out into the ocean, and one can see the Bird Island Lighthouse from the point. Mrs. Pulver, Carl's niece, remembered that the house was located not far from the bluffs, and one could walk down to the water that surrounded the land on three sides. A corner of the house was used as a sighting by the local fishermen. It was a big house, with lots of windows that rattled whenever the wind roared across the point. Charles Henry nailed the windows shut in an effort to stop the rattling but he never succeeded. Later he added a big "music room" on the north side, long and narrow with hardwood floors and a big bay window.

Nathaniel was twelve or thirteen years old when they moved to East Marion. He did not do well in school, and according to Mrs. Pulver, his granddaughter, he never graduated from any school. At various times in his life, he called himself a doctor or a dentist, but he never practiced either profession. In fact, he never worked at anything except farming.

Charles Henry had a fierce temper and liked to rule his home with an iron hand. Carl himself remembered that his grandfather never let his father do anything and kept him as completely under his control as possible. Carl always said Nathaniel's problem was drinking, and probably that is partly true; but Nathaniel loved horses and racing, as his granddaughter remembered, and she should know. Many years later it was this love of horse racing and gambling that caused him to lose whatever money he had inherited, and he had to live with Mrs. Pulver's family when she was a little girl. Thereafter Nathaniel was supported by her father in a small apartment in Boston. She remembered him then as a fat little man, a "five by five," she said. But in his youth, Nathaniel was a good-looking man. He cut a fine figure riding his well-groomed horse and following the races, when and if he could get away from the farm.

We do know that he got as far as Nashua, New Hampshire, where he met and fell in love with Maria Josephine Hodge, a lovely young singer five years his senior, who was born in Francestown, New Hampshire, on February 24, 1842, the fourth of seven children. Her parents were Levi Woodbury (named for a governor of the state) and Marry Longley Hodge. She was a distant relative of President Franklin Pierce. By the time she was eight years old, the family had moved to Nashua, and Levi had set up shop as a harness maker on Merrimack Street. Three years later he died, leaving five children for his widow to care for. Maria Josephine, or Josie, as she was called, was only eleven.

The circumstances of her marriage are interesting and lead one to believe that on this occasion at least, Nathaniel rebelled against his father. It seems quite clear that they eloped. All the Ruggles genealogies (and there are several extant) give the place of the wedding as Nashua, which would have been natural since Josie's home was there. But instead it took place in Milford, New Hampshire, a town not too far west of Nashua. There were three daily trains that made round trips from Boston to Nashua to Milford and Wilton. The young couple could easily have arranged to meet at Nashua and continue on to Milford for their marriage.

The wedding took place on November 9, 1868. On the marriage certificate Nathaniel gave his age as twenty-one, which, according to the genealogies, was correct. But according to his death certificate, compiled with information supplied by his youngest son, Edward, Nathaniel's birth date is actually one year later, March 25, 1848.[3] If that is true, he was not yet twenty-one when he and Josie were married, and he lied about his age. Unfortunately we will never know the truth, for birth records in Peoria were not recorded until 1877. Josie was twenty-six. Also on the marriage certificate, Nathaniel gave Milford as his residence and physician as his occupation. The birthplace of each of his parents is incorrect, too. His father's is given as Rochester, Illinois, and his mother's as Springfield, Illinois. There was no notice of the marriage in the local newspaper, and Nathaniel never paid any taxes in Milford nor was he listed as either a practicing physician or a dentist.

I believe that Carl never knew the circumstances of his parents' marriage. He only remembered that Charles Henry "was always very down on Father—wouldn't let him do anything or think for himself. He treated him like a sailor, giving him orders. He'd never allow Father to drink anything but he'd drink."[4] Sadly, and partly as a result of Charles Henry's treatment, Carl came to have neither love nor respect for him.

After the wedding, Nathaniel and Josie returned to the big house on Butler's Point, and it is easy to imagine the storm that broke over his head when Nathaniel brought his bride home. Charles Henry would have vented the full force of his violent temper on Nathaniel. However, from all accounts, Josie, with Violetta's help, won him over. He may not have forgiven his son, but he soon came to appreciate his daughter-in-law.

Before the Civil War the people of Marion had manufactured salt, built ships, and developed a thriving whaling industry. Now in 1868 it had become a sleepy seaside village, whose main industry was farming. The main part of town lay along the north and west sides of Sippican Harbor with the oldest part along the northern tip. It was called Old Landing and dated back to the 1600s. As the town grew, it moved south along the west side, which came to be called Wharf Village, or Lower Village. The earliest settlers lived at Old Landing and their descendants considered themselves the aristocrats and leaders of the town. By contrast, the people of Lower Village had allowed their homes to become shabby, and many had moved away. Around former bustling wharves there were fields with cranberry bogs and cow pastures.

The Ruggles property was a long way from the center of town, across the harbor, far from the main roads and the general population. If Nathaniel and Josie wanted any outside entertainment, or even if the family went to church, it meant traveling some distance. The recently formed Methodist Episcopal church was located just north of Old Landing and was the nearest to their home. Since Josie loved to sing, she might have joined the church choir; otherwise her music making would have been confined to the music room, where she often played the piano and sang for herself.

In 1870 Mary, their first child, was born, and after a span of six years, on March 11, 1876, Josie gave birth to a son, our subject, Charles Sprague. Three years later Edward Milton was born. Charlie's early years are lost to us except for the few memories or stories he was content to tell and for the anecdotes that Mrs. Pulver remembered hearing from her father, Edward Milton. From her, we learn that Charlie was not very well liked by either his sister or his brother. For six years Mary had been the only child, and it was difficult for her to share the limelight with a new baby, especially a baby brother. Edward resented Charlie, too, and it was more than just a friendly rivalry between brothers. Charlie was a small child, perhaps sickly, and his mother and Violetta doted on him. He returned their love and attention in full measure, but Mary and Edward were very jealous. Charlie seems to have resembled his mother, especially around the mouth, while he took after his father around the eyes. But Charlie always claimed a likeness to his mother, not his father.

At an early age he showed a genuine interest in music, listening attentively to his mother at the piano. Sometimes the whole family gathered in the music room to sing together, and occasionally Nathaniel would play the drums to make the music more exciting. During one of these happy times, at the age of four, as he told it, Charlie took a cigar box and pretended that he was playing the violin. He persisted at it long enough, coaxing and pleading with his family for lessons on a real violin, until they finally agreed to let him study with Mr. Hill, who lived in New Bedford.

Mr. Hill was an itinerant music teacher, who gave lessons to the children in nearby communities when the weather permitted. He also had a band of twenty-five players and regularly gave concerts in the area during the summer months, arranging some of the music himself. Since Charlie was too small to start on a full size instrument, his first violin was three-quarter size.

When Charlie went to the one-room public school in Great Neck in East Marion about a mile and a half from the farm, Miss Cynthia Delano was his teacher. In addition to the other subjects, she was also expected to educate her pupils in music, teaching them the names and lengths of notes and a few songs by rote.

The Robinsons were the nearest neighbors, and the children often played together. Sometimes they walked the four-and-a-half or five miles up to Old Landing, or more often, they went cranberry picking in the bogs closer to home. Sometimes they just watched the big carriages filled with summer guests on their way to the great square wooden hotel with the wide veranda on Great Hill called Marion House, to the east of Charlie's home and farther out on the peninsula. Marion House, the second hotel in the village, was a three-story building that could accommodate three hundred guests. Soon after the railroad was built in 1854, the village had become the summer playground for tourists from New York and Boston, and even from as far away as Chicago. They came and stayed at the hotels or in boarding houses, and then bought or built their own summer homes. By the mid-1880s there was a large colony of summer people, many distinguished in arts and letters, business and government. Their story has an interesting though brief connection with Charlie's.

General Adolphus Greeley, the Arctic explorer and chief signal officer of the army and head of the weather bureau, knew about Marion from his old friend, Captain Emerson Hadley of Old Landing. Since Washington is very warm during the summer, General Greeley and his wife rented the Hadley home for the summer of 1887. Once settled they invited President and Mrs. Grover Cleveland to visit them for some respite from the hot weather. President Cleveland felt he could not leave Washington, but there was no reason why Mrs. Cleveland should not go. So, accompanied by her mother, Mrs. Folsom, Frances Cleveland came to Marion.

The president and Mrs. Cleveland had also heard of the charms of Marion from Richard Watson Gilder, a summer resident and editor of *Century* magazine, who had met Mrs. Cleveland at the Wells College commencement ceremonies in Aurora, New York, that past June. After the ceremonies Gilder had traveled to Washington with the first lady to be presented to the president.

Frances Folsom Cleveland was only twenty-three years old at the time. She had been Grover Cleveland's ward ever since her father, Oscar Folsom, Cleveland's friend and law partner, had died. They had been married in the White House only a year before on June 2, 1886, making her the second youngest wife of any United States president (Dolly Madison was the youngest). Mrs. Cleveland was not only beautiful and young, but lively and charming.

During that first summer in Marion, she often visited with the Gilders. There were lectures and readings, and private parties at the Old Stone Studio, a ruined old stove oil factory behind the Gilder home that had been remodeled by Stanford White and turned into a studio for Mrs. Gilder, who was the painter Harriette DeKay. It was either during this visit or the following summer when she again returned to Marion without the president, this time to stay with the Gilders, that the beautiful first lady and Charlie met.

Charlie's version of the meeting varied over the years, and he is our only source for this event. It seems that he was taken to play the violin for Mrs. Cleveland, and according to him, she herself accompanied him on the piano. In some versions, the president was also there. More likely the meeting took place without the president during those first two summers when Mrs. Cleveland came to Marion with her mother. My own guess is that it was probably during that first summer, when she had not yet settled into the role of first lady. Her Marion friends would have been on the alert for anything in the area that would amuse and entertain her.

Charlie was only eleven at the time, but he had been studying violin for several years already, and if his mother had been active in the local singing groups, as is likely, it is fair to assume that the townspeople would have known about Mrs. Ruggles's talented son. We have no idea what they played; but if true, it was the first big musical event in

Charlie's life, not calculated to endear him to his sister and brother, but one he never forgot or ceased telling. It is very unlikely that this performance occurred with the president in attendance, since he did not come to Marion until the summers of 1889 and 1890 after he was defeated for a second term and was no longer in office. Furthermore, by that time Charlie's home life had changed radically.

There was a dark side to Charlie's boyhood, and it left an indelible mark on him. The tension between his grandfather and his father was never absent, and oftentimes this put both Violetta and Josie in difficult, if not untenable, positions. There were arguments and quarrels and many moments of strained relations. Charles Henry controlled his home with an iron hand, and even the slightest objection brought forth his fierce and explosive anger. As he grew older, that anger turned into rages, sometimes uncontrollable. At times his wrath was so great, he would turn it against himself and pound his head against the walls. Mrs. Pulver remembered the children would tremble, for they could hear and feel the house quiver with the force of his rage.

When such fits were on him, he would be put away into another room of the house—locked away from the women and children, so that he might not harm them, for even Violetta could not help him then. His food would be taken to him, and he would remain apart until he felt well enough to rejoin the family. All that anger and tension within the family took its toll on the children, especially Charlie. Later in life he denied that he had any siblings, protesting that he was an only child; and he always spoke ill of his father, while inventing seafaring stories about his fearsome grandfather.

Then on Friday, May 10, 1889, while Charles Henry was isolated from the family, he died. The notice appeared on the front page of the *New Bedford Evening Standard* under the headline: "Sudden Death in Marion": "Capt. Charles H. Ruggles, who resided on the Point at Great Neck, Marion, died last evening about 7 o'clock, while sitting in his chair at lunch, as usual. His death was so sudden and painless that none of his family, who were at the time in an adjoining room, knew of his death until they found him sitting in his chair, lifeless."[5]

The town clerk gave the cause of death as apoplexy, and burial was in the Ruggles plot in Rochester. Life could have been easier now, but that was not to be. Josie soon became ill, and a little over a year later, on September 11, 1890, she died of heart disease and was also buried in the Ruggles plot. Charlie was fourteen years old.

Now it was Violetta who took charge of the family. There was still ample money, and they owned the farm. But the place held too many sad memories for all of them, and it was so isolated. Violetta decided to move the family closer to Boston where Nathaniel could have a fresh start, and where Charlie and Eddie, still of school age, could get a better education. They would keep the house as a summer place and let others farm the land.

So Charlie moved to East Lexington. He said he never returned to Marion, but, typically, the truth was a different story.

NOTES

1. Harriet H. Carter, alumni secretary of Kents Hill School, kindly provided me with this information.

2. John Kirkpatrick, "The Evolution of Carl Ruggles: A Chronicle Largely in His Own Words," *Perspectives of New Music* 6:2 (Spring-Summer 1968): 146.

3. Waterman & Sons Funeral Service of Boston supplied a copy of Nathaniel's death certificate.

4. Kirkpatrick, "Evolution of Carl Ruggles," 146.

5. *New Bedford Evening Standard*, 11 May 1889.

2

Young Man, Young Musician
1890–1907

In the *Lexington Minute-Man,* a weekly newspaper, the following notice appeared on Friday, November 21, 1890: "The Austin house, opposite the Willard Hotel, owned by Mr. Edward Harrington, was sold last week to Mrs. Violetta Ruggles, of Marion, Mass., who we understand, will occupy the house with her son, Dr. N. S. Ruggles and his family. They contemplate making extensive improvements which will make it an attractive place. As they are a musical family, we hope our village may have an opportunity to hear them."

Six months later, the Ruggleses moved to a new house on North Street (now Trapelo Road) in Waverley. It was a bigger home with a barn, and it occupied two lots. Then within a few months, Nathaniel also purchased the adjoining house and two additional lots, having decided to enter the real estate business, and hoping to profit in the growth of the area. Meanwhile, in the summer of 1891, he took Charlie and Eddie back to the farm for vacation.

The two boys were enrolled in the local schools, but formal schooling held little importance for Charlie, who was too busy working at his music. In January 1892 he was appointed director of the YMCA orchestra for the "Wednesday night sociables" in Boston, and on April 14, he and his sister, Minnie, entertained at the meeting of the Ladies Aid Society held in the vestry of Waverley Hall. For this performance, Charlie received his first critical notice: "A musical program of entertainment was rendered in the church, each number of which received hearty applause. Master Charles Ruggles' violin selections were rendered with much feeling and delicacy. He captivated the audience by his manly bearing, and is evidently at home in the concert room. The zithern playing by Master Ruggles with guitar accompaniment by Miss Ruggles, was a pleasing entertainment."[1]

Charlie's first instrumental group was called The Waverley Five, and on the Fourth of July in 1892 they entertained at Charlie's home for a neighborhood party given by Nathaniel. Lights were strung along the lawn, and between the musical selections a brilliant display of fireworks was set off. That year Nathaniel and Eddie returned to the farm for the summer, but Charlie stayed in town with Violetta and served as scorekeeper for the local baseball team, the Waverleys. All his life, he was an ardent baseball fan.

The Ruggles orchestra, the old Waverley Five slightly enlarged, made its first appearance that summer. They gave two Wednesday evening concerts on August 17 and 24, performing marches, waltzes, and other light pieces. In the fall, Charlie was appointed the sole leader of the YMCA orchestra of Boston, and he brought along his close friend, Harry Bates, to be the first cornet player for the group. Meanwhile he also kept the Ruggles orchestra going, and at one performance he even persuaded Nathaniel to play the drums with them. That evening the orchestra also included Charlie on violin, Harry Bates on cornet, Edward Brown, Jr., on piano, and Frank Bowers on clarinet.

On New Year's Day, 1893, Minnie, Charlie's sister, married Mr. Fred E. Holt. The wedding took place in the Ruggles home with only a few relatives invited, but there was plenty of music, with Charlie playing the violin for the ceremony and the Ruggles orchestra providing music afterward. Unfortunately, Minnie's husband died just six months after their marriage and she returned home.

There was another change in Charlie's home life, too, for Nathaniel had taken a bride. In the same week that Minnie's husband died, Nathaniel married Mrs. Ida Ruggles in Mayo, Tennessee. The family story is that the marriage was arranged through the mails, and that Ida was a redhead. Quite likely she was a distant relative. Now there were three women in the household to look after the boys: their grandmother, their new stepmother, and Minnie, as well as a frequent fourth, Aunt Sophie, Nathaniel's sister. Charlie, meanwhile, was busier than ever with the Ruggles orchestra, which began playing at events even beyond the Waverley area. Not until October could the entire family return to Marion for a month's vacation.

The country suffered a depression during 1893 and 1894, and Nathaniel, like so many others, was caught in it. Unable to pay the taxes on all his properties, at first he sold two of the four lots. Then he had to sell them all, and the family moved to a smaller home in a nearby area called Wellington, now a part of Belmont. Two years later the family had to move once again to even more modest surroundings in Watertown, a much larger community and one more directly connected by trolley to both Boston and Cambridge.

Eddie stayed behind, for he was now working as baggage master at the Waverley train station, but Charlie moved with the family. Violetta was still mother to him and he needed her, for she was his link to the past, and he could not contemplate a life without her attentions. Also, from a more practical point of view, he simply could not afford to live away from home. His income from music was not sufficient, though he worked very hard at it. When he could not find jobs for his band, he sat in with other groups. For a short while he directed a small orchestra in the Park Theater at Waltham. He played at nearby Cotuit, and he continued with the Boston YMCA orchestra. In 1897 he also founded the Waverley town band, which gave open-air concerts from mid-July to Labor Day.

By the time Charlie was eighteen years old, it was apparent to everyone that Nathaniel would not leave much of an inheritance, and Charlie realized that playing in theater orchestras or even having his own band would not bring him much fame or fortune. On the other hand, he had played enough of the popular and semipopular music of the day to understand it thoroughly; indeed, he had arranged the music and perhaps even written some original material for his groups. But gradually he realized that he needed to learn more, especially after The Great Awakening.

During these years, Charlie's second home was with the Bates family. They were all musical, and Harry's sister, Marian, studied voice. One day when Charlie was visiting, he heard Marian singing an art song that was so beautiful that he had to stop and listen. He asked her what it was, and to sing it again for him. When she did, he was once again deeply moved. It was "Feldeinsamkeit" by Brahms. Charlie never forgot that experience, for suddenly he had become aware of the emotional power of music. It turned him in the direction of classical music, and later in life he spoke of it as The Great Awakening.[2]

The combination of that event and his increasing dissatisfaction with his own musical knowledge led him to seek out John Knowles Paine, who was teaching music at Harvard and lived in nearby Cambridge. Paine was a famous composer, and Charlie was hesitant, but Violetta supported his decision and spurred him on. To his delight, Paine agreed to teach him composition as a private student at his home, but also insisted that Charlie take up other musical studies to round out his musical education. So he began to study violin, first with Walter Spaulding and later with Felix Winternitz, and counterpoint with Josef Claus. Spaulding taught at Harvard, Claus and Winternitz at the New England Conservatory, but Charlie studied with each privately and did not enroll at either institution.

More and more of his time was spent in Cambridge. In 1897, he met Inez Haynes, who had just graduated from Radcliffe, and they became lifelong friends. After her marriage to Rufus Gillmore, Charlie was a frequent visitor to their home and later to their summer home in Scituate. Inez, a writer, introduced him to other young people interested in the arts. Mrs. Paine liked the brash young man, too, and often, after his lesson, Charlie was invited to stay for tea or a meal. One time, Paine himself invited him to an evening of music so that he could meet Miss Amy Fay, who had studied with Franz Liszt. When the evening was over, Charlie was invited to escort her home.

Since Paine insisted that he attend concerts, he began going regularly to the Friday afternoon rehearsals of the Boston Symphony. He also began to study scores, buying a few and borrowing more. The performances of Wagner's music stirred him deeply. In later years, he said it "made him burn," and he was excited by the so-called new music. From 1897 to 1902, he could have heard works by such younger composers as Feliz Weingartner, Anton Bruckner, and Richard Strauss. Wagner and Strauss became his heroes.[3]

When he was an old man, Charlie remembered that Paine would give him beginnings of phrases or a group of chords and require him to make short pieces from them. Then at the lessons Paine would criticize his work and suggest alternate ways of writing. Sometimes Charlie would listen and accept the criticism, and sometimes he would argue vehemently for his own way. Grateful as he was to have the opportunity to work with such a distinguished composer, he did not want or intend to become a mere imitator of the older man's style, especially since he began to feel that Paine's music was by now old fashioned and out of date.

In 1899 Charlie had his first compositions published by C. W. Thompson & Co. in Boston. They were a set of three songs: "How Can I Be Blythe and Glad," "At Sea," and "Maiden with Thy Mouth of Roses." Probably written around 1896, they were published under the name he used here for the first time and would soon use for the rest of his life: Carl. There were several Charles Ruggleses living in Watertown then, and Charlie wanted a different name. The fact that he chose Carl, the German form of his given name, shows his admiration for German music. The change also is the first indication that he was getting ready to break with the past. While he stayed with the family, he continued to use both names: Charles S. for everyday affairs, and Carl for musical matters. As soon as he left home, however, he dropped Charles S., though never legally, and became Carl for everything.

Only one song remains from opus 1, "How Can I Be Blythe and Glad," which is a poem by Robert Burns. Charlie designed the cover, too, and in bold script his new name is written large across the center of the page. Underneath in delicate and leafy scrollwork, he has printed the words: "3 Songs"; and underneath that are the words: "with Pianoforte Accompaniment Op. 1," and the titles of each song, which sold for forty cents apiece.

"How Can I Be Blythe and Glad" is not a very good piece, distinguished neither in its melody nor in its accompaniment. Each of the three stanzas is given the same musical treatment, except for the final phrase that brings the song to its conclusion. The words are treated syllabically, and there is no attempt to color them in any way, either through added notes in the melodic line or in the accompaniment, which merely supports and follows the text throughout the entire piece. One wonders whether the other two pieces were similar, or whether Charlie felt this simple style was the one best suited to the Burns poem. We do know that only the third song was sung, at least once by his wife when they lived in Winona, Minnesota, some ten years later. Charlie apparently approved of that one.[4]

The only other song existing from this period, "Thy Presence Ever Near Me," was published in 1901 by Arthur P. Schmidt and Company of Boston. In addition to the printed copy, there also are two handwritten scores by Charlie, one for low voice and one for high. On one he has written the date of composition, 1898, and on the other his address: 6 Adams St., Watertown; Carl is of course the name he used.

The text of this piece is a German romantic poem, originally from the Persian, translated into English by Austin Hall Evans. It has two stanzas to which Charlie put the same melody, but this time the lines are flowing and full of emotion. The melody expresses the text and reaches its highest peak on the words "heavenly radiance" in the first verse, and "risest as tomorrow's sun" in the second. Where the sinuous line calls for it, Charlie repeats words or slides them over several melody notes, and the accompaniment does not follow the text exactly. Instead there is a strong bass line that acts as counterpoint to the melody, and in between are countermelodies that sometimes go with the bass and sometimes support the voice, especially at chromatic points. The piece is a decided cut above the earlier work, but it is still very much in the tradition of turn-of-the-century parlor songs, with no sign of the striking dissonances and extreme tensions of Charlie's mature musical style.

Sometime in the 1920s Charlie set about systematically destroying all of his early compositions, for he did not want any music to survive from this apprentice period. These are the only ones that escaped the trash bin, because they had been published and were therefore on file with the Library of Congress. It is reasonable to conclude that Charlie wrote other songs, but they are lost.

In 1900 Julius Ackeroyd, a violinist with the Boston Symphony Orchestra, moved to Watertown. Charlie arranged a meeting and soon began studying with him. He loved the backstage gossip and stories that Ackeroyd could tell him about working in the symphony. At about the same time, Charlie met Alfred DeVoto, a new and talented young piano teacher at the New England Conservatory. The two quickly became close friends, both being ardent champions of the new music, which DeVoto often performed on his recitals.

To make ends meet during these years, Charlie worked at a variety of jobs. When he was an old man, he said he had studied boat design with a man named Frisbee. Typically he recalled that the classes were at the Massachusetts Institute of Technology and that Frisbee was a professor of Marine Architecture, but neither statement was the truth. There were free evening classes at the Hawes school in South Boston in art, naval architecture, and other subjects, and a John Frisbee was one of the teachers.[5] These were the classes that Charlie attended, after which he worked for a while as engraver and draughtsman, while he tried to keep up with his music.

He had begun to do some private teaching of violin and music theory, but students were hard to find. Charlie finally talked to Paine about his financial situation, and Paine encouraged him to apply for a teaching position outside the Boston area. Although not overly enthusiastic about it, Charlie did send in his application, and in January 1902 Paine himself wrote a letter of recommendation. This was Charlie's first attempt to secure a teaching post, but nothing came of it.

That same year the family moved again, just down the street to smaller quarters at 14 Adams Street. Violetta was growing more infirm, and Nathaniel simply could not manage the family affairs. He had lost most of the real estate in which he had invested, including the Marion property, because he had not kept up with the taxes. For Charlie the situation was especially bitter. The music and artistic world seemed to be slowly opening out to him, but the world of his family still held him. Where he had hoped to find material support, he found instead that such help was dwindling away to nothing. While Violetta loved him as always, she was aging fast, and he knew he would lose her soon. Unlike Eddie, who had gone off and found his own life, Charlie still could not make the break. It would have to be thrust on him.

In November 1902 his luck changed and he began writing music criticism for two weekly newspapers, the *Watertown Tribune* and the *Belmont Tribune,* both edited by Mr. George Stratton. It seemed a great opportunity: he was getting paid; his name was before the public, with each article signed "Carl Ruggles"; and he was able to attend the concerts free of charge. Also, there was the exciting prospect that he might be advanced to more important newspapers.

He wrote twenty-eight columns, entitled "Musical Comments," which appeared between November 27, 1902 and November 7, 1903, and which were printed weekly until mid-May 1903; then there were four summer columns in June and July, and a final one at the beginning of the next season. Most are reviews of the symphony concerts and recitals. A few are notices of concerts in other cities, and the rest are Charlie's commentaries on books, composers, and performers.

He was not at all bashful about expressing his views, whether positive or negative. Of a violinist's performance with the symphony, he wrote: "Take it all in all, it was about the poorest exhibition of violin playing that I have ever heard at a Symphony concert."[6] Charlie did not care for Handel's "Israel in Egypt" when it was given in the spring of 1903 by the Handel and Haydn Society: "It is a great pity that time and energy are wasted on such material, when there are so many modern works one would like to hear. . . . In this work of Handel's there is little which is inspired."[7] If he did not enjoy the music of Haydn and Mozart, he liked Beethoven's Fifth Symphony very much. Schumann, Schubert, and Saint-Saëns did not get the high marks from him that Berlioz, Wagner, and Liszt did, while the music of Richard Strauss received the highest praise of all.

When Maestro Wilhelm Gericke and the symphony gave the first Boston performance of Strauss's "Death and Transfiguration" in February 1903, Charlie's enthusiasm was boundless: "Richard Strauss's 'Tod und Verklärung,' is one of the most marvelous scores ever penned by man. . . . Never have I heard anything that could surpass the conflict with death. The Fever motive, its development, the crescendo of awful sorrowness, in which the death motive is intoned by the brass, the second feverish motive, cutting through the ensemble like a streak of red death, the transfiguration, and death motives again, all this and more is thrown at one in a welter of color, a maelstrom of tone that is thaumaturgic."[8]

Charlie's last article for the season appeared on July Fourth. By that time he had gone off for the summer to Sharon Springs, New York, to play in the orchestra, confident that he would resume the reviews the next season. Furthermore, Paine had promised to help him enroll in a writing class at Harvard as a special student when the fall semester started. Charlie took English composition, English 31, with a faculty that included Professor Barrett Wendell, Dr. G. H. Mayadier, C. R. Nutter and W. R. Castle. It was the only course he ever took at Harvard.

Unfortunately, Mr. Stratton, the editor, decided to terminate Charlie's column after the first one of the new season had appeared. Instead of "Musical Comments," the following week saw a column of local interest by "Willie Watertown" introduced, and Charlie's reviewing days were over. Once more he was reduced to the uncertainty of playing in theater orchestras and community groups, perhaps teaching a few students, and doing odd jobs. In 1904, both he and Nathaniel worked for J. C. Pike & Co. in Boston, doing delicate china repair work.

By the end of the year, Violetta had become so ill that she was confined to a wheelchair, and they all agreed it was time to move nearer to the relatives who lived in Boston. Charlie knew at last that he had to make a break. He grieved deeply over leaving Violetta, but he was not at all sorry to leave his father. When the family moved he stayed behind in Watertown and settled into a boarding house at 26 Whitney Street. Then on May 22, 1905, Violetta died. Now the break with the family was complete. After her funeral, Charlie never saw his father again. He was twenty-nine years old, and for the first time in his life he really stood alone.

At this point, Charlie turned to his friends, and with Alfred DeVoto conceived the idea of making joint appearances in lecture recitals on this new music about which they both felt so keenly. Charlie would deliver the lectures and DeVoto would play the examples. Another advantage of working with DeVoto was the opportunity to meet other musicians, as well as the critic, Lawrence Gilman. DeVoto also talked to Charlie about moving to Lawrence, Massachusetts, a large town with an active music club named in honor of George W. Chadwick, the director of the New England Conservatory, and with churches, which had much good music. He felt sure that Charlie would find music students there, and it was still near enough to Boston that the two of them could continue their collaboration.

Charlie followed his advice, and at some point in late 1905 he moved to 4 Albion Street in Lawrence, a move that signified the end of his life as Charlie. Henceforth, he always called himself Carl, and from now on we shall do the same. The move was lucky for him, for soon after he arrived, a young woman named Charlotte Snell came into his life.

The year before, Frank A. Snell, his wife, Catharine, and their daughter, Charlotte, had returned to Lawrence from Burlington, Vermont. Frank had first come to the town in 1871 to work at the Everett Mills. He married and had two children: first a son, Henry, then a daughter,

Hattie, who was born on March 1, 1880. She did not like her name, and from the time she was a child, called herself Lottie. In 1888, Frank moved his family to Montreal, where his brother lived. Lottie and her cousin, Cora, were sent to Hochelaga Convent School from 1889 to 1891. Lottie, who grew very quickly and looked older than her age, was very bright and loved to sing. She studied music during the years in the convent school and continued her music studies when she left.

At the age of fourteen, she went to work for the Liverpool and London Globe Insurance Company. She impressed everyone there by her intelligence, her pleasing personality, and her sense of responsibility. In 1897, when she had to leave because her father had taken a new position in Burlington, Vermont, the manager and staff presented her with a testimonial letter and a gift as a tribute to her excellent work. Lottie and her parents lived in Burlington until her father retired in 1905. She continued to study voice and developed into a fine contralto, often performing as soloist with the church choir. While they lived in Burlington, her brother, a student at McGill University, was killed in a hockey accident on February 2, 1898.

After Frank's retirement, the family returned to Lawrence, and Lottie, who now called herself Charlotte, lost no time in finding a singing position as alto in the quartet for the Trinity Congregational Church. She also became active in the Chadwick Club, often participating as soloist at their monthly meetings. At the April 5, 1906 meeting Charlotte was introduced to one of the guests, a new musician in town, a short, bald fellow who had deep blue eyes and managed to look directly at her even though she was a foot taller. His name was Carl Ruggles, and they were immediately attracted to each other. Carl always said it was love at first sight. When he played some violin selections that evening, Charlotte was enchanted. A year later she wrote to him: "It was a year ago last night that we met, yet it seems a lifetime. I thought of you playing and in fancy heard the voluptuous swell of your music."[9]

Soon Carl and Charlotte were together as much as possible, and they made an interesting-looking couple. She was tall and stately with very black hair, and spoke softly with a low, cultured voice, appearing confident and sure of herself. Carl, on the other hand, often spoke brashly, sometimes too loudly, with a raucous laugh, and under his blustery exterior longed for another strong woman to take Violetta's place. They went to concerts, to socials, and to parties with Charlotte's friends. Charlotte even tried to teach him to dance, and Carl introduced her to his friends.

In the fall he persuaded her to resume vocal studies, and she commuted to Boston once a week to work with William L. Whitney. Carl was so impressed with her voice that he arranged for her to sing for Lawrence Gilman, who advised her not to try for an operatic career, feeling that she should concentrate on the art songs and oratorios that would be more suitable for her talent.

Meanwhile Carl and DeVoto had begun to give their lecture-demonstrations on modern music, and one engagement was before the Chadwick Club. The presentation was entitled "Modern and Ultra-Modern Music," and it took place on November 13, 1906. Carl spoke about Wagner, Tchaikovsky, Rimsky-Korsakoff, Verdi, Puccini, Reger, Brahms, Richard Strauss, Franck, Lekeu, Loeffler, D'Indy, Charpentier, and Debussy, while DeVoto and another pianist, Homer Humphrey, performed the musical examples. According to the review published the following day, and quite possibly written by Carl himself, it was "the most satisfactory lecture on music ever given in Lawrence."[10]

Now more than ever, Carl longed for a real position, for he and Charlotte wanted to marry. Once more, he sought a teaching position, but it was to no avail although this time DeVoto wrote a letter of recommendation. Carl did not get the position, and marriage was quite out of the question until he could find some kind of steady employment. But where? and how? Once again living in Lawrence was to prove lucky. Mr. and Mrs. Edmund Choate were active members of the Chadwick Club and good friends of Charlotte, who soon introduced them to Carl. The Choates had a relative who lived in Winona, Minnesota. Among other business activites, he was a dry goods merchant, and his store, located in the center of town, was in one of the largest buildings, which he also owned. In the upper floors were offices for rent, and in January 1907 the Mar D'Mar School of Music moved to the fourth floor.

At that time the school was looking for a violin teacher, and Mr. Hannibal Choate, the landlord and patron of the school, offered to help find the right person for the position. He wrote to his Lawrence relatives, whom he knew to be active in musical circles, and who brought up Carl's name almost immediately. Winona, Minnesota, was a long way from Lawrence, but if the job turned out to be as favorable as the letters indicated, Carl would have a start on a promising career. He was frightened, but encouraged and excited. Charlotte promised that she would follow him to Winona, and that, once he was established, they could be married. At last he wrote his acceptance. His new position began on February 1, 1907.

NOTES

1. *Belmont Bulletin*, 23 Apr. 1892.
2. Conversation with author, Bennington, Vermont, 24 Feb. 1967. This

and all subsequent conversations with Carl took place in his room at the Crescent Manor Nursing Home in Bennington, where he lived from 1966 until his death.

3. Weingartner's Symphony in G Major, opus 23 was given its first Boston performance on 12 Apr. 1901; Bruckner's Fourth Symphony was given on 10 Feb. 1899, and his Fifth on 27 Dec. 1901. Richard Strauss's "Thus Spake Zarathustra" was first performed on 29 Oct. 1897; "A Hero's Life" on 6 Dec. 1901; and the "Feuersnot" love scene on 7 Mar. 1902.

4. Charlotte sang "Maiden with Thy Mouth of Roses" in 1910, and Carl orchestrated the accompaniment for the occasion. According to the program notes written by Charlotte, the song was originally written in 1897.

5. I am indebted to John Kirkpatrick for this information, which he forwarded to me from Mr. John Gardner, Associate Curator of Small Craft, Mystic Seaport Museum, Mystic, Connecticut.

6. *Belmont Tribune,* 6 Feb. 1903.

7. *Belmont Tribune,* 18 Apr. 1903.

8. *Watertown Tribune,* 12 Feb. 1903.

9. Charlotte H. Snell to Carl Ruggles, 6 Apr. 1907.

10. *Lawrence Telegram,* 14 Nov. 1906.

3

The Winona Symphony Orchestra
1907–12

When Carl arrived in Winona, the population was slightly over 21,000, but it was not a typical small town, for, as one of Carl's early pupils reported, there were at that time more millionaires per capita in Winona than anywhere else in the country. Founded around 1851 and situated on the Mississippi River, Winona became the nation's second largest port for exporting wheat, and during the late 1800s became equally important for lumbering. It was also an important center for the northwest railroad, whose stops once employed 1,200 men.

There were broad avenues lined with large Victorian homes, many with special architectural features such as towers and turrets, added as their owners moved up the financial ladder. The house owned by the Lambertons, for example, had sixteen-inch brick walls, imported French bas-reliefs, and a handcut Czechoslovakian chandelier in the music room. The mansion had been built in 1857 by Charles Huff, but the Lambertons, who had lived in it since 1872, had made the luxurious improvements. Shortly after Carl arrived in town, Henry M. Lamberton and his wife, Jeanette, moved into the house after the death of his father. Henry was a huge, portly man, a banker and lawyer, while Jeanette, eight years younger than he, was a soprano and an important figure in musical circles, whom Carl soon met.

Two newspapers, the *Winona Independent* and the *Republican-Herald,* carefully reported the activities of the town, and there were two or three small café orchestras whose members also played for the silent movies, given first at the opera house, then at the Capitol and the Bijou. The opera house, seating 1,200, was jointly owned by A. B. Youmans and Hannibal Choate. O. F. Burlingame was the manager. Since Winona was situated between Chicago and Minneapolis, Burlingame was often able to bring star performers for one night appearances as they made their way to one or the other larger city. Once Carl and Charlotte had arrived in Winona, they could have seen "Uncle Tom's Cabin" with a company of "twenty men, women, and children," or

Charles Frohman's production of "Peter Pan." Carl remembered going to see the boxer Fitzsimmons, who appeared in a show called "The Country Gentleman."

In 1907 the Musical Literary Society was twelve years old and numbered more than 215 members; it had monthly meetings for study purposes and also sponsored lectures and recitals. A season ticket to all the programs cost one dollar and a half. In addition, the largest churches—St. Paul's Episcopal, the Baptist, the First Congregational, and the Central Methodist—regularly gave concerts. In 1906, for example, the choir of the First Congregational Church celebrated Mozart's 150th anniversary. Winona also had two colleges: Winona Seminary, its name later changed to the College of St. Theresa, and the Normal School. Miss Caroline Smith, head of the music program at the latter, often performed for the community, and was active in the Minnesota State Music Teachers Association.

In 1905 there were seventeen automobiles in Winona and the first garage was opened. The trolley car ride cost five cents, and Earl Wood, one of Carl's violin pupils, bought one of the first motorcycles in 1907. During the summers there were boat rides to Fountain City, Wisconsin, across the river, and in the evenings band concerts on the levee or in one of the parks.

The Mar d'Mar School of Music was founded by Marc D. Lombard, an organist who had studied in Germany, and who started his career by giving private lessons in piano, organ, and theory in 1900. By 1905 he had successfully developed a full-fledged music school at 401-3 West Wabasha, with a full-time faculty of eight-plus assistants. The subjects taught included piano, organ, voice, elementary theory, harmony, counterpoint and composition, ear training, musical analysis, and ensemble playing, as well as Italian, French, German, and English. Mr. E. W. Cameron was the business manager, and the seventy-five patrons who supported the Mar d'Mar included such community leaders as Congressman James A. Tawney, Hannibal Choate, Judge A. H. Snow, Paul Watkins, who was a patent medicine manufacturer, and Mrs. Augusta Rising, wife of one of the bankers.

Carl replaced Arthur E. Burke as head of the violin department when the school moved to elegant quarters on the fourth floor of the Choate building on 51 East Third Street, where rooms on the east side had fireplaces with glazed tile hearths and mantles. In addition to an office and reception room, there was a large recital hall and even a music store. Elevator service was available at all hours, day and night, as long as the school was in session.[1]

Even before Carl arrived, he had made his name known through the newspapers, and immediately on his arrival he became active in the musical life. In the article announcing his appointment, which he doubtless wrote, Winonans were given a detailed account of his background, some of it true and some not. The story lists his teachers, George Hill and Claus, and suggests that he studied with Paine and Spaulding at Harvard. Other violin teachers, Julius Ackeroyd and Eugene Grauenberg, are mentioned, and there is a statement that for two years he had been in charge of the Cambridge School of Music, which was not true.

By the end of February he was busy teaching violin at the school and active as a soloist. On Sunday, February 24, accompanied by Arthur Tolleson, another teacher at the school, Carl performed Godard's "Berceuse" from *Jocelyn*. On the same program Jeanette K. Lamberton was soloist in a song entitled "Face to Face," and the program was repeated on March 15. Meanwhile Carl also gave weekly violin recitals at the school.

Carl's first appearance at the Opera House took place on Friday, April 5, at the Antiphonal Concert that was given to raise money for furnishing the basement of the Free Baptist Church. This was a big event, with four choirs, the YMCA quartet, and three soloists: Carl; Professor S. W. Mounty, baritone; and Jeanette Lamberton. Benz and Clausen's orchestra provided music as the audience assembled, and in addition, there were three speeches on the "Bay Problem." Carl performed Anton Dvořák's "Romance in D Major" and Schumann's "Traumerei" with great success, the review saying that he played with "the most delicate feeling."

On Monday, April 15, the *Republican-Herald* announced, "Manager Cameron of the Mar d'Mar School has secured the services of Boston's famous contralto, Miss Charlotte Harriet Schnell [*sic*] to assume charge of the vocal department. Miss Schnell will arrive this week." Carl had worked hard for this, and so had Charlotte. When she finally obtained singing engagements with the Minneapolis Symphony Orchestra and at the May Festival at Grand Forks, North Dakota, Marc Lombard and Mr. Cameron were persuaded to hire her. On Friday morning, April 19, 1907, Charlotte began her duties as head of the vocal department at Mar d'Mar.

Carl and Charlotte were soon in the midst of preparations for the May Festival on May 30 and 31. Various artists would present solos on May 30, and a performance of "The Holy City" by Gaul, with soloists, chorus, and orchestra, was scheduled for May 31. Both performances were at the Opera House, and a ticket for the two events cost one dollar and a half. In the meantime Charlotte left to keep her other singing engagements, performing as contralto soloist in "The Messiah" and appearing in another work, entitled "Hiawatha's Wooing." On May 23 the newspapers proudly announced that she would be the contralto soloist at the May Festival, and the *Winona Independent* carried her picture. Her dark hair is piled high on top of her head, her ears showing. She looks very serious with her long face and dark eyes. All that is visible of her apparel is a high lace collar.

The Winona Symphony had its beginnings in preparation for the May Festival, for on April 20 the *Republican-Herald* announced that Carl had been engaged to train the Gerlicher orchestra and that on Sunday at 2:00 P.M. in the music hall, "Choate Block" (the Mar d'Mar school), the regular rehearsal of the Winona Symphony Orchestra with "Mr. Carl Ruggles, conductor" would take place.[2] The orchestra would take part in the performance of the "Holy City," though Marc Lombard also accompanied on the piano, but Carl now had his first opportunity to conduct the Winona Symphony in public. With Charlotte's help, he prepared both the chorus and orchestra for the program.

In spite of rehearsals and concert preparations, Carl and Charlotte and other members of Mar d'Mar found time to perform for the elite Saturday Night Club at their dinner meeting on May 25 at the Hotel Winona. The forty-five members dined lavishly on a meal with a main course of "Boiled Tenderloin with Mushroom Sauce." Carl played the Dvořák "Romance in D Major," while Charlotte sang "Goodbye" by Tosti, and "Nur wer Sehnsucht Kennt" by Tchaikovsky, for which Carl played the violin obligato and Marc Lombard the piano.

The May Festival was a great success. There were large and enthusiastic audiences at both concerts, and at the conclusion an ovation was given to all the participants. Both Carl and Charlotte received excellent notices for their solos in the first program: "Mr. Carl Ruggles, the violinist, is a master upon the queen among instruments. . . . Miss Charlotte Harriet Snell is a welcome addition to the musical circles of Winona, her deep rich contralto voice being listened to with much pleasure upon this her first public appearance in the city."[3]

Carl's appearance as director also brought forth a complimentary notice. In his first appearance as musical director he had "acquitted himself ably in the part as he has on other occasions as a concert violinist of high order."[4] As a testament to the high place Charlotte and Carl had already achieved in Winona musical society, the closing event of the festival was a reception given at the school to honor them.

During that first year Carl had lived at Grafton's Boarding House while Charlotte roomed with the Reverend Thomas and his wife. Until Charlotte arrived, it had been a lonely place for Carl. Money had been tight. Carl was used to that, but in the beginning before he began to collect his salary for lessons and performances, there had been so little that he had come to know real hunger. On occasion he would take a table at the Hotel Winona and eat the bread and crackers at the set-up, then remember he had a prior engagement and abruptly leave without ordering and, of course, without paying.

Yet good things happened, too. Even though he was direct and demanding, and on occasion loud and coarse, he always sought his friends among the rich and the influential. Old Hannibal Choate with his high collar and black bow ties liked his ways. They both loved colorful language and off-color stories, "man-talk," as it was called. Since Choate was one of the most powerful men in Winona, it did Carl no harm if people knew that he occasionally dined at the Choate home. Choate collected violins and various objets d'art, too—some fake and some authentic—and he let Carl use one of his violins when he gave public performances.

Carl could be charming, as well, and Mrs. Choate came to like him, too, especially after the arrival of Charlotte, with her refined manners and distinction, as well as a gentleness that Carl lacked. She smoothed the rough edges and the wounds that his sharpness left, a job she was to do for the rest of her life. Mrs. Choate liked Charlotte. Everyone liked Charlotte. The old couple even began to help financially.

Carl and Charlotte returned East for the summer, and Charlotte stayed with her family in Lawrence. Carl visited as well, and they may have gone to Scituate to see Inez and Rufus Gillmore, Carl's old friends.

When they returned to Winona in September, they were abruptly notified that the Mar d'Mar no longer needed their services. The newspaper simply stated that the voice and violin departments were being dropped because they were not profitable, and Carl and Charlotte were suddenly without jobs. It was a terrible blow to both of them, and it was not good for the school. Within a year the Mar d'Mar closed, and both Cameron and Marc Lombard left Winona. But what were Carl and Charlotte to do?

Now friends came forward to help them. In less than a month, it was announced that Charlotte would be the new "choir mistress" of the First Baptist Church, and Carl had been hired to conduct the YMCA orchestra and glee club at a salary of fourteen dollars a month. In addition each of them took private students at a fee of seventy-five cents for a half-hour lesson. In these times we wonder how they could have lived on so little money. But in those days rooms could be had for between three and five dollars per week, movies cost ten cents, and if one chose to eat at a restaurant, a chicken dinner with all the chicken one wanted was available for twenty-five cents. Still, it was essential to be careful with living expenses, and without help from their friends the going would have been very hard. Carl's lifelong dependence on support from patrons dates from these early days in Winona.

The orchestra progressed slowly, in spite of Carl's plea for members in the local papers. By December he had been able to recruit only about sixteen, which meant that their repertoire had to consist of light music, with Carl arranging the parts. Knowing that the orchestra needed broader support, he went to the Choates, the Snows, the Risings, and others who were influential in town, and as a result, in January of 1908, the Musical Literary Society of Winona agreed to sponsor the Winona Symphony Orchestra with Carl as director. He would be paid five dollars a rehearsal, and the first rehearsal would take place on January 30. Carl was elated, and with good reason. He had the largest and most influential cultural organization in the town supporting the orchestra. They would pay for the music; they would raise additional money for the orchestra when he requested it; and they would see to it that there would be good audiences for the concerts, which he was confident would take place soon.

Meanwhile Horace Seaton, the organist at St. Paul's Episcopal Church, to which the Choates belonged, had formed a Choral Society, and the Musical Literary Society sponsored their first concert. Carl was one of the soloists, playing the Franck sonata, for which he was paid fifteen dollars. The reviewer said he was "indisputably a past master of his violin."[5] This was good publicity for Carl, who announced that the first concert of the Winona Symphony Orchestra would take place on Wednesday, April 29, 1908, at the Opera House, with tickets at fifteen, twenty-five, and thirty-five cents. By this time there were thirty-five players in the group.

That last week in April was one Carl would never forget: the first symphony concert and his marriage! Carl and Charlotte were married on Monday, April 27, just two days before the concert. It was a small, noon wedding at St. Paul's Episcopal Church, with the Reverend Percy E. Thomas officiating. Horace Seaton improvised on the organ through-out the ceremony. Carl was thirty-two years old; Charlotte was twenty-eight.

Two days after the wedding Carl conducted his first symphony orchestra concert. Oboe, bassoon, and French horn players were not available in Winona, so these were imported from the St. Paul orchestra and arrived in time for the final rehearsal in the afternoon. All the other players were Winonans. The auditorium was full, with most of the women of the Musical Literary Society decked out in jewels and long dresses and the men in tuxedos. The Youmans sat in a box on one side of the auditorium, the Choates in a box on the other. The concert was not only a musical highlight but also one of the social events of the season, and Carl had rented a white tie and tails for the occasion. The program included: Prelude to *Faust* by Gounod, orchestrated by Carl; Suite, "Un Giorno in Venezia" by Nevin; Micaela's Air from Bizet's *Carmen;* "Negro Episode" by Gilbert; and the Prelude and Siciliana from *Cavalleria Rusticana* by Mascagni. Mrs. H. M. (Jeanette) Lamberton was the soloist.

The concert was a great success. An editorial, which appeared two days later, read: "The initial appearance of the Winona Symphony Orchestra Wednesday was so good that it might be well to have more of these high-class musical programs. That Winona has talent was clearly shown. And that Carl Ruggles is a leader no one present that evening will dispute."[6]

So the orchestra was successfully launched, and Carl, too. He and Charlotte were the musical stars of Winona, along with Jeanette Lamberton, his soloist. Jeanette McKain Lamberton, born in 1869, was older than Carl by seven years. A good cook and the mother of two children, she was married to one of Winona's rich men, who was extremely proud of her vocal achievements, and she herself was very serious about her singing. According to her daughter, she had studied in Bloomington, Illinois, and Chicago, and even for a short time in Paris. Her major voice teacher was Madame Marchesi, and all through her years of singing in Winona, she went regularly to Chicago for coaching.

Mrs. Lamberton, a big woman, nearly six feet tall with a large bosom, was always well-dressed, and she towered over Carl. Considering herself a prima donna, she behaved like one. Possessed of a violent temper that at the slightest upset would be turned loose, it was rumored that in her anger she threw china vases and plates at the servants. But she could sing. By all accounts, she had a beautiful soprano voice. She and Carl were worthy adversaries. They could not have liked each other, for each wanted the spotlight, and each wanted to be known as the leading musician of the town. On the other hand, each honestly recognized the other's ability and knew that it was to the advantage of both to work together. It was a prickly relationship that developed between them, and sometimes it threatened to burst apart.

When Carl and Charlotte returned from the East in the fall of 1908, they rented a little house of their own on Century Street, and also an upright piano for their private lessons. Soon Charlotte was busy with the church choir and Carl with the orchestra. Carl planned six concerts for the 1908–9 symphony season, with an orchestra of forty-two players. A vigorous campaign was launched to sell season tickets for three dollars. Single tickets cost twenty-five, thirty-five, and fifty cents each. Announcements for the ticket sales indicate that the orchestra members would be paid from the proceeds, but in fact, none were. More likely the money went to pay for the St. Paul Orchestra players, who were still needed to fill in the gaps. Rehearsals continued at the YMCA until that organization decided to charge them a fee of two dollars a week. They then moved to the Odd Fellows Hall over John Von Rohr's drugstore, where they could rehearse free of charge.

Carl took care of the publicity, writing articles for the newspapers discussing the music to be performed. That season the young Belgian composer, Guillaume Lekeu, was Carl's favorite. The Musical Literary Society took care of the advertisements and the concert programs. Carl also spent a great deal of time arranging the music, which was obtained by mail either from St. Paul or Chicago. Lacking a complete instrumentation, he had to arrange the works to fit his players, and he found that his theater orchestra experience came in handy. In addition, either he or Charlotte wrote the notes for the programs, which consisted of short orchestral works, or single movements from symphonies. Suites, preludes, and dances from larger works were the main items. In the case of Lekeu, his "Étude Symphonique No. 2" was given on the second concert, and on the third, his "Étude Symphonique No. 1."

There were soloists, too, oftentimes local artists; Charlotte sang on the fourth concert, and Mrs. Albert W. Hodges, another Winonan, on the second. Sometimes the orchestra would accompany the soloists; at other times they would have only the piano. On the third concert, Mr. George Hamlin, a tenor from Chicago, was the guest artist, performing art songs for the entire second half of the program.

Certainly one of the highlights of that season was Carl's own "Valse de Concert," performed on December 1, and dedicated to the Musical Literary Society. The newspapers raved: "a splendidly spirited waltz." . . . "very sweet . . . full of fine climaxes, excellent use of the horn motives, and with a harmonious enthusiasm, and one's only criticism, was in fact that it was not repeated."[7] The music is gone. Carl either lost it when they moved, or destroyed it as he insisted he had done with all his early works. Judging from the reviews and the earlier songs that are still available, we can assume that he had not yet turned his back on his early style, with no harsh dissonances to disturb audience or players.

He and Charlotte continued to do some solo work, and one of

Carl's few appearances took place on November 8, 1908, when he played the violin obligato for Mrs. Lamberton's "O Divine Redeemer." Charlotte, on the other hand, often did solo work in the churches, and was the alto soloist in "The Messiah" given by the Choral Society under the direction of Horace Seaton on February 4, 1909.

For the 1909–10 season, although the orchestra gave only five concerts, the orchestra management was put on a more solid basis, with officers, directors (which included Carl), a Ladies Auxiliary Board, (including Charlotte), and a Winona Symphony Orchestra Guarantee Fund to which an ever growing number of Winonans contributed. Membership in the orchestra continued to grow, too. News of the orchestra had gone beyond Winona, and Oscar Hatch Hawley, from Minneapolis, wrote about Carl and the orchestra for the December issue of the *Musical Courier*.[8] Carl arranged reprints for the local newspapers.

On the fourth program Charlotte was soloist and her selections included one of Carl's early songs: "Maiden with Thy Mouth of Roses," which he had orchestrated for the occasion. The program notes, also written by Charlotte, stated simply: "This song was composed in 1897 and orchestrated by the composer in 1910."

The orchestra expanded its activities that season, giving a special children's concert in February, and assisting with the public school music program. Caroline Smith from the Normal School also enlisted the orchestra to provide the music for their spring production, "Heart-ease." That spring Carl started an auxiliary orchestra, and according to the newspaper, there were twenty interested players at the first rehearsal on March 4, 1910.

Meanwhile, in January Charlotte had accepted a new position as soloist and choir mistress at the First Congregational Church. However the First Baptist Church persuaded her to stay on, at least through the spring. She agreed to keep the choir, but gave up being their soloist, so for several months she was training two church choirs.

On the final symphony concert of that season Mrs. Lamberton was the soloist, her first appearance with the orchestra since the initial concert two years earlier in 1908. By now Carl's stature had grown considerably. He knew he didn't have to put up with any of her temperamental tantrums, and he was prepared for her. She too realized what was in store, for Carl was a dictator on the podium. Knowing exactly what he wanted, his rehearsals were a special combination of cajoling, swearing, and shouting to whip the musicians into shape. Soloist and conductor got along fine as long as they agreed on interpretation. When they didn't, both erupted. More than once, Mrs.

Lamberton stormed out of rehearsals with Carl swearing at her as she left. But she returned and the final concert of the season went off on schedule.

The annual recital for their private students took place on June 1 at the parish house of the First Congregational Church. One of Charlotte's pupils, Hazel Strong, sang "Thy Presence Ever Near Me," an early song of Carl's published by Arthur P. Schmidt and Co., and Carl presented four violin students. Then the Ruggleses returned East for their summer vacation.

When they returned to Winona in the fall of 1910 they rented another little house, and in its living room to the right of the front door, they installed the old upright piano. Once again lessons were resumed and Charlotte began her work at the church. For Carl it was also a continuation of prior duties: arranging music for the orchestra, doing publicity, and conducting rehearsals. As before there were five programs during the season, but without a doubt the highlight was the First Annual May Festival, under the auspices of the Winona Symphony Orchestra, assisted by the St. Paul Symphony Orchestra at the Opera House on May 1, 1911.

Travel by train was easy in those days, and when Carl and Charlotte wanted a special outing they went to St. Paul for the symphony concert. In the spring of 1909, along with some members of the Musical Literary Society, they had also traveled to LaCrosse, Wisconsin, only twenty-eight miles down the river, to attend Chicago opera presentations of both *Faust* and *Carmen*. That trip had started an idea in Carl's mind. If the orchestra ever became good enough, he wanted to conduct an opera, and shortly after their return to Winona, Carl decided that this was the year to attempt it. He asked the board of the orchestra for their support, which was given wholeheartedly. By the time of the performance nearly every prominent family had at least one member singing in the chorus.

As a way of insuring an orchestra competent and large enough, Carl proposed that the entire St. Paul Symphony come to Winona and give a concert of their own in the afternoon. Then they would join forces with the Winona Orchestra, and, under his baton, perform the opera in the evening. Walter Henry Rothwell, conductor of the St. Paul group, accepted the proposal. *Faust,* by Charles Gounod, was selected, and in January Carl began rehearsals with the chorus. All of Charlotte's pupils sang, but Carl took charge of rehearsing. There were 111 singers: 56 sopranos, 24 altos, 12 tenors, and 19 basses. Several members still remembered that experience when I spoke with them some sixty-three years later. "Carl was not a show-off on the podium," one woman said.

"He was not dramatic except when the music called for it." She added, "His language was terrible! And he was so demanding. It was Jesus this, and Goddamn that—all the time."

Carl's use of colorful language was famous throughout Winona. Young boys would creep into the back of the rehearsal hall just to watch and hear him shout. One such young lad, now a very old man, remembered that Carl "could say shit so you smelled it! 'Shit, start that passage over!' he would say and strike the baton on his music stand." One time he waved the baton so energetically that it got caught in a woman's hairdo. Rehearsals were never dull, but everyone agreed that he inspired them to work hard and to do their very best.

For soloists, Carl had Charlotte sing the mezzo-soprano role of Siebel, and it seemed prudent to invite Mrs. Lamberton to sing the part of Margarita. She accepted. Moreover, she helped to find the two male leads through her vocal coach in Chicago. They were George Harris, Jr., tenor, who sang Faust, and Charles Champlin, bass, who sang Mephistopheles.

By spring there was a frenzy of activity connected with the May Festival. At one rehearsal, just as Carl raised his baton to give the downbeat, Jimmy Rice, the French horn player, jumped the gun and beeped into his horn. Carl turned to him, "Jimmy, did you do that?"

"Not me," Jimmy answered, "the horn did."

One time, Mrs. Lamberton was late for rehearsal, and Carl remarked audibly so that everyone could hear, "She's probably throwing something at her servants."

Tensions grew as the time for the performance drew near. Charlotte tried to calm Carl and keep the peace, but it was not always possible. At the end of the final dress rehearsal, at which Carl had put out four chairs for the soloists close to him and at the front of the stage, Mrs. Lamberton insisted that her chair be larger and more ornate than the others. Carl refused. She demanded. They went back and forth. He swore absolutely no. She shouted back, and they began to call each other names and to swear in front of chorus and orchestra. Finally, she stormed out, shouting that she would not sing at all.

The St. Paul Symphony arrived Sunday morning on the day of the performance for a joint orchestra rehearsal. Then in the afternoon Mr. Rothwell conducted his own group in their concert, while Carl got himself ready for the evening performance and worried whether Mrs. Lamberton would keep her threat. Finally, it was time to assemble at the Opera House. Everyone was there except the leading soprano. Was she really not going to appear? People began to whisper and wonder, while Carl swore and paced up and down. He smoked his cigar furiously and spilled ashes on his rented suit. In desperation he turned to Charlotte, "What shall I do?"

She put her arms around him and said he mustn't be so upset. She would sing both parts, if Mrs. Lamberton didn't appear. Carl protested "You couldn't do that," and Charlotte replied, "Try me." Just then, Mrs. Lamberton arrived — one half hour late.

The performance went off smoothly and triumphantly to an overflowing and enthusiastic audience. Mrs. Lamberton used her chair, but she had not forgotten her anger. She left as quickly as possible, almost before the performance was over, avoiding Carl and the others. Later that night, when Carl was making his way home alone after a jolly after-concert celebration from which Charlotte had left early, someone accosted him in one of the alleys and beat him up. He finally arrived home with a bruised face and black eyes. The assailant was never found, and an ugly rumor was circulated that he had been hired by Mrs. Lamberton's husband to retaliate for the insults that she had suffered from Carl during the rehearsals.[9]

The reviews of the concert were glowing:

The part of Marguerite gave to Mrs. Lamberton numbers splendidly suited to the delicacy and beauty of her voice, and in the final trio, that trying and difficult number, brought out its full power and range.

It was a cause of regret that the part of Siebel gave so little opportunity of hearing Mrs. Ruggles, tho [*sic*] the two numbers for Siebel are each a gem and were given fitting setting in Mrs. Ruggles' interpretation of them.

Mr. Ruggles had his forces under such excellent control that voice and instruments sustained a fine balance throughout the evening.[10]

To Mr. Ruggles' tireless efforts in shaping and drilling the orchestra and chorus, and his broad musicianship in the interpretation of the opera, which was so clearly manifested last night as he led the combined forces of the great orchestra and singers, to him must be given the credit for the greatest musical event in the history of the city.[11]

For Carl the issue was what the professional musicians of the St. Paul Orchestra, not the public, thought of him. It was the first time he had ever conducted a truly professional organization, and he wanted their approval. Christian Timner was concert master of the St. Paul Symphony. An older man who had played in the Amsterdam Concertgebouw Orchestra under Willem Mengelberg, he was a fine violinist, and in the afternoon concert he had been soloist with the orchestra in works by Wagner and Glazunov.

In the evening Carl and Timner shared the same dressing room. When the performance was over and they had both returned to the room, Timner turned to him and began to criticize him in no uncertain terms. "He told me I didn't know a damn thing about conducting. Oh, there had been a few good things—but damn few," Carl remembered. Hurt but undaunted, Carl asked Timner if he would take him on as a conducting student, and to his surprise the older man agreed. "But you probably won't show up," Timner growled. "That's the way you Americans are." He was wrong. Carl did go for lessons, and shortly afterward, he began going up to St. Paul once a week until it was time for summer vacation.

That summer of 1911 was special, for during it Carl and Charlotte took their only trip to Europe. After *Faust,* a group of Winona businessmen that included Hannibal Choate and John Booth, a Winona banker, decided to show their appreciation to the Ruggleses for their contribution to the musical life of the town, and they provided enough money for a six-week trip. Once before when Carl had been working with Paine, he had almost gone abroad. A banker named Beal, according to Carl, had promised to send him. But Mr. Beal had died unexpectedly, putting an end to the plan. Now Carl and Charlotte would go together; it would be their honeymoon trip. They sailed from Boston on July 8, aboard the SS *Canadian,* under Captain Bullock, and both of them performed for the passengers during the voyage.

Wednesday, July 19, Carl and Charlotte were in London at Covent Gardens, where they saw *Madame Butterfly.* Then they went to Paris for a day or two before traveling to The Hague. They remained there for the rest of their stay in Europe, and Carl traveled by trolley every day to Scheveningen, the summer resort nearby. According to the *Republican-Herald,* which reported on their trip, Carl studied conducting with Dr. Ernest Kunwald, conductor of the Berlin Philharmonic, and Charlotte coached with Thomas Denys, bass of the Royal Opera of Berlin.[12]

Equally as important for Carl must have been the talk about the revolutionary changes taking place in music. The young Igor Stravinsky had upset the musical world with his two ballets, *Firebird* and *Petrouchka,* produced by Diaghilev in Paris in 1910 and 1911. Scriabin's *Prometheus, Poem of Fire* for large orchestra, piano, organ, chorus, and the keyboard of light with its new quartal harmony, had been given its first performance in Moscow on March 15, 1911, with Serge Koussevitsky conducting and the composer at the piano. That same year, Arnold Schoenberg had completed his *Gürre-Lieder,* and Ravel's first suite from the ballet, *Daphnis and Chloë,* had been presented in Paris. Mahler's *Das Lied von der Erde* had been given in January 1911. Harmony, melody, rhythm, the use of instruments, all the elements of music were being used in new ways. Changes were occurring in the musical world, and Carl and Charlotte would certainly have encountered them, even if they did not hear the new music.

They remained in Europe until August 5, when they boarded the *Pennsylvania* at Hamburg, Germany, and arrived in New York on August 18.[13] The next two weeks were spent with Boardman Robinson and his wife, the former Sally Whitney, whom they had met in Scituate. Boardman Robinson was a painter and his wife a sculptor. At that time he earned his living mainly as a cartoonist for the *New York Tribune* and other newspapers and journals. Robinson, or Mike as he was called, was born in Nova Scotia in the same year as Carl, and his father really had been a ship captain. Mike was six feet tall with red hair, a beard, and bushy eyebrows. He had studied art in Boston and Paris, loved Emerson and the heroic, was well read and a thinker. He also had a reputation as a wit and a fervent left-wing liberal. Carl admired the big man enormously, and Mike and his wife were to remain his close friends for many years.

On their return to Winona in September 1911 Carl and Charlotte moved into the larger side of a big duplex house on Main Street. This was a good location for Charlotte, since the First Congregational Church was just down the alley; and Charliebelle Paris Hillyer, her friend and the organist of the church, lived across the street. Central Park was also nearby. Carl and Charlotte didn't have much furniture but they did at last get a grand piano for the living room. Years later Carl explained that they had been given the piano. The company, MacPhail in Boston, had shipped it out for one of the soloists performing with the symphony, and afterward they told Carl he could have it, if he would note on the concert programs their name. It's a good story, but it's not true. There were no piano soloists with the orchestra and none of the programs ever mentioned a piano. Probably it was a rented instrument or one that had been given to them by a friend.

Carl resumed his weekly conducting lessons with Timner. Whenever it was possible, he would go in the morning so he could attend the St. Paul symphony rehearsals; then in the afternoon he would have his lesson. They studied the scores that Timner was playing in the orchestra. Timner would play the violin and Carl, pretending there was a full orchestra before him, would conduct. At every point, Carl remembered, Timner would stop and criticize him. Baton technique and interpretation went hand in hand at the lessons, which continued throughout the year.

For this season, there were only four concerts, but two were opera programs. Carl presented Mascagni's *Cavalleria Rusticana* at the second concert in February, and for the Spring Festival he chose *Carmen*. By this time the orchestra numbered around sixty and its reputation was growing. They gave a concert in Rochester, Minnesota, the first and only out of town performance, and Carl orchestrated Hollmann's "Chanson d'Amour" so Charlotte could be soloist. Rochester received them well.

The Spring Festival took place on April 25, 1912. This time the chorus numbered 107: 48 sopranos, including Charlotte, 22 altos, 13 tenors, and 24 basses. To avoid problems, all the soloists came from out of town. The St. Paul orchestra as before, performed in the afternoon, and the opera began at 8:15 P.M. It was a stunning success, and this time even Timner was satisfied. His pupil was doing admirably.

The newspapers raved: "Winona music lovers were present to enjoy the treat of the musical season, and their anticipations were fully realized. . . . The Second Annual Festival was epoch making in every sense of the word."[14]

Once again there were the student recitals and final church duties before Carl and Charlotte could leave for the summer. And this summer was different.

NOTES

1. Much of the information on Winona came from Jan Saecker, "Carl Ruggles in Winona" (Master's thesis, Winona State College, 1967).

2. *Republican Herald,* 20 Apr. 1907.

3. *Republican-Herald,* 31 May 1907.

4. Ibid.

5. *Winona Independent,* 8 Apr. 1908.

6. *Winona Independent,* 1 May 1908.

7. *Republican-Herald* and *Winona Independent,* 2 Dec. 1908.

8. Oscar Hatch Hawley, "Music in Winona," *Musical Courier,* 1 Dec. 1909, 15.

9. Several people who had participated in the festival told me the story when I was in Winona doing research.

10. *Winona Independent,* 2 May 1911.

11. *Republican-Herald,* 2 May 1911.

12. *Republican-Herald,* 31 Aug. 1911.

13. I am indebted to John Kirkpatrick, Carl's music executor, for the exact dates of their trip.

14. *Republican-Herald* and *Winona Independent,* 26 Apr. 1912.

4

The Opera
1912–18

Carl and Charlotte had been spending part of their summers at Scituate for some time, and this summer was no exception. When they returned to Winona at the end of the summer, the *Republican-Herald* reported: "While at Scituate they were the guests of Inez Haynes Gillmore, the novelist.... They were also guests for a week of Boardman Robinson, cartoonist on the New York Tribune."[1] But that is only part of the story.

Over the years the Gillmores had become the center of a small group of artists who annually gathered for their summer vacations on the second cliff over the causeway in Scituate in an area known as "The Writers' Roost." They worked and played, and talked and argued over politics, art, or any other subject, after noisy and hard-hitting games of tennis. Those who visited were divided into two classes: the "regulars and the once-in-a-whiles." According to the *Boston Sunday Post*, in the former class were: "Mr. and Mrs. Rufus Gillmore, Samuel Merwin and Mrs. Merwin, Will Irwin, Mrs. Jacques Futrelle, Ralph Renault and Mrs. Renault, Carl Ruggles, the composer, Franklin Clarkin and Robert Hale and his wife, Mrs. Beatrice Forbes-Robertson Hale. The once-in-a-whiles, who manage to creep out from New York for a week or two at a time, include Franklin P. Adams, Samuel Hopkins Adams, Boardman Robinson, the cartoonist, Gelett Burgess, Maude Radford Warren and Miriam Finn Scott."[2]

That summer there was much talk about the the revolutionary changes taking place in the arts. At the time, Boardman Robinson was a contributing cartoonist to *The Masses* and a friend of John Sloan, art editor of the magazine and member of The Eight, a somewhat notorious group of painters who believed in painting scenes from the everyday life of the poor people of the cities, a view that Robinson shared.[3]

Carl in turn held forth on the new developments in music—the breakdown in tonality and the new sounds.[4] Others contributed from their knowledge of the concerts in Boston and New York during the previous season, mostly decrying the lack of adventure and excitement in the programs. This was a heady atmosphere for Carl, and it fueled his desire to return to composition, something he had been hankering to do more and more. The orchestra had taken much of his time and energy these past years, but it had not satisfied his creative need. He wanted to tackle something big and important, and all that artistic talk only increased his yearning to work anew at the problems of composition.

During their visit with the Robinsons in New York before they returned to the Midwest, Carl renewed his friendship with the artists he had met the previous year, and Robinson introduced him to George Bellows and John Sloan. Carl also met Dr. Frederick H. Bartlett, the distinguished pediatrician and close friend of the Robinsons. A Harvard graduate of the class of 1895, Dr. Bartlett delighted in the company of artists and he and Carl immediately liked each other.

At another gathering that week, Carl and Charlotte met Charles Henry Meltzer, a writer who was also known as a journalist, music critic, author, and translator of works from French and German. Meltzer, who was older than Carl and Robinson, was an English native, son of Russian-born parents, and he and his wife, Anne, had come to the United States in 1888. He had been drama and music critic for the *New York Herald* and the *New York World,* and he had also been assistant and secretary to Maurice Grau and Heinrich Conried at the Metropolitan Opera Company. Several of his translations of plays had been produced and favorably received in New York and his English translations of opera librettos had also been acclaimed.

Meltzer was most proud of his translation of Gerhart Hauptmann's play "Die versunkene Glocke" (The Sunken Bell), which Hauptmann had written in 1897. Two years later, with the personal approval of Hauptmann himself, Meltzer had made an English version of the play, "freely rendered into English verse," which E. H. Sothern, the famous actor-producer, had produced in New York in March 1900 with himself and his first wife, Virginia Harned, as the leading characters. It ran for only two weeks to mixed notices, but Meltzer's verse was praised.

Meltzer was convinced that "The Sunken Bell" would make a fine opera, if only he could find the right composer; and because he knew both Grau and Conried, he was sure he could interest the management of the Metropolitan to produce it. All he needed was an exciting composer, and that night Meltzer found his composer. Carl and he must have talked for long hours and doubtless met several times during the Ruggleses' stay. By the time Carl and Charlotte left for Winona, several decisions had been made. He and Meltzer were to meet again, soon, for further discussions, and Meltzer was to discuss a possible production with the management of the Metropolitan Opera. Meanwhile Carl was to begin work on the opera immediately.

This decision was the crucial one in Carl's life, the turning point. There is no question that he could have continued conducting the orchestra in Winona. The previous season had been highly successful, and there were plenty of financial backers to help the orchestra grow and improve. For that matter Carl himself might have had a successful career in conducting, but that was not what he wanted. His one ambition was to be a famous and successful composer. He was thirty-six years old. If he did not make the attempt soon, it would be too late.

To Carl and Charlotte it seemed such a fortuitous opportunity that they could not fail. A libretto written by a famous German playwright, translated by an experienced writer who knew all the right people at the most important opera company in the United States, and distinguished friends in New York who were sure of its success. It was almost too good to be true, and there were moments when Carl worried and wondered if he was up to the task. But Charlotte had no doubts. She believed in him and his talent absolutely. By the time they arrived in Winona, they had agreed that Carl would devote all his energies to the composition of the new work, except for giving a few private lessons. He would give up the orchestra, and Charlotte would bear the brunt of supporting them. Perhaps this is the period in their lives when she coined the phrase that she would often voice throughout the difficult years ahead: "Let genius burn."

On their return they moved quietly back into their house at 321 Main Street. Charlotte resumed her activities as choir director and soloist with the First Congregational Church, and they both began their private lessons. There was no official announcement that Carl would not direct the orchestra, but everyone soon knew, for once Carl had told one person, the news spread rapidly by word of mouth. His decision was further confirmed when he went to New York for another series of conferences with Meltzer in early November 1912. Five years later, again in New York, he sent a postcard to Charlotte in Winona, reminiscing about the 1912 visit: "Do you know it was just 5 years ago election night that I was in N.Y. and stayed with M- [Meltzer] at Staten I? Five years on the Bell. Five years of sacrifice on your part. Let us pray to God that it will prove worth it all."[5]

Shortly thereafter he returned to Winona to resume the huge task of writing the great opera. In February 1913, after six months work, he apparently decided that a public announcement was in order, and the *Winona Independent* carried the story with great fanfare: "Winona Man as Composer Gains Fame" was the headline. The subheading continued: "Carl Ruggles Composing A Grand Opera Under Contract of New York Company To Require Two Years Liberetto [*sic*] Being Written By One of Nation's Foremost Literary Leaders": "Already Mr. Ruggles has spent two years on the music of this opera, and last November, it has been learned, he submitted the music in its embryonic form to the New York producers. It was thought so highly of that the contract was immediately drawn up. The work is to be competed [*sic*] two years from the date of the contract."[6]

Typical of Carl, exaggerations and misinformation abound in the article. He had not been working on the opera for the past two years. He had not submitted the music, even in "embryonic form," to New York producers, and there was no contract. He would also live to regret his own public promise to complete the opera in two years, for he was to work on it far longer. A minimum of seven or eight years would have been closer to the truth.

The Ruggleses lived as cheaply as they could and kept their social life to a minimum. Charlotte had far more students than he did, so he scheduled his pupils when she was not busy. One student remembered that he took his violin lessons early in the morning, and once arrived when Carl was having breakfast. Carl told him to go into the living room, tune up, and begin playing his lesson. Meanwhile Carl continued eating in the kitchen and shouted corrections and criticisms between mouthfuls. He could work on the opera only when he had access to the piano, so he spent many hours walking or sitting in the park just across the street, sometimes drawing the scenes in black and white in his sketchbook. And he began to take his drawing seriously.

In the spring of 1912 another artist had come to Winona from the East. Rockwell Kent, the painter, then working for the architectural firm of Lord, Hewlett and Tallent, was sent from New York to supervise the building of twin homes for the Prentiss and Bell families, whose wives were sisters. Mr. Prentiss was a banker, and Mr. Bell was head of the local lumber mill. Kent lived simply and sparsely in Winona, riding a horse to and from work and painting whenever he had spare time. Like Carl, he was considered an eccentric in the town; but unlike Carl, he chose his friends from among the workers. Still, Mr. Prentiss liked him, and in May of 1913 he offered Kent an opportunity to show his paintings in the rotunda of the town library. In his autobiography Kent wrote about that show: "I really thought that the show looked grand: I did . . . so did just one man, a strange, intense little man, a bald egg-headed little man, with eyes that were alight with fervor, and a protruding lower lip that could betoken such conceit and arrogance as might defy the world, or tremble with emotion close to tears. He was alone in the rotunda of the library when I entered. He walked straight over to me and reached out his hand. 'You,' he said, 'are a *great* painter.'... He was the Carl Ruggles so widely known in the music world today."[7]

For Carl it was the beginning of a long and fruitful friendship. Through their letters we can glimpse the ups and downs of Carl's moods as he struggled to complete the opera, which he had been working on for a year and a half. Carl hoped to go to New York in June 1914 to meet with Meltzer again, but the trip was too costly and he was not feeling well that summer. Instead they went to Charlotte's parents, who were running a boarding house in Lawrence, where they could have their own quarters. In July Meltzer met him in Boston to discuss the work, since it was nearly time for its completion if Carl intended to have it finished in two years. Afterward Carl wrote to Kent: "Did I tell you what they said of my work in the East? Well, I told them that telling me that I was better than any ones [*sic*] here, amounted to nothing. It was how it compared with the best in Europe."[8]

It is important to remember the phrase, "compared with the best in Europe," for it is crucial to an understanding of Carl's attitude toward his work. It was to Europe he looked for his equals, or if these were dead, possibly for his superiors. With few exceptions, and there were a few, he looked with disdain on his fellow American composers. He wanted his music on the world stage, and for the rest of his life he would insist on rating composers, with himself close to the top.

Carl and Charlotte's life took a happy turn that year when they learned that Charlotte was pregnant, with the baby due in the late spring. Even though they had to live frugally, these years in Winona were not altogether unpleasant for them. Their rich friends and patrons often invited them for meals or for events at the Opera House. When the weather was balmy, on Sunday afternoons they were invited for boat rides on the Mississippi River, and sometimes were taken for drives outside of town. Carl and Charlotte were especially close to Hannibal Choate and his wife, whom Carl now called "Mother Choate." He and Hannibal would trade stories with each other, the more salacious the better, and the big house would be filled with their laughter.

All his life Carl sought his friends among the rich or the artistic, and if a person combined both traits, he or she was especially sought after. With his cigar in his mouth or waved about in his hand, he could be charming. He was a good storyteller; everyone attests to that. He could quote at length from the nineteenth-century poets and put on grand airs with a great flourish. There was, and perhaps still is, a traditional interest among the rich in being a patron of the arts and in helping struggling artists. Of course the artists were thought to be eccentric and slightly outside the structure of society, but if they were good fellows and fun to be with, then it was quite all right to befriend them. In Winona, Carl and Charlotte, especially Carl, suited the role exactly.

Charlotte was more than an eccentric artist to these people, and they recognized that. She was a tall, striking-looking woman and a real lady. Her students adored her and everyone respected her. She had such a lovely singing voice that even people who did not belong to the First Congregational Church would attend services there if Charlotte was going to sing a solo.

Anne Ahern, one of Charlotte's favorite pupils and friend, was often helpful to both of them. Sometimes she would borrow a car from her fiancé, Dr. Sam Schaefer, and drive Carl up the river for a little way or out to Lake Winona on the other side of town. Then she would leave him there to draw; when he was ready to return, he went to a nearby house and telephoned for her to come and get him. When he didn't like the drawings, he would tear them up, or give them to her by way of thanks. The sketches were all in black and white, she remembered, and of varying sizes, including some very large ones.

Charlotte was a "terrible" housekeeper. Neither she nor Carl minded living in a messy home. For one thing, Charlotte was too busy, and Carl was not very helpful around the house. There were always big sheets of music paper on top of the piano — Carl's manuscript, and music of other composers; sheet music and books lay strewn all about the rooms. Over all these papers were dust and ashes from Carl's cigars or cigarettes, for they both smoked, and the ashtrays were always full. Often before their return in the fall, they would write to Anne, asking her to clean their house on Main Street so it would be ready for them. Once she went into the basement to check on the furnace and discovered that instead of taking the ashes outside during the cold weather, Carl had simply dumped them beside the furnace there in the basement. The pile had grown so large it interfered with opening and closing the furnace door.[9]

Charlotte worked at the church until Sunday, April 18. She and Carl presented their students in recital on May 10, and on May 25, 1915, their son was born. He was named Micah Haskell after his great-great-grandfather. "Mother Choate" was his godmother. Dr. Tweedy delivered the baby, and Mrs. Schaefer remembered being at the hospital with them. While Charlotte was in labor, Carl stood outside the room playing his violin to soothe and comfort her, and probably himself as well. Afterward he said that Micah, when he was born, had "pink hair."

The next two years went by much as the others, though now Carl had to help take care of Micah. On Sundays especially, while Charlotte was in church, it was his job to care for the baby. When the weather was good, they would go across the street to the park where Micah could play while Carl read or sketched. Private lessons and Charlotte's church job continued to be the mainstay of their existence. As before, Carl put together a small orchestra for the annual Christmas and Easter cantatas that he conducted. Carl's rehearsal and conducting techniques hadn't changed a bit. At one Easter service he swung his baton so wildly that it clipped one of the lilies in the floral arrangement and sent it flying through the church.

Through it all, of course, work was continuing on the opera. The number of large pages with the ruled staves continued to grow. Carl was already several years past the two year deadline he had set for himself, and doubtless he was now under pressure from Meltzer, his librettist, as well as from his friends, to put the finishing touches to it. Nineteen sixteen–nineteen seventeen should have been the year of its completion, but it was not; he just kept on working at it.

The United States officially declared war on April 6, 1917, and while Carl was too old to enter the service, many young men from Winona, including several of their students, rushed to enlist in the armed services. Unhappily the anti-German sentiment that swept the country reached irrational proportions. Artists and musicians from Germany working in the United States were suspect. Even Karl Muck, conductor of the Boston Symphony, encountered problems; and of course all music by German composers, living or dead, was banned. Carl and Meltzer must have wondered about the fate of their opera, but Carl slogged on.

On the first of July the Ruggleses took the train to Boston to spend their summer in the East, and when autumn came, another crucial family decision had been made, doubtless influenced by friends. As the *Republican-Herald* wrote: "Mrs. Carl Ruggles has returned from the East, having spent the most of the summer in study in Maine. Her little son Micah accompanied her back. . . . Mr. Ruggles did not accompany her back, as his work the coming year connected with the publication of the opera upon which he has been working for the past six years, will keep him in New York City."[10]

Let us stop now and look at *The Sunken Bell*. The libretto of *The Sunken Bell* is a strange mixture of myth and folklore that moves back and forth between the world of humans and the realm of elves and witches. Heinrich, the hero, is a young Silesian bell-founder who has fashioned his most beautiful bell, which he is moving up the mountain to be placed in the belfrey of a new forest chapel. Since the wood sprites are opposed to the world of humans, especially to their religions and the sounds thereof, they cause the bell to fall off the wagon and roll deep into a lake. Heinrich tries to save the bell and narrowly escapes drowning. Ill and distraught, he wanders into the home of the elves. A beautiful elf named Rautendelein, the heroine, sees him and falls in love with him, though she is warned about the world of men by Nickelmann, the Old Frog in the Well, who wishes to marry her himself. The neighbors find Heinrich and bear him home to his wife, Magda, and their two small sons. Rautendelein follows him and without his wife's knowledge, casts a spell that brings him back to health and strength.

Heinrich, who now loves only Rautendelein, goes with her back to the mountains. They live in a mountain cave, and the goblins are pressed into service to help him cast sweeter sounding bells than ever before. Not even the pleading of the village pastor who finds their home can persuade Heinrich to return to the world of men. But when he sees a vision of his two little sons carrying a heavy urn filled with their mother's tears, and when he hears the tolling of the sunken bell struck from the depths of the lake by Magda, his wife, who has drowned herself, his illusion is shattered. Heinrich dies in the arms of Rautendelein, who cannot save him and who becomes, at last, the consort of Nickelmann.[11]

Opera libretti, it is true, are often illogical and full of bizarre accounts, and this one is surely no exception. The problems of staging might be overcome, but to make the world of humans and the world of wood sprites equally believable and not comic would present the most serious difficulties. Perhaps Meltzer felt that with music this could be solved.

What is fascinating is that he chose Carl to do the music without ever having heard any of Carl's compositions. He chose him because his friends, especially Boardman Robinson, said he should. Meltzer admired Robinson's work and independence. When Robinson introduced him to Carl and told him that Carl was a strong modern composer, Meltzer was impressed. And once they had become acquainted, it is clear that they liked each other; that was enough for the librettist.

As far as we know, Carl had never written or even attempted any large compositions before this time. The only instrumental piece we know about is the "Valse de Concert" that he conducted with the orchestra in Winona. The music is not extant, but from the reviews of the concert there is nothing to indicate that it was strikingly original or modern. His only other compositions were the art songs. One wonders why his friends, not only Boardman Robinson, thought of him as a modern composer, and the answer is simply that Carl said so. None had heard his music, but he spoke so eloquently and persuasively about his art, and so knowingly, that each assumed this little man with the big voice really composed the way he talked.

For Carl, the offer to collaborate on the opera with Meltzer must have seemed an opportunity of a lifetime. Meltzer's accomplishments, his European background, and all his travels and worldly knowledge impressed Carl, who was honored to be associated with this man. The opera would be his introduction to the artistic world of New York where he felt he belonged and where he hoped to gain fame and fortune. Carl had an exalted view of the artist as not only set apart from society but slightly superior to it, and with the opera he hoped to join this august group.

The music came slowly. In fact, it was never finished, though he worked at it exclusively from 1912 to 1918, and intermittently until 1921. Boardman Robinson may have been the catalyst that started the project, but it was Rockwell Kent in whom Carl confided most frequently about his work. In November 1913 Carl wrote to Kent that his work was "getting on splendidly."

"I too am working ceaselessly," he wrote the next month. "We think now the opera will be ready for production by next October." Several weeks later Carl wrote: "I have just made a new Bell motive. It is like nothing in all the world. Will send it to you *written plainly*." By April 1914 Carl was beginning to have some misgivings about the project. It was hard work, and he wrote that the "labor of composition is most fatiguing. I rather think it will be, when finished the best and most original music since Wagner. But it is a hard grind at times, and then I become dispirited, but then again when I see what the other[s] have done, and are doing I take heart."[12]

But the opera was by no means finished. In May 1915 Carl wrote: "The 'Bell' is deepening, and growing sharper in character," and again in September, "I have been trying to finish the 'Bell.' " By the fall of 1917, pressure from Meltzer and other friends, and encouragement from Charlotte persuaded him to take the fateful step and move to New York. Though the opera was still not finished, it was far enough along to be shown to opera managers, and he struggled to complete it during that year. In October he went to visit Meltzer at his home on Staten Island, and he wrote to Charlotte: "We have cut out III Act and saved about an hour and 6 months work. . . . Today I made some of the most wonderful harmonies for the very last strains, mystic and symbolic bells, heard way up in the wings."[13]

Meltzer wrote to Carl the next month that he had spoken to Arthur Bodansky at the Metropolitan Opera Company, and Carl reported that Bodansky was interested and wanted to see the score. In early February Meltzer read the opera to Gatti and told Carl that he could play it to the "powers that be" whenever he was ready. Finally, by April Carl felt sufficiently finished to ask his old friend, Alfred DeVoto, to come down from Boston to play the work for Otto Kahn.[14] Unfortunately Kahn was in England on matters related to the war effort, so Meltzer arranged for Carl to see another businessman, named Wigham, who might be able to influence Kahn to produce the work. But now Carl admitted that the anti-German sentiment was a problem.

He told Charlotte that Meltzer and he felt that they would have to change the names of the characters in the opera. Rautendelein was to become Rose Eglantine; Magda became Martha; and Heinrich, Harold. Carl found Rose Eglantine acceptable, but had reservations about the name of Harold for the leading male role. Meltzer, too, was beginning to feel discouraged, and in a letter to Carl, he wondered gloomily if they would ever get a hearing. In fact, they did not. The opera was never produced and Carl never finished it. He continued to work at it occasionally, but gradually he turned his attention to other compositions and soon the "Bell" was completely ignored. Later he destroyed most of it, telling everyone that the strong anti-German sentiment in this country had precluded a production. That is certainly part of the truth, but the rest is that Carl simply could not complete it. It was too big for him, and he never again attempted to compose a work of that magnitude.

Though Carl insisted that he had destroyed the "Bell," small pieces of it were found among his papers after his death. In addition he sent snatches from it to Kent and to Charlotte while he was composing. Enough remains to give us an idea of his struggle and what the opera might have sounded like.

The early fragments, say from 1912 to 1913, show his style firmly rooted in the late nineteenth century: tonal with chromatic harmonies, and seventh and ninth chords. The later sketches from 1918 show real changes: with a marked increase in dissonances, in the use of polychords, and a genuine break with tonality. For example, here are two Heinrich motives only a year apart from each other, yet they show major differences. Both were sent to Kent, the first in December 1913 (example 1), the second in November 1914 (example 2).

Example 1. A Heinrich motive from the "Bell" (1 Dec. 1913 letter to Kent). Here and elsewhere, Ruggles's notation has been copied as exactly as possible.

Example 2. A second Heinrich motive from the "Bell" (11 Nov. 1914 letter to Kent).

We should note a number of things. The most obvious is the enormous increase in chromaticisms in example 2, and the two large dissonant skips: a major seventh and a diminished octave. The range is much wider in example 2, and it is written in octaves to give it even more force. This latter sketch already exhibits two characteristics that were to remain a part of Carl's new ultramodern style: the use of extreme ranges (note the peak A flat octave) and the contour of his melodies, which moved wave-like, as he wrote, "from the depths to the heights, and again to the depths."

The first sketch moves from the D flat major triad to the B flat seventh chord. The high C flat suspended note resolving at last to the B flat is very Wagnerian, recalling one of Carl's heroes. If we could hear the two examples, the differences would become even more obvious. Example 1 sounds yearning and romantic; example 2 infinitely more anguished and dramatic.

Here are two more examples from December 20, 1913, and February 1918 (see examples 3 and 4). Example 4 was sent to Charlotte: "This is the finale of Act II the first draft. Subject to changes, but isn't the chord marked ( ) wonderful. You keep rolling the top notes so that they can sound through. Be sure to play the low E flat."[15]

Example 3. From pp. 84–85 of the libretto for the "Bell" (20 Dec. 1913 letter to Kent).

The differences between these two examples are apparent even to the eye. Example 4 is more complex, has a larger range, and is much more dissonant. Example 3 shows Carl still writing in the late-nineteenth-century style of chromatic harmony. Notice the string of seventh chords from beat two of the second measure through to the end of the example, and the obvious chromatic line from the high G in measure one down to the final B flat. Only the D sharp or E flat, its enharmonic equivalent, is missing. Also, the rhythm is much simpler and more obvious in the earlier example—though we cannot discuss rhythm too much with these as examples, for they were hastily written out and Carl was lax about writing exactly what he meant. What interested him at that time were the new sound combinations he was creating.

Example 4 shows him well on his way toward those new sounds. The chromatic lines are still there but are less obvious. See the middle voice in measure two, and note the major seconds (whole steps) right together. See, too, in measure three, the last held notes in the middle part of the top score, the B, C, E, F sharp, and G sharp, while the melody provides the E flat (D sharp) and D flat (C sharp) and the bass G. Here are dissonant sounds, generally though not always, approached linearly, that is, without skips. This was to be another characteristic of his modern style.

The chord that pleased Carl so much shows us some more char-

Example 4. Finale of act II, first draft curtain, for the "Bell" (10 Feb. 1918 letter to Charlotte).

acteristics of his new style. The notes as he wrote them from bottom
upward are: E flat, C natural, G sharp, F, B natural, C sharp with G
and B flat tied over from the previous measure. If the sharps are changed
to their flat equivalents (or vice versa) thus: E flat, C, A flat, F, B natural,
D flat, G, B flat, it is immediately apparent that the chord is made of
several triads, a polychord: F minor, A flat major, E flat major, to name
only a few of the possibilities. One can also see it as a series of thirds,
or a thirteenth chord starting on F with the eleventh, both B flat and
B natural, thus: F-A flat-C-E flat-G-(B flat-B natural)-D flat. Now of
course we don't know how Carl thought of this combination except
that he particularly liked it. In fact, he liked it so well that he continued
using similar chords for the rest of his career. It was the ambiguous
nature of the sound that he liked, the combination of several triads.
He even chose one such combination as his musical signature and used
it on greeting cards to friends.

The use of thirds, too, was another trait that stayed with him. He
still liked that sweet sound, and it nicely offset the harshness of some
of the other dissonances. Moreover, the traditional system of harmony
is based on thirds; Carl was nurtured on that system, and it continued,
underneath, as a part of his style. Long tied or held notes were also
a trademark of his style. Often he approached his dissonant combinations by this means, and in this example we may note how long the
top third is held, the G and B flat. These are the final high notes, too,
but an octave higher, the extreme range from the low E flat in the
bass to the high B flat in the soprano.

One more vocal example (see example 5) will suffice to show us
how far he had come. He sent this to Charlotte and wrote of the notes
encircled: "this is fine so far, the other must come."[16] Those four notes
show us a hint of Carl's newly developed sense of melody. The motion
from the F sharp down to the F natural in the lower octave, the
augmented octave, a dissonance, is emphasized, along with a touch of
word painting by using "deep" on the lowest tone. By comparison the
notes that follow are indeed commonplace. His judgment was correct.

None of this was a system for Carl. We would be very mistaken if
we believed that he had rules for writing. He did not. All his life he
worked by trial and error. Pounding on the piano, singing, shouting,
trying first one sound combination, then another and another. On and
on it went, painfully and slowly, until at last he had the right notes in
the proper places; not because they obeyed certain rules of harmony,
but because they sounded right to his ear. Sometimes he couldn't be
sure. Then he was beset by doubts; as we have seen, he finally gave
up on this work. Still, composing the opera was not really a failure.

Example 5. A vocal example from the "Bell" (10 Feb. 1918 letter to Charlotte).

In those years of such hard work Carl gradually forged his own dissonant style of writing. He had learned to write in an ultramodern way and in his own unique voice. The "Bell" was central to Carl's life as a composer and by no means unsuccessful, even though it was neither completed nor produced.

Carl came to New York City at the end of August 1917, and after visiting briefly in Forest Hills with Eugene Schoen, whom he had met through Robinson, he moved into the city to live at the home of Dr. Fred Bartlett.[17] Carl could use the piano and work there undisturbed during the day, since the doctor's wife was out of town, but it was only a temporary solution until he could find other living and working quarters.

Dr. Bartlett belonged to the Harvard Club, and he immediately arranged for Carl to make use of it as well. During that year Carl went there nearly every day either for lunch, or to read, relax, and write letters on Harvard Club stationery. He did this so often and to so many of his friends and correspondents that it gave rise to the conviction that he himself had graduated from Harvard, something that Carl never denied.

Three main threads run through Carl's life during this year: the opera, the need for money, and, especially, loneliness. It was the first time he and Charlotte had been separated for such a long time, and he missed her and Micah, now two-and-a-half years old, very much. They wrote to each other at least once a week, often more frequently, and their love and their loneliness, as well as their determination to sacrifice everything for Carl's work, come through clearly as one reads their correspondence: "Worked 3 hours this morning, but it was so hard to be alone and the house was cold. It seems more difficult for me each day to be away from you and Micah, but I'm going to stick it out. We will both be brave won't we darling? Do write as often as you can, it is the only thing that is worthwhile."[18]

Bartlett, Schoen, and Robinson were already arranging for Carl to meet the people of wealth who were the art patrons in the city. Before the month was out he had been introduced to Mrs. Harry Payne Whitney, and when Charlotte heard the news she wrote: "You are flying high. Mrs. H. P. Whitney is up in the solar system, isn't she?"[19]

Charlotte and Micah were living at Mrs. Bannon's Boarding House, and while she did her teaching, Mrs. Bannon looked after Micah. If Mrs. Bannon had other commitments, then Charlotte hired one of the older boys to care for him. This year most of her students were girls, for most of the young men had gone into the service.

Money was the main problem, and Carl was determined to find something that would enable him to stay East and to bring Charlotte and Micah to him. When he talked with Robinson and "Dr. Fred" and Schoen, the latter thought he might be able to help. The American Socialist Society, in which Schoen was active, published the *New York Call* and operated the Rand School of Social Science. Since Schoen was on the board of directors of the school, he thought he might be able to secure employment for Carl through the society.[20] By a happy coincidence the *Call* was looking for a new music critic, and Schoen urged Carl to apply for the job. He did, confident that he would get the position given Schoen's influence, but much to his disappointment he was not hired.

Meanwhile Charlotte wrote that she too was working hard. She had given six lessons in one afternoon; another time she taught from 3:00 to 9:15 P.M., and she was trying to keep up with the bills. What should she do about the insurance? she asked, and sent Carl ten dollars. To save money, Carl gave up cigars and began to smoke a pipe. She promised that she would send him more money and added that she had been "very extravagant." She had "bought some chrysanthemums 75 cts yellow ones. I just got hungry for some flowers."[21]

In the meantime Carl wrote more about the Rand School. He had gone to see some plays there and he thought they were fine. And Schoen had another plan for Carl, one that pleased him even more than being a music critic. "We are going to start the orchestra," Carl wrote. "There is no doubt about that. And it will be great."[22] The Rand School did offer cultural courses along with their other subjects in political and social sciences. There were classes in poetry and literature, in dancing and art; and there was the Rand School Chorus directed by Sigfried Jacobssohn. It was Schoen's plan to persuade the board of directors to establish an orchestra with Carl as the director, but first the board would have to approve.

"Dr. Fred" also had a scheme for helping Carl. Among his patients were the children of Mr. and Mrs. Joseph Grace of the Grace Lines.

He knew that Mrs. Grace was an accomplished musician and interested in composition. He asked her if she would like to study with Carl, and to everyone's delight, she replied in the affirmative. "Think of the Graces," Carl wrote happily: "Dr. Fred spoke to her yesterday telling her I would be glad to teach her. And for her to fix the time. Dr. says $25.00 for the afternoon. It seems a lot doesn't it? What do you think? Shall I abide by Dr. Fred's decision? Lessons here are always $10.00 per hour, that is by the heads of departments. I will have to give up my whole afternoon, it takes an hour to go in there in an auto. Mrs. Grace is to send the *Rolls Royce* for me [the Graces lived in Great Neck, Long Island]."[23]

Charlotte's reply was ecstatic:

It really seems to [*sic*] good to be true, and I walked over to the window then looked in the mirror afraid that I was dreaming— Could you really charge her $25.00 for one lesson—I will be on pins and needles until I know that you have really gone—

I had a balance of $1.15 in the bank—this morning I deposited $16.25—I paid out 3.00 for Micah shoes

7.50 for board
1.75 to Barbara

12.25. Olive Schultz owes 6.25 and Harriet Gillett 6.25.[24]

Before Carl could reply, Dr. Fred's wife, Lieska, returned home, and Carl moved to share an apartment on Madison Avenue with Harry Andrews, another friend of the doctor. Carl assured Charlotte that Andrews was a fine man, and certainly one of the kindest, for he refused to allow Carl to pay anything toward the rent on the apartment, saying that he was lonely and grateful for the company.

Meanwhile it was agreed that lessons with Mrs. Grace would begin in December, and if she came to town for them, Carl would only charge fifteen dollars, but if he had to go out to Long Island, she would pay the twenty-five dollars. Before they started Carl sent a financial report to Charlotte: "Have been in N.Y. 3 months, and it has cost me $58. 2 checks $25 each and 8.00 in bills. Some record—what? .60 cents a day. *I think I can plan for the dinners. You must pay on the insurance*. In the meantime I will get on some way."[25] Mrs. Grace's fee was surely going to be welcome, but Carl explained that she would be paying by the month. He would have to teach through December before her check would arrive in January.

The holiday season was a sad time for both of them. They had hoped that Charlotte would be able to come East for Christmas, but clearly that was too costly for them. They had to be content with sending presents to each other and planning for the summer. "One of my disappointments at not coming to New York is that I cannot meet Harry Andrews," Charlotte wrote: "Any one that could live with you Carl dear this long and not at times want to poison you is a person after my own heart—I hope you don't wear his clothes and borrow his laundry—I must write him and warn him."[26]

Still, they began the new year with hope. Schoen once again talked with Carl about the plans for an orchestra at the Rand School, and he indicated that it was a real possibility. Carl was so excited about the prospect that he wrote to Charlotte and asked for the orchestral scores that he had left behind. The lessons with Mrs. Grace had begun and Carl was enjoying them. "You should hear Mrs. Grace's piece, it is fine," he wrote. "Of course, I made it so, but never less [sic], it is a fine first attempt, and Joe [Mrs. Grace's husband] is *delighted* about it all. *It all helps.*"[27]

Meanwhile Charlotte wrote that she was now giving twenty-eight voice lessons a week in addition to her work at the church. For Valentine's Day she sent a valentine to Carl and one to Harry Andrews as well. Carl had forgotten about the holiday and begged forgiveness. She forgave him, but in the last week of February she reminded him that her birthday was on March 1, "and woe to you if you forget— I don't care what you send something that cost a nickle [sic] but I don't want to be forgotten."[28]

As the months went by, the separation did not get any easier. They tried to express their love, and when Carl wrote that she was wonderful, Charlotte replied, "I loved your last letter. It is wonderful to be thought great and beautiful whether you are or not." When she wrote an especially loving letter to him, he said that he would carry it with him always. Sometimes he asked her to send him a love letter to help ease his loneliness, and hoping to bolster his spirits, Carl invented a saying: "*Adage:* 'who so bloweth not his own horn, the same shall not be blown.' "[29]

Whenever the Boston Symphony Orchestra performed in New York, Carl attended with Lieska. He was not very fond of Lieska, whom he thought rather scatterbrained and inefficient, but he could not dismiss her completely because she was good to him, and because she sincerely enjoyed music, even his. Lieska often invited musicians to their home, and thanks to her he was meeting other musicians in the city. "She [Lieska] has been very sweet to me for a long time," Carl wrote. "I suppose she thinks I have the stuff. Her ear is quite good for modern music. You would laugh to hear her go for anybody who criticizes my music. . . . Henry Cowles [*sic*] praise, she says, is what she knew all the time. . . . Anyhow she has the faculty to feel and pick out the finest pasages [*sic*]."[30] This letter contains the first mention of Henry Cowell, and from the misspelling of his name we can assume they had met only recently. Cowell was to play a very important role in Carl's career, and this is one more instance of the chain reaction brought about by Carl's friends, from whom so much of his good luck flowed.

Charlotte, always the more practical of the two of them, was not content to put all their hopes for the future on the opera or the Rand School orchestra, which had still not materialized. When she urged Carl to think of the future and begin to make plans for some kind of financial security, he reluctantly went to the Fisk Teachers Agency. He wrote her that he had told the manager he would accept no salary less than three thousand dollars, and that he hoped for a university position. This was the third time he had tried to find a teaching position, and as before, he was not successful. Either the agency was unable to offer him anything because he lacked the college degrees that are generally considered essential for a university position, or he would not accept what they offered, since he did not want to leave New York.

Through all the activity Carl continued to compose. He rented a piano on 61st Street, nearer to his living quarters, and worked sometimes from 9:30 A.M. to 12:30 P.M., and again in the afternoon from 2:00 to 5:30. The music was pouring forth. He sent little snatches to Charlotte, and for Micah's third birthday he sent a musical sketch: "My darlings: This is for precious sonnie's birthday. A cluster for each year" (see example 6).[31] This may have been the beginning of Carl's thinking about a song for Micah, because the next year he wrote his only art song in his modern style, "Toys," for Micah's fourth birthday.

At the end of June Charlotte and Micah were due at last to come

Example 6. A musical sketch for Micah's third birthday (22 May 1918 letter to Charlotte and Micah).

East, and there was much excited discussion about where they should meet. Finally they agreed that it was best for Charlotte and Micah to go straight through to Lawrence and for Carl to meet their train at Albany. The family was joyously united, but the reunion was brief, for soon Carl returned to New York to find a place for them to live.

Just across the George Washington Bridge in New Jersey was a little community called Grantwood. It was not an expensive area then, and one could live cheaply and still have access to the city. There Carl found a little house that he thought would suit them and that they could afford. When he wrote to Charlotte about it, she replied: "Is there a gas stove in the kitchen or an ice chest — Very important factors, and do our neighbors realize the strength of your lungs and your technique on all bravura passages — Please make that very plain to them — ."[32] At last they were together.

NOTES

1. *Republican-Herald,* 29 Aug. 1912.

2. *Boston Sunday Post,* 24 Aug. 1913.

3. Albert Christ-Janer, *Boardman Robinson* (Chicago: University of Chicago Press, 1946), 23.

4. Jacques Barzun wrote: "it is evident that by 1911 . . . the European system of major-minor harmony and total enharmony had yielded all it could possibly give. It had been exhausted in a few centuries by an extraordinary number of composers and their patrons. After Richard Strauss any further exploiting of it could only fall into meaningless repetition, clever allusiveness, or deliberate pastiche. From every derived hint the accustomed mind could call up the great original from which it sprang. . . . And what had happened to music was also happening to the other arts." Introduction to Joan Peyser, *The New Music: The Sense behind the Sound* (New York: Delacorte Press, 1971), x. Reprinted in Jacques Barzun, *Critical Questions on Music and Letters, Culture and Biography, 1940–1980.* Selected, edited, and with an introduction by Bea Friedland (Chicago: University of Chicago Press, 1982).

5. Carl Ruggles to Charlotte Ruggles, 14 Nov. 1917.

6. *Winona Independent,* 16 Feb. 1913.

7. Rockwell Kent, *It's Me, O Lord* (New York: Dodd, Mead & Co., 1955), 269–70.

8. Carl Ruggles to Rockwell Kent, 11 Nov. 1914.

9. Interview with Mrs. Anne Ahern Schaefer, San Francisco, California, 22 Mar. 1975.

10. *Republican-Herald,* 1 Sept. 1917.

11. Born on 15 Nov. 1862, Gerhart Hauptmann was one of the most distinguished German dramatists of the late nineteenth century. "The Sunken

Bell" was written in 1897 and presented in its original language version in 1898 at the German theater in New York with Agnes Sorma as Rautendelein.

12. Carl Ruggles to Rockwell Kent, 1 Dec. 1913; Carl Ruggles to Rockwell Kent, 20 Dec. 1913; Carl Ruggles to Rockwell Kent, [mid-Apr. 1914].

13. Carl Ruggles to Charlotte Ruggles, 14 Oct. 1917.

14. Otto Kahn was an influential banker and on the board of the Metropolitan Opera from 1907 to 1934. Giulio Gatti-Casazza was general director of the Metropolitan Opera from 1908 to 1935. These two could make the decision about producing "The Bell."

15. Carl Ruggles to Charlotte Ruggles, 10 Feb. 1918.

16. Ibid.

17. Eugene Schoen, a distinguished architect, met Carl in 1914, and they remained lifelong friends.

18. Carl Ruggles to Charlotte Ruggles, 9 Sept. 1917.

19. Charlotte Ruggles to Carl Ruggles, 18 Sept. 1917.

20. The Rand School of Social Science is now defunct, but in its day it was a focal point in the lives of many, especially new immigrants who were struggling to make their way in the new country. The school officially opened on 1 Oct. 1907, and was named after Mrs. Carrie D. Rand, who left a bequest of $200,000 to the society for its educational program. By 1915 the school had grown so large that new quarters had to be found. When the YMCA building at 7 East 15th Street became available, the Rand School purchased it, and in the fall of 1917 the school opened in the new building.

21. Charlotte Ruggles to Carl Ruggles, 10 Nov. 1917.

22. Carl Ruggles to Charlotte Ruggles, 14 Nov. 1917.

23. Carl Ruggles to Charlotte Ruggles, 20 Nov. 1917.

24. Charlotte Ruggles to Carl Ruggles, 27 Nov. 1917.

25. Carl Ruggles to Charlotte Ruggles, 24 Nov. 1917.

26. Charlotte Ruggles to Carl Ruggles, 20 Dec. 1917.

27. Carl Ruggles to Charlotte Ruggles, 14 Jan. 1918.

28. Charlotte Ruggles to Carl Ruggles, 23 Feb. 1918.

29. Charlotte Ruggles to Carl Ruggles, 14 Feb. 1918; Carl Ruggles to Charlotte Ruggles, 18 Feb. 1918.

30. Carl Ruggles to Charlotte Ruggles, 15 Mar. 1918.

31. Carl Ruggles to Charlotte Ruggles, 22 May 1918.

32. Charlotte Ruggles to Carl Ruggles, [summer of 1918].

The Ruggles family, 1893. Father
Nathaniel and sister Mary are
seated; brother Edward Milton is
standing on the left; Charles
Sprague (Carl) is on the right.
Author's collection.

Carl Ruggles, 1910. Photo by
Dobbs. Author's collection.

Charlotte Ruggles, 1912. Author's
collection.

The interior of the Opera House in Winona, Minnesota, ca. 1911. Author's collection.

The schoolhouse home of Charlotte and Carl Ruggles, from a postcard ca. 1926. Author's collection.

Portrait of Carl Ruggles by Boardman Robinson, 1913. From *Arts
& Decoration* 14:3 (Jan. 1921):
236.

Harriet Miller, Carl's patroness.
From *Arts & Decoration* 14:4 (Feb.
1921): 296.

Bust of Carl Ruggles by Sally
Whitney Robinson, ca. 1918. Photo
by Whitney Robinson. Author's
collection.

Carl Ruggles, Betty Madden, and Charlotte Ruggles, in Coral Gables, Florida, 1941. A gift from Mrs. Betty Madden. Author's collection.

Carl Ruggles in Florida, ca. 1941. Author's collection.

Carl Ruggles in his Arlington, Vermont, studio, ca. 1951. Photos by John Atherton. From Photographs of Artists, Collection I, Archives of American Art, Smithsonian Institution.

Carl Ruggles and Robert Frost, at the Southern Vermont Art Center, 1952.
Photo by Clara Sipprell. Author's collection.

This photograph, by Bill and Gwen Gloan, was part of a New York Public
Library exhibit in 1957. Note the inscription to Henry Schnakenberg. A gift
from Mrs. Betty Madden. Author's collection.

Carl Ruggles receiving an honorary degree from the University of Vermont in 1960. Author's collection.

5

The Rand School
1918–21

Money problems continued to plague the Ruggleses. Charlotte was unable to help now, for she had neither church position nor private pupils. Though Carl continued to teach Mrs. Grace, he needed something more, and he hoped it would be the conducting position at the Rand School. He kept after his friend, Eugene Schoen, who in turn continued pressuring the board of directors to take action. Finally, on Tuesday, December 10, 1918, in an article clearly written by Carl, the Rand School announced plans to organize a "Workers' Symphony Orchestra": "The school has been fortunate in securing the services of Carl Ruggles as organizer and director. Ruggles was an infant prodigy with the violin. . . . He went to Harvard to prepare for a literary career, but the call of music eventually proved too strong, and on graduation he joined the Boston Symphony orchestra as a first violinist. Subsequently, he moved to Minnesota, and established a workers' orchestra there. . . . Ruggles is a composer of the modern school, ultra-radical in his musical ideas; but is schooled in all forms."[1]

By mid-January 1919 the orchestra was well underway, though the group still needed brass and string bass players, and the Rand School suited Carl well. Two of his closest friends were there. Schoen was on the board, and Robinson gave lectures at the school and published his cartoons in the *Call*. Carl was not a socialist, nor even interested in politics, but he would argue vehemently on the subject with his friends, taking first one side and then the other. His arguments with Harold Kellock and Eugene Schoen at the latter's home in Forest Hills lasted most of the night, as they discussed a wide range of subjects, their voices gradually getting louder and louder, with Carl's generally the loudest.

The sentiments of the country had turned ultraconservative after the First World War, and there was an unreasoning fear of foreigners and radicals. In early 1919 the congressional committee, headed by

Senator Clayton Lusk, authorized a raid on the headquarters of the Rand School, and on May Day of that year, "four hundred soldiers and sailors devastated the New York office of the Socialist daily *Call*."[2] Files were destroyed and records were confiscated, but none of this seemed to concern Carl, who continued to work with the orchestra. By April there were forty members who rehearsed every Sunday morning at the school.

Carl was also working at his music, giving up the opera for new works. Among his papers John Kirkpatrick found sketches for a short violin and piano work entitled "Mood" and subtitled "Prelude to an Imaginary Tragedy." Kirkpatrick believed the work was written in 1918.[3] For Micah's fourth birthday on May 25, 1919, Carl wrote a song, "Toys," in his modern dissonant style. He wrote both the text and the music, and it is dedicated, "To my little son Micah." The text reads:

> Come here, little son, and I will play with you.
> See — I have brought you lovely toys —
> Painted ships,
> And trains of choo choo cars,
> And a wondrous balloon, that floats, —
> And floats, — and floats, way up to the stars.

The vocal range of the song is an octave plus a sixth from D above middle C up to high B. The melody follows the text as the balloon floats up to the stars. It is to be sung "quasi recitative," and the rhythm is very fluid, with the meter indications changing in every measure to allow for the speaking quality of the words. The vocal line consists mostly of skips, many of them dissonant, with only a few stepwise progressions.

There is very little support from the piano part, which is also difficult and has its own profile. Full of dissonances, it requires large stretches of the hands. Before each line of text the instrument has rhythmic figures or long runs, so that the full range of the keyboard is used (see example 7).

Even though the piece is only sixteen measures long, it is difficult to perform. While the music does follow and enhance the meaning of the words, it is too compact and too intense for the text; and perhaps too short for the difficulty required to learn and perform it. On the other hand, if the performers are very good, the song can soar and become a tiny gem.

Carl probably had to send the song to Micah, for once again the family was separated. Charlotte was enduring a difficult pregnancy. Indeed she was so ill that they decided that she and Micah should go

Example 7. "Toys," mm. 9–11 (© 1920 by Theodore Presser Co. Used by permission of the publisher).

to Lawrence, where her mother could help with Micah, and she herself would be given care and attention. They gave up their little place in Grantwood and Carl moved back into the city to the apartment with Harry Andrews. The song is all the more touching, for it expresses more what Carl would have chosen to give to Micah for his birthday than what in fact he was able to offer.

Rehearsals with the orchestra continued throughout the spring. Carl wrote to Charlotte that "the orchestra played better than it ever has this morning. Schweiger, the oboe said 'Some conducting this morning. I would like to hear you with a real orchestra.' . . . I'm going now to have tea with Inez [Inez Haynes Irwin] and from there to the Meltzers for dinner."[4]

By mid-summer Charlotte felt well enough to join Carl, and they returned to Grantwood, New Jersey. Also that summer Rockwell Kent and his family had gone to Vermont to look for a place of their own. Kent's classmate at Columbia, John Fisher, and his wife, the writer Dorothy Canfield, lived in Arlington, Vermont, and when Rockwell found the place he wanted near Mount Equinox in Sunderland, the Fishers loaned him a thousand dollars to help purchase it. In addition, while he worked on the new home, Kent and his family stayed in the South Wing of the brick house in Arlington that belonged to the Canfield family.

Rockwell wrote to Carl:

> Carl! Will you do me a favor? Dorothy Canfield Fisher, who is our hostess here has organized a little troop of farmer-actors — of whom I am one — and we give a show in Manchester this month. I am to sing a couple of old songs with a quartet as chorus. Wont [sic] you, wont you Carl set the few short lines of the chorus of these songs into four part harmony for me? That will only be a few minutes work for you, wont it? I am sending you the book with the songs marked. If you will do it do it soon, please, for we have to learn the damned things. . . . I wish I could hear your music to Walt Whitman! But what a thing to undertake, how can it be done?[5]

This letter was Carl's introduction, as it were, to Arlington, Vermont, and its surroundings, an area that he was eventually to call home. It is also the first mention of a new vocal piece using a Whitman text. Several years were to elapse before he actually got around to it, but later he did use "On a Clear Midnight" by Whitman as part of his *Vox Clamans in Deserto* for voice and instruments. Meanwhile he complied with Kent's request and sent the arrangements back to him in four days. "I just sent the music," he wrote. "I enriched it a bit, the harmony I mean; it should sound well. Good luck!"[6]

Carl had not forgotten Micah's birthday song. He had submitted it to the H. W. Gray Publishing Company in New York and they had accepted it. Now it was his turn to ask Kent for a favor. He wanted him to design the cover for the song. Unfortunately Carl also had a piece of bad news to communicate. In early November Charlotte, ill with the flu, suffered a miscarriage. She recovered slowly, and the event cast a shadow on their life for the rest of the year. Kent responded as sympathetically as he could. He invited them for Thanksgiving in Vermont and readily agreed to do the cover design for the piece, which at that time was entitled "A Birthday Song."

They did not accept Kent's invitation. Charlotte and Micah went back to her parents' home, where she could rest and regain her strength, and Carl stayed on in New York to work with Mrs. Grace and the Rand School orchestra, which by now numbered around fifty players. In the meantime Carl was alone in the city and working with Kent, by mail, on the song. They finally agreed to call it "Toys," and Kent, sensing Carl's loneliness, once again issued an invitation to join him in Vermont, for the city was gearing up for the holiday season and Carl had neither money nor family to share in the fun and excitement.

On New Year's Day of 1920 Kent wrote that he could not do the cover of "Toys" right away. He was too busy with a new book and his paintings, for he was to have a show in early spring. Once again he issued a cordial invitation for Carl to visit them in Arlington, adding: "I wish you more happiness and all good things in your life finer even — than you've ever dreamed of—and all so that you get to work and make another grand opera. Carl, for heavens sake begin the new great work. . . . You're one of the few great men I've ever met or seen."[7]

Now Carl was at it again—talking about his next work in grandiose terms and quite probably well before he had written even a note of it. He did this all his life, and the works sometimes came into being, sometimes not. On more than one occasion this presentation before the fact would create problems for him but that never made him hesitate. He needed to speak about the work as if it were real before he could in fact begin the arduous task of actually composing it.

At last the Rand School Symphony Orchestra was ready for its first concert on Saturday evening, February 28, 1920, at 8:15 in the school auditorium, with Louis Torres, baritone, as soloist. Tickets were thirty-five and fifty cents, and readers of the *Call* were promised a program of the "world's best music." What is interesting is that the actual program for this first concert was not given in any publicity prior to the concert. Carl may very well have been unsure of the contents right up to the final dress rehearsal. But the concert did come off, and here is the program:

Overture from Suite "L'Arlésienne"	Bizet
Aria "Dio Posente" from *Faust* Louis Torres	Gounod
Symphony in B minor (Unfinished)	Schubert

Songs with Piano	Selected
Louis Torres	
Angelus from "Scenes Pitturesque"	Massenet

Carl had already conducted the Bizet and the Schubert in Winona, so only the Gounod and the Massenet were new to him. It was a triumphant evening. Charlotte was there, along with many of his New York friends, including Boardman and Sally Robinson, and Gene Schoen and his wife, Elizabeth—Kent, too, perhaps, for by then he and his family were in New York for his exhibition.

The orchestra played to a full house and won much praise for its performance. The auditorium was "packed" (it seated 575) according to the review that appeared in the *Call,* the only newspaper that even noticed the concert: "Judged by its premiere," the reviewer wrote, "the orchestra gives promise of becoming one of the finest organizations in the city."[8] That was a bit exaggerated, to be sure, but without doubt Carl had proved his ability, and the Rand School was not long in showing its appreciation. At the meeting of the educational council two weeks later on March 12, he was also given the post of director of the Rand School Chorus, succeeding Lochner, who had moved away.

Those were good months for Carl. There was not much money, and that was a constant worry, but Charlotte and Micah were back with him and he was moving ahead at the school. Kent was in New York, so they could see each other often, and through Kent he met more and more people in the arts. In addition, Henry Cowell, the young composer whom Carl had met at the Bartletts', brought a friend of his, Charles Seeger, out to Grantwood for a visit, and Carl and Seeger immediately liked each other.

Like Henry Cowell and Carl, Charles Seeger was a composer, but he had given up composing in any formal way; though as he himself said many years later, "There was always a tune running around my head."[9] A graduate of Harvard, he had been chairman of the music department at the University of California in Berkeley, where he taught the first musicology course in this country. Now he was teaching at the Institute of Musical Art (later Juilliard School of Music). He and Henry Cowell were close friends, and soon Carl became a third member of their circle, all three joined by a common and overriding desire to write and support truly modern music.

Cowell was the youngest of the three. Born in 1897, he had come East to make his mark in the musical world. He was also the one who had the organizational skill and the energy to carry out his plans. Seeger was the intellectual of the threesome, the teacher and theoretician. And Carl? Carl was the talker. A bombastic speaker, he could out-talk nearly everyone with his wonderful plans, mostly about his own works; and he loved to damn everyone beyond his immediate circle. But he respected Seeger for his academic training, and he admired Cowell because of their shared interest in modern music. When they got together they sat up most of the night shouting about music, composers, and other subjects. Carl would regale them with his stories, and they never failed to have a wonderful time. They loved each other, and, though they might become mutually exasperated at times, their friendship lasted throughout their lives. After Carl died, Seeger characterized this devoted friendship as "kind of a love affair." They were never offensive to each other, and "each party was more concerned with the happiness and well-being of the other."[10]

Meanwhile Carl was trying to take advantage of his new prestige at the Rand School. He wrote a long letter to Schoen, asking him to persuade the board to allocate money for music, and he hoped to do the *95th Psalm* by Mendelssohn with Charlotte as soloist. Schoen certainly had some influence and he did his best to bring Carl's plans to fruition.

In the meantime the first orchestral program was repeated in mid-April with slightly reduced ticket prices and once again it was a great success. One member of the audience was so moved by the concert that he handed Mrs. Mailley (Mrs. Bertha Mailley, executive secretary of the Rand School) a ten dollar bill as he left the hall, saying, "That concert was worth far more than 30 cents. I want to give what it was worth."[11]

All through the spring Carl was busy preparing the score of "Toys" for publication, and at last really working on the new piece that was to be a three movement work for orchestra. When the cover was finally completed, Carl was delighted with it, except for the fact that, as he wrote Kent, it was not signed by the artist, and he wanted Kent to get credit for it. Kent replied with some scorn, suggesting that his signature was unimportant, that if Carl wished it signed, *he* could put Kent's name to it. This Carl did, and the song was finally published later that summer.

Kent also put forward another plan for getting Carl to visit Vermont without any expense on Carl's part. Kent proposed to Mrs. Gilchrist, a woman prominent in Arlington and active in the Poetry Club, that Carl lecture to them about art and modern music. In return they would pay Carl's fare. He would stay with Kent and they could have a good visit. At first Mrs. Gilchrist was delighted, but when she brought the subject before the Poetry Club and gave Carl's background, she was mortified to find vehement objections raised to his appearance on the grounds of his connection to the Rand School. She relayed the information to Kent, and he in his turn was outraged, immediately withdrawing Carl's name

"Here, read this enclosed letter," he wrote to Carl:

> Copy of one I've sent to Mrs. G. Called there last night and learned that there had been some objection raised against you for your connection with the Rand School. On MORAL GROUNDS! Can you beat it? Said some of the members would be angered at the appearance of a man who could be suspected of "Free Love"—whatever that means! But it was not at all Mrs. Gilchrist's attitude—for her own sake it could not be. Well, she was to take the matter up at the next meeting and get a final decision. I told her that I was quite sure that you would have as serious "moral" objections to appearing before such people as they might have to you. I assured her that I would have.[12]

Poor Carl, caught in the middle of a ridiculous situation not of his making! And in truth, when it came to matters of love, he was totally devoted to Charlotte and nearly as conservative as his nameless accusers. It is a nice bit of irony that it all happened in Arlington, where he and Charlotte ultimately made their home and where Mrs. Gilchrist became one of their good friends.

Kent did not give up, however. He had another scheme for bringing Carl to Vermont that summer, and this one seemed more likely to succeed. He wanted Carl and one or two other musicians from the school, such as Samson or Alexander Bloch, to give a benefit concert in Manchester for the little North District school. Kent planned to enlist the support of some of the prominent people in the area who would bring in the summer people, and he hoped that there would be a large audience for the event. Accordingly, he approached his old and generous friend, Dorothy Canfield Fisher, who gave her enthusiastic support. The artists would have all expenses paid.

This plan should have worked, but it didn't. Kent simply could not get Carl to commit himself. Perhaps he could not get the others; perhaps he did not want to make the trip without Charlotte; perhaps he just wanted to work on his music. Whatever the reason, he did not go to Vermont that summer. This was just one example (we shall meet others) of Carl's not taking advantage of opportunities that were offered to him. At such times he seemed almost afraid. One senses a deep insecurity in him that recurred at other points in his life.

After a summer break in August the entire family returned to Grant-wood. Now Carl was a member of the regular staff and head of the newly established Music Department of the Rand School. With the exception of a concert series run by the School Music League, and a few music lectures by Mr. Herman Epstein, Carl had charge of all the musical activities. These included, in addition to the orchestra and chorus, a junior orchestra, and "If the demand warrants it, courses of instruction in composition, harmony, counterpoint, and orchestration. . . . conducted by Mr. Ruggles from a modern viewpoint."[13]

The orchestra, which now numbered sixty, gave its first concert on October 15, 1920. There were two soloists: Abraham Haitowitch, a blind Russian violinist, and Mrs. Carl Ruggles. Charlotte had regained her strength by now, and her selections for the concert were, "Hark Hark the Lark" by Schubert and "Sleep and Sorrow" by Tchaikovsky.

Charlotte made a fine impression when she sang in October, and soon after the concert she was asked to train the chorus for an international dance pageant planned for New Year's Eve at the great ball held at Madison Square Garden. The pageant would consist of folk dances from different nations: England, Finland, China, Russia, and India. The chorus would provide music from each of the countries. Teachers from the physical education department were to coach the dancers.[14]

The New Year's Eve celebration to ring in 1921 was going to be a gala occasion, and Carl and Charlotte were right in the center of it. The doors would open at 8:00 P.M. Dancing to Schiller's orchestra would start at 9:00, and the pageant at 10:30. The Grand March, led by Helen Keller and Art Young, would begin promptly at midnight, after which Miss Keller would say a "few words of greeting." At 1:00 A.M. a beauty contest would be held with Willy Pogany, Ryan Walker, and Art Young as judges. By 2:00 A.M. the prizes would be awarded. All this was solely for the Rand School faculty, students, and guests, who paid seventy-five cents for tickets if purchased early and one dollar for those bought at the door. From the reports following the ball, it was a huge success, with 10,000 in attendance. The pageant was stunning, and the chorus that Charlotte had trained sang the most stirring of "labor's revolutionary hymns."[15]

In the meantime Carl was steadily working on his new work. In October he wrote to Kent: "I have called my new work: *The Sun-Treader* Rhapsody for 6 horns and Orchestra. Can you imagine the golden throated glory of those six horns mounting to the heavens?"[16]

A few days later in a postcard to Henry Cowell, he wrote: "I have just finished rhapsody for 6 hns and orch. It is superb. You should see the writing for the Hn. All in unison. . . . Seeger thinks it splendid. Damrosch has written me about it." Then across the side of the card: "Can't you get some of your friends to order Toys?"[17]

The lessons with Mrs. Grace were a continuing source of income for Carl but hardly a steady one, since they did not take place on a regular basis, and following the summer break in 1920 did not resume until December. Around mid-December, in a letter to Kent, Carl wrote gloomily: "We send you all our love, which is about all we have to send this Christmas." The country was in the midst of a depression that winter of 1920-21, and Carl and Charlotte felt its effects. Fewer students were available for private lessons, while the students and supporters of the Rand School were less and less able to sustain the cultural activities offered by the school.

The first orchestra concert of the new year took place on January 14. The program included the Prelude to *Faust* by Gounod, Bizet's "Suite L'Arlésienne," the "Prelude and Siciliana" from *Cavalleria Rusticana* by Mascagni, and the "Largo" from Dvořák's "New World Symphony." In addition, Maurice L. Seifstein, tenor, sang one aria from the Mascagni opera. None of these were new works for Carl; he had conducted all of them in Winona. Unfortunately the concert was poorly attended. But it was not just the orchestra concert that had a small audience; the programs of the Rand School Music League, the chamber music concerts, and the recitals were also given to half empty halls. It was clearly a result of the depression.

At the same time the school was trying to raise $35,000 to build permanent buldings at its summer camp on Lake Tamiment in Pennsylvania, and Carl's friend, Eugene Schoen, was the engineer and architect in charge of this project. In an attempt to raise some of those funds, the school sponsored a series of "Tamiment nights," which were mostly musical entertainments. The orchestra performed on the second Tamiment night, January 27, 1921. This time the soloist was a young violinist named Cyril Towbin, who, in addition to several solos with piano accompaniment, performed the Bruch violin concerto with the orchestra. The other orchestral selections were the same as those on the previous program, with the Dvořák omitted. Evidence suggests that this concert, too, was no better attended, for on January 30, the *Call* carried a scathing article by Max Endicoff, excoriating his fellow workers for not supporting the cultural events at the school.

These were clear danger signals, and a final solution was soon arrived at. On March 28, 1921, at a board of directors meeting of the American Socialist Society, which ran the school, the orchestra was discussed, and the following was reported in the minutes: "Comrade Heller reported on the Orchestra. It was moved to advise the Orchestra that unless it can formulate some plan for raising funds, the Orchestra would be discontinued. Schonberg instructed to write a letter of appreciation to Mr. Ruggles."[18]

Thus ended Carl's contact with the Rand School and his serious attempts to make his way as a conductor. We can put the blame only partially on the depression. He was a difficult and demanding conductor and the school itself was changing. Though Carl maintained his close friendship with the Schoens for many years, the Rand School had nothing more to offer him. It was time to move on. But where? The loss of even a small income was difficult for the family.

NOTES

1. *New York Call,* 10 Dec. 1918.
2. Elizabeth Stevenson, *Babbitts and Bohemians: The American 1920s* (New York: The Macmillan Co., 1967), 58.
3. *Boston Globe,* 3 March 1976.
4. Carl Ruggles to Charlotte Ruggles, 1 June 1919.
5. Rockwell Kent to Carl Ruggles, 3 Aug. 1919.
6. Carl Ruggles to Rockwell Kent, 7 Aug. 1919.
7. Rockwell Kent to Carl Ruggles, 1 Jan. 1920.
8. *New York Call,* 29 Feb. 1920.
9. Interview with Charles Seeger, Bridgewater, Connecticut, 20 Nov. 1974.
10. Ibid.
11. *New York Call,* 17 Apr. 1920.
12. Rockwell Kent to Carl Ruggles, 17 July 1920.
13. Rand School Bulletin for 1920–21.
14. *New York Call,* 23 Nov. 1920.
15. *New York Call,* 2 Jan. 1921.
16. Carl Ruggles to Rockwell Kent, 27 Oct. 1920.
17. Carl Ruggles to Henry Cowell, 1 Nov. 1920.
18. Minutes of the board meeting and other material on the Rand School are deposited in the Tamiment Library of New York University.

6

Men and Angels
1921–22

Through all their problems, Carl continued to work at his new composition. Charlotte would not have it otherwise. Carl was her genius, and she never let him forget it. In a letter to Kent he wrote: "thank you for all the splendid things you say and have said about me. I hope I have lived up to them in my new work, 'Men and Angels.' It is for orchestra in 3 movements."[1]

Men and Angels was the title that remained for the new work, and "Sun-Treader" became the name of the last movement. But the work was going slowly, and there was constant worry about finances. Once the Rand School position was ended only the lessons with Mrs. Grace kept them from being penniless. This was the time of their greatest poverty, but Carl was lucky in his friends.

In the early spring of 1921, Seeger and his first wife, Constance, took a trailer trip south. Although it was to have lasted for many months, their resources ran out, and the trip had to be cut short. At about the same time Carl wrote that they, too, were in serious financial straits. Seeger replied almost immediately, inviting them to Patterson, New York, where his mother lived and where he and his wife were soon returning. The Ruggleses were urged to visit by the end of May or early June. Carl's postcard had started Seeger and his wife thinking about how they could refit the big "barns" at Fairlea (the property in Patterson) for living quarters, so that they and their friends would be independent of his mother, who was living in the house. Then it would be a base of operations for Seeger himself, and Carl, Charlotte, and Mike could stay throughout the summer. The offer was an answer to their prayers, and as soon as possible they made the trip to Patterson. Their quarters were not lavish, but they could manage since so much of living went on outdoors during the summer months.

There was a piano, and Carl was able to work. When Seeger was at home (often he was in New York), the two men sat up well into the night discussing music. Then Carl would show him what he had written, and they would go over every single note. Seeger remembered that Carl almost always talked about "notes," not about the architecture of the work, for he had no vocabulary for phrases or forms. Seeger did not want to interfere with Carl's creative ideas; he was, Seeger felt, an "autodidact." But Carl was having trouble with the new work. He wanted to talk about it; he wanted advice. In the end the piece was much changed from his original vision, and one wonders how much of the change was due to Seeger's influence.

Once when the Ruggleses were still living in Grantwood, Carl and Seeger made a trip into the city together. They had such a good time that when they parted back in Grantwood, Seeger wrote that it almost brought tears to his eyes. He added: "I would rather talk things over with you than anyone I can think of—partly because we are in very similar situations, partly because I don't know what is in your mind and partly because I cannot make out just what is in my own." Then he also wisely cautioned that they must be careful about mixing their ideas: "I felt very much as if I were muddying up a clean thing when I stood dallying with the voice idea at your home that first evening."[2]

Remembering their friendship many years later, Carl told me: "My style began with Seeger. Cowell brought him out to me at Grantwood, New Jersey." There was a long pause, then: "It was 'Angels' that did it, you know." In those days, he said, Seeger had a Stanley Steamer, inside which he had installed a portable organ. He would drive over to Grantwood, and he and Carl would "work all night on that organ." They worked until the milkman came around in the morning, and then they would buy a quart of milk from him. They tested out "sounds and other things," Carl said, and that led to the theory of dissonant counterpoint.

At Seeger's home in Patterson they would improvise together, Carl remembered. Constance was a violinist, and Seeger would get at the piano: "I would take my viola, and his wife would take the violin, of course. And we would start a composition—doing it free. Did it time and time again," he nodded. "That's how we used to do." Then there was a long pause while he remembered it. "That's something, huh?"[3]

All those talks with Seeger were stimulating for Carl, and he kept on writing and erasing, scratching out and writing again. In August he wrote to Kent: "Oh Rockwell, you should hear my episode for *Seven Muted Trumpets*. It is a marvel, nothing like it in the whole world. So serene, and on so beautiful a level."[4] The "episode" was to be the completed work, "Angels," but first he had to drop the idea of combining it with orchestra, and gradually he did.

Kent, too, was actively engaged in Carl's cause. He urged them to come to Vermont to stay with him, and more and more it seemed the only thing to do. By mid-summer Charlotte, ever the practical one, was pushing Carl to think about where they would live in the fall when they could no longer lead a semi-outdoor life. Kent's urgent offers of a visit were really their only possibility. "Received your kind letter with your more than kind invitation," Carl finally replied. "Nothing would please us more and I think we may be able to go up to Arlington in a week or two. Will write you a letter soon as I know for sure."[5]

By the end of August it was clear they would have to leave Seeger's, for the weather was becoming too cool, especially at night. Once this was decided, they moved quickly, and, perhaps out of embarrassment at their lowly financial straits or out of inability to express their gratitude, they left when Seeger was away. He remembered his surprise at their departure when he returned to Patterson, though he knew they expected to leave sooner or later. They had packed and left so quickly that some food was still on the table and one of Charlotte's shoes was left behind. Seeger thought they probably had spent the last of their money on the train fare to Arlington.[6]

Kent met them at the station and took them up the mountain to his place in Sunderland, Vermont, just north of Arlington. Kathleen and the children were there to greet them, and Carl and Charlotte and Micah must have felt that it was a regular homecoming. With two hundred acres of land, horses and other farm animals, and a wonderful view of Mount Anthony off in the distance, they had really come to the country. There was a piano for Carl, and living quarters were reasonably comfortable. They were thrilled.

It seemed like paradise, there at Kent's "Egypt," as he called his property. Carl worked at his music and then talked for hours with Kent about all the ills of the world. They compared their respective arts, and one story told by Carl has it that they bet each could not produce a work in the other's field. Carl did, we know — it is a view of Mount Anthony — but no music by Kent has surfaced. Of course, Carl had been drawing and painting for some time, so it would seem the advantage was on his side.

The new piece was moving along slowly, but Kent drew a cover for it anyway. "Men and Angels Symphonic Suite by Carl Ruggles," it said. In the middle of the page was a picture of a glorious sun rising above the mountains and the ocean, with the rays of the sun reaching to the heavens where two clouds floated. This time the cover was signed: "Rockwell Kent. 1921." There are other pages that show Carl using stencils to print. On one practice page he printed: "Men and Angels by Ruggles the Great illustrated by King Kent." Two other title pages show his indecision about the exact nature of the new work. One reads, "Men and Angels Three Symphonic Improvisations," and the other, "Men and Angels Symphonic Suite in Three Movements." Both pages have the movements listed: "Men, Angels, and Sun-Treader," in smaller capital letters.

This was in October 1921, with winter and storm clouds approaching. For one thing, Kent's marriage was breaking up.[7] And for the Ruggleses, there were the serious problems of money and once again a place to live. They could not stay forever with Kent, who was busy with his own life, but they underestimated his concern for them. He wrote from New York:

Heres [*sic*] what's settled with Mrs. Grace. . . . I called her up immediately on my arrival in the city and was asked out for dinner on the night of the next day. I had a talk with Dr. Bartlett before I went and, fully armed, launched an overwhelming gas attack. But, by God, it had to be overwhelming to get by with her! She is *HARD*. However, you get $100.-a month for six months. You're to live with me in Arlington and Charlotte to settle where she can get pupils—*students*—I mean. You're to give Mrs. G. 2 lessons a month and are to be paid your round trip fare each time from Arlington. If things go well this is likely to be continued. You are to give Mrs. G. a lesson next Wednesday, leaving New York on the *9.11* train for Great Neck. But I must see you first I'll meet the train from Arlington . . . Tuesday night.[8]

Charlotte did not move away to find students, but Carl renewed the lessons with Mrs. Grace, as Kent had outlined. Often he stopped in Croton-on-Hudson to stay with the Robinsons or went into the city, where he stayed with Dr. Bartlett. Sometimes he would remain an extra day to see Henry Cowell, who was back from California, or Charles Seeger. Those were especially important reunions, for he heard about the latest developments in music, and all three men went over his scores. So they stayed in Arlington throughout the winter, with Carl commuting to New York, while Charlotte and Micah, who was in school, bore the brunt of the cold, harsh weather. Fortunately Charlotte was a good seamstress, and with the help of hand-me-down clothes she was able to keep them all reasonably warm and presentable.

There is an unfinished song of thirty measures from this period that John Kirkpatrick found among Carl's papers before he died. When asked about it, Carl replied that he had written it around 1921. "I was thinking of Mike when I did it—Mike on a horse," he said. It is a

literal setting of Robert Louis Stevenson's poem "Windy Nights" from
A Child's Garden of Verses.[9]

The piano accompaniment follows the voice exactly, playing the
voice part in the right hand, mostly an octave below or at the same
pitch. The piano part is generally in the bass clef, and is dark and
somber. The range for the voice is not high, either: from B below
middle C to F an octave and a fourth above. What distinguishes the
piece is the intense chromaticism and the resulting dissonances, which
can be seen in examples 8 and 9. In example 8, while the left hand
plays octaves, the right hand plays dissonant major seventh intervals,
and Carl uses this combination at several points in the piece. Example
9 is a chromatic chord progression that is a variant of the brief introduction as well as the climax of the piece, when the voice sings its
part one octave higher. Another point of interest is Carl's use of sharps
and flats interchangeably in his score; obviously it was the pitch that
mattered to him, not the spelling of the note.

Example 8. "Windy Nights,"
m. 12 (manuscript, ca. 1921).

It was not a finished work. There were pencil indications for possible
corrections and transpositions. Quite probably it was a result of leftover
musical thoughts from the Symphonic Suite that was continuously
occupying him at this time. But it is easy to imagine Charlotte and
Carl performing this music at the end of the day in the late autumn
while Micah, only a little boy of six, fell asleep.

Around this same period, and again thanks to Kent, Carl became
associated with the Whitney Studio Club on West Fourth Street, which
had opened in 1918 as an outgrowth of the Whitney Studio and the
Friends of Young Artists. It was generously supported by the famous
art patron and sculptor, Gertrude Vanderbilt Whitney, and run by her
invaluable assistant and friend, the redheaded Mrs. Juliana Force.[10]
Mrs. Whitney was well known for her largesse toward artists, and
Kent, who was one of the charter members of the club, was not shy

about telling her of Carl's plight and of his need for support. Although she was already giving a stipend to Edgard Varèse, both she and Mrs. Force were sympathetic, and by the end of the year they began to give Carl financial help as well.

Example 9. "Windy Nights," m. 16 (manuscript, ca. 1921).

In the spring of 1922, the Whitney Club announced that Carl would give three lectures on modern music. The first, to be presented on Friday, March 31 (all were at 9:00 P.M.), was entitled, "The Present Situation in American Music"; the second on Thursday, April 13, was on "The Historical Background of Music"; and the final lecture on Thursday, April 27, covered "Technique and Phantasy in the Study of Composition." Admission was by card only, but these could be obtained at the club on the day before the lecture.

There are incomplete notes on the first two lectures among Carl's papers, and programs from the second and third. From them we can get a fairly good idea of their substance. At the first lecture Carl began by reading from a newspaper clipping in which Ernest Newman decried the state of American music as represented by Edward MacDowell, Walter Damrosch, and John Alden Carpenter. Then Carl went on in his own words to continue the drubbing of these three: "I have never been able to see in MacDowell more than a talent. . . . Fat-Heads always imitate the surface things. . . . It is all a reflection of the black-walnut marble top period, Venus de Melos [*sic*] with a clock in her belly. Tiddies, the gilding of everything from False teeth to coal hods. Now think of Walt Whitman coming clean out of that mess. . . ." He said it was "unnecessary to comment on Damrosch's music. He is not to be taken seriously." And Carpenter's was "a re-iteration [*sic*] of all the clichés of the past. Every damned bromide ever pulled." He did have some good words for Charles Griffes, but Carl reserved his unquestioning admiration for his good friend Henry Cowell, who was present and who subsequently performed one of his own pieces.

For the second lecture, the pianist Walter Golde assisted Carl by performing: Fugue in C sharp minor by J. S. Bach; Sonata in E minor, op. 90 by Beethoven; Prelude to *Tristan und Isolde* by Wagner; Intermezzi by Brahms; selected works of Debussy; and op. 2, no. 2 of Schoenberg.

Carl spoke first about the music that would be heard. The notes are incomplete, but at one point he said: "I wish to stress this matter of speed in music, because I believe most of the modern music suffers from the lack of it. This slowing down began with Wagner. He never wrote a really fast movement . . . Stravinsky seems to be the only modern with a fast pulse. And it is his greatest strength. Schoenberg is another slow one. To return to Beethoven: I think that in the final reckoning, he will be judged by his fast movements, not the slow ones, beautiful as they are."

There are no notes for the third lecture, but we do have copies of the musical program, which was certainly an interesting one. Three pianists participated: Madame Artur Nikoloric; Mrs. Alexander Bloch, one of Carl's friends from the Rand School; and Mr. Frederick Bristol. Presumably the program began and concluded with a performance by Madame Nikoloric and Mr. Bristol of the first movement, "Men," from Carl's new Symphonic Suite, *Men and Angels*. In between was a complete performance by Mrs. Bloch and Mme. Nikoloric of Stravinsky's *Le Sacre Du Printemps;* and a solo performance by Mrs. Bloch of "The Fountain" by Ravel.[11] But there were changes in the program after it was printed, and instead, the second movement, "Angels" was given, performed with stringed instruments under the direction of Alexander Bloch. We know this from two sources: a letter written to Carl two years later, and from his own reminiscences.

Mrs. Louise Vermont Chapin wrote in 1924 that she had heard his Whitney Club lectures on modern music and at the time questioned his right to speak as he did. She changed her mind, she continued, after hearing the string arrangement of "Angels" at the club. In our conversations, Carl, too, confirmed that "Angels" had indeed been played in an arrangement for strings at the Whitney Club.

Meanwhile the nagging problem of where and how they were to live continued, and once again a solution was at hand through the good offices of Rockwell Kent. During their stay with him he had introduced them to Dorothy Canfield Fisher. The Canfields were longtime residents of Arlington, and Dorothy's unmarried aunt, Martha Canfield, had left Dorothy the Canfield home that had belonged to Dorothy's great-grandmother. Situated next to the Town Hall, it was called the Brick House, and part of it was given to the town for use as the Community House. But Dorothy had kept back an apartment that the Kents had used, and now on April 25 she wrote to Carl and Charlotte, offering them the use of it.

They quickly accepted this generous invitation and were soon comfortably settled in the south wing. On the first floor there was a living room with a fireplace, a small bedroom and a kitchen; upstairs was another bedroom. Carl could work on the piano in the Town Hall. The Fishers lived about two miles outside of town on the Canfield farm. It was a good summer for the Ruggleses. They all entered into the life of the little town, adding their own special flavor. Charlotte let it be known she would take pupils, and Micah made friends with the children in town. Arlington was accustomed to artists and accepted them easily, and they stayed on into early fall.

Charlotte was so grateful for their little house that she wrote a poem in an attempt to express her feelings:

To Dorothy

A little house, four walls
An attic sleeping quietly
With grey perfume of dusty books
And glint of color'd glass
And little boxes filled with golden dreams
And treasures of poor dear hands
So long forgotten.

I am happy here
The memories are so fond and true
My heart is singing a quiet requiem
For all the hopes and dreams
Shrouded so preciously
In grey perfume and sifted sunlight.

—Charlotte R

By October the Ruggleses were in New York at 159 West 74th Street, as indicated by a letter from Dorothy to Charlotte. They renewed old friendships and often visited with Eugene Schoen and his family. Forest Hills, at that time just a small and growing community, had its own little fortnightly newspaper. In one of the columns there is a story of a farewell party for Mr. and Mrs. Wm. P. McCulloch, at which two groups of songs were "exquisitely rendered by Mrs. Carl Ruggles of New York."[12]

NOTES

1. Carl Ruggles to Rockwell Kent, 31 Jan. 1921.

2. Charles Seeger to Carl Ruggles, n.d.

3. Conversation with author, 10 Apr. 1967.

4. Carl Ruggles to Rockwell Kent, 19 Aug. 1921.

5. Carl Ruggles to Rockwell Kent, 2 Aug. 1921.

6. Interview with Charles Seeger, Bridgewater, Connecticut, 20 Nov. 1974.

7. David Traxel, *An American Saga: The Life and Times of Rockwell Kent* (New York: Harper and Row, 1980), 125.

8. Rockwell Kent to Carl Ruggles, [fall 1921].

9. A copy of this song was given to the author by Kirkpatrick, who had edited it.

10. See Avis Berman, *Rebels on Eighth Street: Juliana Force and the Whitney Museum of American Art* (New York: Atheneum Macmillan Publishing Co., 1990).

11. It is interesting to note that the first performance in America of Stravinsky's *Le Sacre Du Printemps* had only recently taken place on 3 and 4 Mar. at the Academy of Music in Phildelphia, with Leopold Stokowski conducting. Carl had obtained a copy of that program with the program notes by Lawrence Gilman, who may even have sent the program to him. Clearly he was keeping up with the latest in the musical world.

12. *Forest Hills Bulletin*, 28 Oct. 1922.

7

The International Composers
Guild: Part 1
1922–24

The International Composers Guild was started in 1921. It was an organization devoted to the cause of modern music, and once again Mrs. Whitney was one of the important financial supporters. While both Edgard Varèse and Carlos Salzedo were the founders, it was Varèse who, with the invaluable help of Salzedo, was the guiding light, the beneficent despot, who kept it going throughout its six years of existence. The first concerts took place in the spring of 1922, and Carl was not a member that first season, but he certainly heard about it. Perhaps he attended the concerts. After the first one there was a party at the Whitney Club, and after the third, when Varèse's songs were performed, Mrs. Force gave a reception at her home on Eighth Street. No one seems to know exactly how the two men met, but meet they did that spring of 1922 and became fast friends, though not without some rocky times. (Carl told me that he had heard about Varèse and the Guild, so he "just went right down there and introduced myself. Told him I was a modern composer and I wanted to join.")

So Carl joined the International Composers Guild in its second season and soon became an active member. When the new season was announced, Carl's "Angels" for six trumpets, billed as the second movement of a symphonic poem entitled *Men and Angels,* was scheduled for the first concert, on December 17, 1922, at the Klaw Theater on West 45th Street. All the New York newspapers carried the announcement, and in the *Times,* the critic Richard Aldrich wrote: "Ravel's sonata for violin and cello written this year will be heard, as well as a symphonic movement for 6 muted trumpets by Carl Ruggles, an unknown American, reported by the Guild to be an extraordinary 'find.' "[1]

In addition to the Ravel and Carl's piece, the program included music by Honegger, Dane Rudhyar, Lazare Saminsky, Marius Gaillard, and Arthur Lourie. Of them all, it was "Angels" that put the concert into the annals of American musical history, and surely it was a remarkable and noteworthy first New York performance. The six stout trumpeters had to play it twice to a vociferous and mixed reception.[2]

Then the critics had their fun. The reviewer for the *Times,* probably Richard Aldrich, wrote: "a symphonic movement, 'Angels' by an American Carl Ruggles, . . . [was] repeated amid calls for 'speech.' "[3] Another critic, William J. Henderson, wrote that the trumpeters "played with about the same conscious joy and delight as does the Luxor Silver Cornet Band in the triumphant scene of 'Aida.' "[4]

A more thoughtful review, written by Winthrop P. Tyron, appeared in the *Christian Science Monitor.* He carefully explained to his readers that the appearance of the six unaccompanied trumpeters and not Carl's music was the cause of the humor. "Ruggles, who is an American, may be considered as introduced to the public by his 'Angels,' if not yet understood by the entire public."[5] Only one critic, the perceptive Paul Rosenfeld, felt differently about Carl's piece: "the fragment of Ruggles' suite is distinguished by the loveliness of the sound of the six close dissonant silversnarling trumpets; and by an inner homogeneity."[6]

For Carl it was a triumphant evening, and how he loved the controversy that raged over his little piece. He remembered that the Guild had to pay the first trumpeter, named Capodiferro, an extra ten dollars because his part was so high. And one of his favorite stories from that event concerned a well-dressed couple who sat beside him and Charlotte and were violently divided in their reactions to "Angels." The wife did not like it; the husband did. Carl remembered: "He told her 'Shut up! You don't know a thing about it.' Then he leaned over and gave me a five dollar tip. Told me to go out and buy myself some cigars."[7]

After the concert there surely was much merrymaking, perhaps at Romany Marie's café-restaurant in Greenwich Village, Varèse's favorite place, which soon became Carl's. Charlotte used to say that whenever they traveled by train she always knew where Carl was by the laughter. Wherever he went he would entertain his companions with his never-ending fund of stories or limericks—mostly scatological. That night, following the concert, Carl held forth with great gusto, and Charlotte was proudly at his side—perhaps even gently giving him cues for the stories. Notwithstanding her regal presence, she, too, enjoyed his jokes.

Let us now take a look at "Angels." It is a slow-moving short piece, only twenty-two measures long, lasting not much more than three minutes, and in simple ternary form ABA, with a short coda. The first part, A, consists of two phrases, the second more active but only slightly longer than the first. The second part, B, beginning at measure five, is longer and more complex. It consists of a series of overlapping phrases, each reaching a higher point until the climax at measure twelve, after which there is a long descending line. The third part, A, then returns and is exactly like the first except for an additional measure at the end of the second phrase. The coda uses the opening motive of B to conclude the piece.

Two things made the work so unusual, so jarring, and so controversial. The first, alluded to in the reviews, was the instrumentation: six muted trumpets all in a row, playing without benefit of other supporting instruments of the orchestra, not even other brass instruments such as French horns or trombones. Along with that unusual homogeneity of tone color was the unremitting use of dissonances. At every downbeat (the first beat of a measure) the notes contained at least one major seventh, for example, B up to A sharp (see example 10). The inversion of a major seventh is a minor second or half-step, for example, A sharp—B. These half-steps were used, too, both within the measures and on the downbeats, especially in the B section. Moreover, because the piece was in close harmony, there was little open

Example 10. "Angels," mm. 1–2 (© 1960 by Theodore Presser Co. Used by permission of the publisher).

space between the notes. As a result, the dissonances were especially harsh to unaccustomed ears. At one point in the climax at measure twelve, Carl combines two half-steps and moves them loudly along for a beat and a half, that is, D sharp-E-F to C sharp-D-E flat to B-C-C sharp (see example 11). The only relief provided is the use of thirds and sixths harmonized with the top voice. These are generally considered sweet consonances, but in this piece they are used simultaneously with the dissonances.

Example 11. "Angels," m. 12 (© 1960 by Theodore Presser Co. Used by permission of the publisher).

Each section begins in an imitative fashion, and there are little segments of imitation throughout. In his later works Carl would develop both the use of dissonance and imitation much further, but this little piece remains an excellent example of his musical style, with its uncompromising dissonances and burning intensity.

The final chord of "Angels" created some real brouhaha (see example 12), and Carl was very proud of it. Note that the top F sharp ties over

Example 12. "Angels," final chord (© 1960 by Theodore Presser Co. Used by permission of the publisher).

from the previous measure and that the chord contains both the major seventh, E up to D sharp, and the half-step, F sharp to G, as well as two thirds: D sharp to F sharp, and E to G; and two sixths: F sharp to D sharp, and B to G. B of course is the note common to both triads used, if one looks at the notes traditionally: E-G-B — B-D sharp-F sharp. The issue of what it meant harmonically and how to view the music of "Angels" was the subject of a controversy in print between Dane Rudhyar, fellow composer and member of the Guild, and Charles Seeger, to whom the piece is dedicated.[8] Carl was not at all concerned about these theoretical questions, but he was greatly pleased that his little piece had generated the whole affair.

Carl's method of composition was, as it had always been, trial and error. He sat at the piano and moved his fingers around, listened hard to the sounds and chewed at his cigar, shouting out some of the lines. Then he would talk about them with his musical friends — in this case, Seeger — and they would provide the encouragement, advice, and intellectual theory for what he was hearing and writing. It was his music, all right, but for all his life he needed those friends to legitimize, as it were, his musical efforts.

Carl was now a member of the inner circle of the Guild and a member of the board, whose meetings were generally held at the home of Mrs. Claire Reis, at that time the executive secretary of the organization. At one meeting, she remembered, Carl shouted that if attendance figures for the concerts were rising, it meant the Guild was not holding to its ideals and was catering to the public. This prompted such a violent discussion that the meeting ended in disarray.[9]

In January, Dorothy Canfield Fisher wrote to Charlotte inviting them back to the Brick House in Arlington, which would be available any time after June 8. There was a piano for Carl now, right next door in the main part of the house, and Dorothy promised Charlotte that this time she would have a proper dishpan. They were delighted by the invitation, for it meant that they had only to get through to June, and they could be sure that the summer would be fine.

Carl spent his days drawing, trying to decide on a new piece of music, and visiting with other artists or friends. He and Charlotte often went to art galleries, and were sometimes invited to parties at the Whitney Studio Club, which moved that spring to larger quarters at nearby 10 West 8th Street. More than once, as the story is told, Mrs. Force would telephone Carl in the middle of the night and urge him to dress and come down to the club, because the party was getting dull, and she wanted him to entertain the guests with his ribald stories. So he would go, and at first may even have been amused by her request, perhaps even a little proud. But soon he and Charlotte realized that playing the court jester was the price he had to pay for the stipend he was receiving from Mrs. Whitney.

For the third and last concert of the Guild's season on Sunday, March 4, 1923, Carl asked that his song, "Toys," be performed. It would be a first performance. Lucy Gates, soprano, was scheduled to sing three songs by Lord Berners, and she agreed to add Carl's song to the group. Varèse's *Hyperprisms* was also on the program, and like "Angels" before, it stole the show. Kenneth Curwen, the music publisher from England, attended that March concert, and after the concert he met Carl, a meeting that ultimately resulted in the publication of "Angels" in 1925.

Meanwhile Carl had been present at the first American performance of Schoenberg's *Pierrot Lunaire,* which took place at the second Guild concert on February 4, 1923. Schoenberg was already a famous composer, and since *Pierrot* had been performed in Europe, but not in America, this was a real coup for the Guild. There were twenty-two rehearsals for the work, with Greta Torpadie, the Swedish-American singer, in the role of Pierrot. Carl remembered: "They all talked about Schoenberg's music. When *Pierrot Lunaire* came out, we all got scores." And he was impressed by the work. "*Pierrot Lunaire* is a good work of his," he said. "There are places in it that are fine." He preferred singing to that "half-sung half-spoken part for the voice," but "it is an amazing work."[10] Carl had mixed feelings about Schoenberg himself, but he respected his compositions, and *Pierrot* seems to have had some influence on him. In casting about for his next piece he decided to do a cycle of seven songs (*Pierrot Lunaire* was "Thrice seven") with small chamber ensemble, and with Charlotte's help he set about picking his texts.

During this same period Carl and Charlotte made an inventory of all their furniture stored at various places, a record that gives graphic evidence of their nomadic existence:

At Seegers [in New York], 1 M. Table, 2 Slat back chairs, Piano bench. At Patterson, 1 blue dish with feet, 1 blue Suga [*sic*] bt,

1 mple desk, 1 m sofa, 1 Pembroke table, 1 Duckfort table, 2 Wicker chairs, 2 S. Windsor chairs, 1 L.M. Sowing [sic] table, 1 M. Bureau. At Burdett's, 1 M. table (2 leafs), 1 Pedestal table, 1 table [a drawing of it is included], 1 cherry table. At Fred's, 2 G clocks, Un Oclock [?] 1 M. bureau, 1 mirror an draws [sic]. At storage, 1 copper coffee pot and stand, 1 cut glass vase, 1 Luster pitcher, 1 bran [sic] bed, 1 cot with m, 1 G *Piano*, 1 pair B Candles, 1 candelabra, 1 pewter CS, 3 pewter Platters, 2 pewter teapots, 1 pewter Coffee pt, 1 iron candle stick.

In early June they returned to Arlington and promptly joined the Arlington Neighborhood Club, which sponsored a choral group. Funds collected by the club were used to light the kerosene street lamps and to help with the library and the upkeep on the Community House. In those days the post office was right next to the Thompson and Howard store, a general store with a potbellied stove around which the men would congregate in the winter. In the front were big wide steps where people met if the weather was fair.

Horses and wagons were still in use, and the mail was wheeled down to the post office from the railroad station in a two-wheeled cart; twenty or thirty townspeople would be waiting and chatting together while it was sorted. The old ice wagon and vegetable carts stood nearby. In the twenties, one of the old-timers remembered, a family could live comfortably in Arlington for twenty dollars a week. Carl walked over to the post office and to the store several times a day to chat with the townspeople, often telling his stories or learning new ones; and sometimes arguing and quarrelling over politics. In fact, when he was not working at the piano or doing some painting, he was most often found at Thompson and Howard's.

It was a good place for Micah, too, who was now eight years old, and especially interested in sports. In addition to the tennis courts right behind the Brick House, there was swimming and fishing on the nearby Battenkill, and plenty of boys for baseball, which was soon to become his favorite sport, and one that he and Carl could share—he as participant, Carl as spectator or umpire.

The Ruggleses were already known to quite a few in the village, and they settled in easily. Charlotte immediately became active in the St. James Church choir and the choral group; she also gave voice lessons. Before long they both were busily engaged in putting on the first of several musical entertainments for the town. They decided to do Gaul's "Holy City" with the neighborhood choral group enlarged to become the Arlington Community Chorus. With the help of Grace Buck, a piano teacher in town, Charlotte began to train the chorus. As in Winona days, once the chorus had learned the music, Carl took over as conductor, and Charlotte sang the solos. The performance took place on September 16 in the high school auditorium and it was a resounding success. More and more they were reluctant to leave Arlington, and luckily this year they could stay on in the South Wing. When it was necessary, Carl took the train into New York and stayed with friends. They both dreamed of finding a place of their own somewhere in the little village, and Charlotte began to look for one.

Carl had been working all through the summer and fall on his new composition, a work for mezzo-soprano and chamber orchestra entitled *Vox Clamans in Deserto*. They had picked the seven songs: Browning's "Parting at Morning," "Son of Mine," by Charles Henry Meltzer, Whitman's "A Clear Midnight," and "As If a Phantom Caress'd Me," Shelley's "Lyric," Keat's last sonnet, "Bright Star," and Carl's own "Premonitions." As it turned out, only the first three were ever completed, and the Guild was waiting for them. Carl's songs were scheduled for the second concert of the new season on January 13, 1924.

Greta Torpadie was the singer, and Salzedo conducted the small ensemble for Carl's three songs, which were given just before intermission. The brief program notes stated that the songs were "written during the past summer at Mr. Ruggles' home in Arlington, Vt. and are scored for flute, oboe, clarinet, bassoon, horn, two trumpets, a string sextet and piano." On a separate insert the poems were given.[11] Varèse's *Octandre,* also on the program, stole the show, but Carl's songs created enough of a furor for the third one to be repeated, and a few critics also showed some enthusiasm for them.

Carl had his own memories of the concert. The singer had not done well, he reported. At the rehearsals, Salzedo had to go over the pitches with her many many times, playing her part on the piano while she struggled to learn it. Then, when they began rehearsing with the instrumentalists, she was so overwhelmed by the difference in sound, that she could not sing at all, and Salzedo had to encourage her by softly singing her part along with her. He did this at the performance, too, and that is how they got through it.[12]

Once again he had turned to Seeger for advice. In fact, it was Seeger who named the work. "We worked a little bit together," he remembered, and Seeger had felt that *Vox Clamans in Deserto* was the proper title. "The first one begins this way — 'Round the Cape of a sudden came the sea,'" and he orated it with great pomp to me. "That's Browning, too," he said. The second song was about Micah with the poem by Meltzer, and the third, — "Wait a minute and I'll get the title," he said, " 'The Clear Midnight' by that great American poet, you know," meaning Walt Whitman.[13] On another occasion he said that *Vox* was connected with Gertrude Vanderbilt Whitney, and that the first song by Browning was dedicated to Mrs. Julianna Force.

The songs remained in manuscript form, and periodically Carl would think about revisions. The third one was all right, and Varèse had liked it. Salzedo, he remembered, had liked the music to the second, but not the text, and Carl felt he was right. But in his lifetime there was only that one performance, and with that he had been so disgusted that he withdrew the work, in spite of the fact that later it was listed by his publisher, Ray Green, for rental.

The manuscript score that Salzedo used for the Guild performance certainly does show that there were problems; problems in pitch for the singer and problems in rhythm for the instrumentalists. In fairness to the singer, it should be pointed out that the vocal range of the songs is nearly two octaves: from B flat just below middle C to an A above the next C, with a voice line of difficult intervals (see example 13). Moreover, since the vocalist does not receive much support from the instruments, it is no wonder that she had problems. At one point, Carl had added in pencil a doubling of the voice part for the second trumpet, asking him to play "ppp" (triple soft) (see example 14).

Example 13. "Son of Mine," from *Vox* (© 1977 by Theodore Presser Co. Used by permission of the publisher).

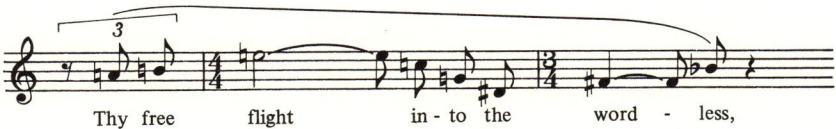

Example 14. "A Clear Midnight," from *Vox* (© 1977 by Theodore Presser Co. Used by permission of the publisher).

These songs show him continuing to work out his modern style. "Angels" had indeed been dissonant, but was more homophonic in style, more vertically oriented, and, of course, there were only six parts. In *Vox* he had fifteen parts (including voice) to draw on. Oftentimes many of the instruments are silent; in fact at no point do they all play together. But he was making more of an attempt to be linear, and at the same time was trying to notate more and more complex rhythms. Odd numbered notes span several beats, and these were to be played against other irregular figures. He was attempting to write out *tempo rubato*, a problem that would remain throughout all his compositions.

Notation is almost always a problem for composers, especially in terms of rhythm and dynamics. The markings one finds on the printed page are after all only symbols for the sounds and silences that the composer hears and wishes reproduced. In Carl's case this was a severe problem, since he was trying to notate different rhythms, with at least one of them unusual, occurring simultaneously. Often after trying out the music in rehearsal or having his friends look over the score, he ended by making it more nearly regular and easier to execute. As one of his friends said, "We smoothed out the rough edges," and Carl was willing to allow them to do this, for he was not that sure of himself.

In *Vox*, for example, he almost never used bar lines in the sketches, though he marked the triplets as opposed to the regular eighth notes. He would also write "fine" by a small passage he particularly liked, and then often as not the next time he returned to the piece, it would be that very passage that he continued to change and reshape. In the fair copy used at the Guild performance, there are five-note figures used against regular four-note figures, and often three against two. If these are performed within one beat, they are not as difficult to play as when they are spread across several beats, and it was here that Carl ran into trouble. The final measures of "A Clear Midnight" point up this difficulty in several cases. For example, originally Carl had the time signature simply 4/4 at measure thirty-one, and within that measure there was a triplet on beat one, sixteenth notes (or four to a beat) on beat two, and two layers of triple rhythm enclosed in beats three and four: (1) three equal quarter notes (a triplet) covering the two beats, (2) two eighth notes for each of the first two notes of the triplet, and three eighth notes (a quicker triplet) for the final note (see example 15).

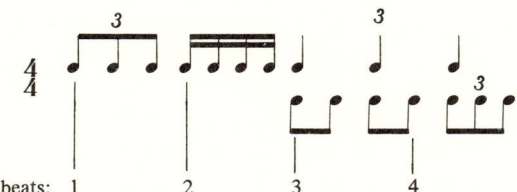

Example 15. "A Clear Midnight," original m. 31, from *Vox* (© 1977 by Theodore Presser Co. Used by permission of the publisher).

The singer was supposed to sing on the final two notes of the quarter note triplet, but obviously, from the change in the score, she had difficulty with it. Carl "straightened it out," as it were, making the whole measure into two measures: one of 2/4 and one of 3/4 with the longer triplet becoming simple quarter notes (see example 16). It was almost the same, but not quite, and it certainly was easier to read and to perform.

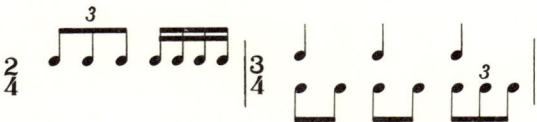

Example 16. "A Clear Midnight," revised mm. 31–32, from *Vox* (© 1977 by Theodore Presser Co. Used by permission of the publisher).

Again in the two penultimate measures Carl had marked the meters 4/4 and 5/4; and once again it was triplet figures used against each other that created difficulty. Because there was a triplet covering the last two beats of the 4/4 bar, Salzedo, the conductor, has marked the score to indicate that he gave five beats, changing the triplet to quarter notes. In the 5/4 measure Salzedo changed it to six for the same reason. Nowadays these rhythms would not be considered insurmountable, but this was 1924, and for the performers as well as for the audience it was a very new and bold experience. So Carl withdrew the piece, but he had learned both from it and from his talks with Seeger. Now he was ready to tackle an instrumental work; *Vox* was his last composition for voice.

Two days after the performance of *Vox*, Nathaniel, Carl's father died. He was seventy-eight years old, and had been living in Boston, where Edward Milton's family had looked after him. Carl had neither seen nor made any effort to keep up with any members of his family except for the one summer when he tried to teach the violin to his niece. However, when he was notified of his father's death, he dutifully went to Boston for the funeral, then rushed back to Arlington and Charlotte.

At last, they found a house in Arlington that they thought would suit them. The old schoolhouse down on School Street had been sold by the directors of the Arlington Town School District in November 1922, after the new school was built. The owners, Gilbert M. Vaughn and Arthur H. Smith, had indicated that they might be willing to sell, and Carl and Charlotte were very much interested. It was a good location, away from the main street, but still close enough for Carl to walk to the post office and the store. There was a good lawn around it, and in the big backyard you could look down on some farms below and the Battenkill. On clear days you could even see far across the river. There were outbuildings on the property for storage, and while it was true that remodeling was needed, some things had been done already. Best of all, the price seemed almost within their reach.

They looked over the inventory of all their possessions and considered long and hard. Charlotte could make all the curtains and other furnishings. Friends would help them; they were sure of that. Everything seemed to suggest that they ought to go ahead with the purchase, and so with much excitement they decided to buy the schoolhouse. Charlotte wrote to Dorothy of their decision, and she quickly answered from France that they could stay in the Brick House until the schoolhouse was ready, and, typically, that she would help them in any way that she could.

On June 2, 1924, the transaction officially took place. The total cost was $1,200, which Carl and Charlotte promised to pay at the rate of $100 annually with 5 percent interest. It was a busy summer for them. Carl was already working on a new piece, and Charlotte was teaching. Both of them were preparing for another community oratorio performance, the *95th Psalm* by Mendelssohn, and at the same time they were having the schoolhouse remodeled. Carl turned for help to Schoen, who gave advice and, more to the point, money and materials.

They put the kitchen in the north entrance (the girls') to the schoolhouse and closed off the south entrance (the boys'), designating that section for the bathroom. One entered through the kitchen into the huge main room. With windows on the north and west, and an enormously high ceiling, it took up half the house and was to be Carl's studio and their main living quarters when he was not working. On the south side opposite the main room, they made a narrow hall and two small bedrooms. The ceilings were eventually lowered in the bedrooms, and slowly the new owners addressed the problems of plumbing and heating, as well as furnishing the house.

Dorothy gave them some furniture, including, according to Carl, a two hundred year-old table. For ten dollars, Charlotte, he said, had managed to buy from the Episcopal Church the chandelier that hung in the main room. He had found the "big huge stove" that sat there, but "you can't heat that place. It was like living in the suburbs away from the stove."[14]

Meanwhile the oratorio was given on Sunday, September 7, to a large and delighted audience. Carl wrote to Schoen that the performance went "splendidly." He also wrote that they were now ready for the plumbing: "all we've got to do is to put in the toilet and the sink. The bathtub can wait. . . . You said you could get one for cost. I think a good one is cheapest in the end, don't you?"[15]

Less than two weeks later Carl wrote again, this time bluntly: "Say, for Christ's sake what's the matter with you, where's that shit house?"[16] Schoen was not at all perturbed, and shortly the plumbing arrived. They moved into the schoolhouse in mid-November, and at last they were home.

NOTES

1. *New York Times,* 17 Dec. 1922, sec. 7.

2. See Louise Varèse, *A Looking-Glass Diary* (New York: W. W. Norton & Co., Inc. 1972).

3. *New York Times,* 18 Dec. 1922.

4. *The Sun,* 18 Dec. 1922.

5. *Christian Science Monitor,* 18 Dec. 1922.

6. Paul Rosenfeld, "Music Chronicle," *The Dial* (Feb. 1923): 222–23.

7. Interview with author, 22 Sept. 1966.

8. For a further discussion of "Angels" see: Marilyn J. Ziffrin, "Angels—Two Views," *Music Review* 29:3 (Aug. 1968): 184–97. The Rudhyar review can be found in the *Christian Science Monitor,* 23 Dec. 1922; the Seeger reply in *Eolian Review* 3:1 (Nov. 1923): 12–23; the Rudhyar reply to Seeger in *Eolian Review* 3:2 (Feb. 1924): 29–31.

9. See Claire R. Reis, *Composers, Conductors & Critics* (New York: Oxford University Press, 1955). For another view of the board meetings and Mrs. Reis, see Varèse, *Looking-Glass Diary,* 177ff.

10. Interview with author, 28 Jan. and 17 Apr. 1967.

11. The author of the second poem, "Son of Mine" was erroneously listed as Rowland Wood on the insert. It should have been Charles Henry Meltzer.

12. Interview with author, 27 Sept. 1966.

13. Interview with author, 7 Apr. 1967.

14. Interview with author, 17 Oct. 1966.

15. Carl Ruggles to Eugene Schoen, 30 Sept. 1924.

16. Carl Ruggles to Eugene Schoen, 9 Oct. 1924.

8

The International Composers Guild: Part 2

1924–27

Carl's new composition, on which he worked throughout the summer and fall, was scheduled for the first concert of the Guild's 1924–25 season, on December 7. It was dedicated to Schoen by way of thanks for all his help and was called *Men and Mountains,* from Blake. The slow movement for seven strings was entitled "Lilacs." As Carl wrote to Schoen: "Lilacs is the symbol for desolation, abandoned farms, cellar holes etc. The first movement is: Marching Mountains."[1] By November 7 he had sent Varèse the first two movements, "Men" and "Lilacs." "Marching Mountains" was now the third and final movement. The piece was scored for a "Symphonic Ensemble" with the following instrumentation: one flute—piccolo, one oboe, one English horn, one clarinet, one bassoon; two horns, two trumpets, one trombone; two violins, two violas, two cellos, one contrabass, and piano.

Carl was feeling good about his music, and with reason. He had recently received a letter from Richard Hammond, acting chairman of the Program Committee of the International Society for Contemporary Music, requesting the score of "Angels" for performance at the Chamber Music Festival to be held at Venice in early 1925, and his new work was going to be ready on time. When it was finished, he sent copies to Varèse, who was anxiously waiting for it, and to Cowell. They both responded with glowing remarks, although Varèse had a few reservations. He thought "Lilacs" was beautiful, but he felt the other movements needed a few changes, and he urged Carl to come to New York so they could go over the score with Seeger and attend rehearsals.

The concert was Eugene Goosens's first appearance in New York, and he made every effort to be sure that it went well. He and his wife came down from Rochester, New York, where he was conductor for half the season, and Carl was soon charmed by both of them. At the rehearsals Carl again met Kenneth Curwen, the music publisher, who agreed to consider "Angels" for publication. Some of the critics attended the rehearsals, too, including Lawrence Gilman, whom Carl came to know and respect. He often spoke of him with great fondness, in part influenced by Gilman's enthusiastic reviews of his music.

It wasn't all work during those days before the concert. Carl remembered with great glee that one time, when they were feeling especially good after a rehearsal, he and the Goosens went out together, and drank considerably more than usual, with the result that the three of them ended up falling asleep together in one bed. He laughed uproariously as he told the story.

Since the work had been written in Vermont, Carl had talked a great deal about it with Kent. In fact, Kent had called the work *Men and Mountains,* after Carl had played part of it for him. Kent also suggested the Blake quotation and gave the title to the first movement. Carl had named the others. "Lilacs," he told me, came from Walt Whitman's "When lilacs last in the dooryard bloomed," while "Marching Mountains" was his own creation. "They really do look like marching mountains up there," he said, motioning with his finger toward Arlington.[2]

The concert took place in Aeolian Hall, which was larger than the Vanderbilt Theater where the previous concerts had been held. It was a packed house. Charlotte was there, and Kent, as well as the Schoens and the Robinsons, and of course Cowell and Seeger. Carl was surrounded by friends and supporters, though many in the audience still came out of curiosity or to laugh and jeer.

Dorothy Canfield Fisher had written a highly complimentary article about Carl and the new work, which he hoped would be quoted in the program notes. But Louise Varèse, who wrote the notes, only used Dorothy's description of "Lilacs," and the headings for each movement that Carl had chosen. He was especially proud of the first one: "plangently," and boasted that it was the first time any composer had ever used that word. When I asked him where he had found it, he answered disdainfully, "Pooh, I suppose I have a vocabulary of 20,000 words at least." Then he added, "To be a writer, you should have 50,000."[3]

Men and Mountains, as we have seen, was scored for a chamber ensemble, to which Carl added a cymbal. The entire piece is not very long. The first movement has only twenty-nine measures; the second, thirty; and the third, forty-two. But it is a dense piece, and the unrelenting dissonances and uneven rhythms give it a feeling of strength and make it seem longer than it is.

"Men," the first movement, is subtitled "Rhapsodic Proclamation for Horns and Orchestra," and the horns have three long, somewhat broken lines of recitative, while the rest of the orchestra provides dissonant commentary. Interestingly, each recitative begins on the exact pitch with which the previous one ended. Thus while the first ends on G flat, the second begins on F sharp; and while the second ends on A flat, the third begins on G sharp. Throughout the piece, wherever there are held chords there are sharp dissonances; but this is predominantly linear music, and the lines rise and fall like waves.

It is interesting to compare the first movement to its model, the third, entitled "Sun Treader," of that earlier *Men and Angels,* which Carl never really completed. That first work was scored for a very large symphony orchestra: piccolo, three flutes, two oboes, English horn, two clarinets, bass clarinet, three bassoons and contrabassoon, six horns, three trumpets, three trombones and tuba, tympani, cymbal, and strings. He had even written in space for two harps at the beginning, but there is no music for them.

The musical material, however, remains much the same in both pieces. In fact, except for the amalgamation of two measures into one in the newer movement, "Men," it is exactly the same. Still, in "Men" Carl has focused the work and given it a clear shape. Now it is clearly a three-fold proclamation for the horns. The much reduced texture permits the lines to sound more sharply; there is space between them, and the material shines forth with a brightness and a clarity that the original did not have. Now one hears the uneven rhythms, the triplets against the sixteenth notes, or the eighth notes against the triplets. The dissonances, the major sevenths and the minor ninths, are clearer, too, for there is more space between them. To get that tonal space, he has the instruments often playing at their extreme range, and this helps to produce that extraordinary tension we hear in his music.

The final chord of "Men" is typically as dense as he could make it, with the simultaneous sounding of eight notes of the chromatic scale: C sharp, D, D sharp, E, F, F sharp, A and B flat. The latter four notes are played once, while the first four are doubled, either in unison or at the octave, so these are the notes one hears most clearly. Carl always insisted that what mattered most was not so much the notes themselves but the voice leading to the main notes. If we look at the notes of the last two chords, we can see what he meant by the movement of the lines: how they move either by steps or skips to their last note (see example 17). Notice the open spaces between the notes, and how easily each instrument moves smoothly to its final note by either consonant skips or by steps. This is a clear indication that Carl was on his way to mastering dissonant contrapuntal technique.

"Lilacs" is a direct descendant of "Angels." Like its predecessor, it

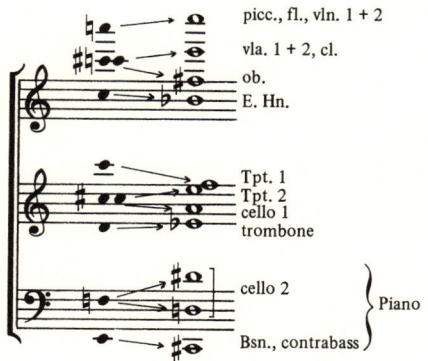

Example 17. "Men," final chord, from *Men and Mountains* (© 1971 by Theodore Presser Co. Used by permission of the publisher).

is the slow middle movement and written for one group of instruments, this time for two violins, two violas, two celli, and contrabass. But the similarity does not end there. Both movements are in ABA form, and both have their climax in the B section. In fact, there are even melodic likenesses, with both movements using a similar melodic figure (see example 18).

Example 18. "Lilacs," m. 6 (left), from *Men and Mountains* (© 1971 by Theodore Presser Co. Used by permission of the publisher), and "Angels," m. 19 (right) (© 1960 by Theodore Presser Co. Used by permission of the publisher).

There are differences, of course, and these show how much Carl had mastered his technique. While "Angels" was mostly homophonic with the instruments generally moving along together in close dissonant chords, "Lilacs" is truly linear and more open. There are musical question and answer responses, and these give rise to perhaps the most notable difference between the two movements, which occurs in the middle of the B section. In "Angels," Carl has the high point occurring toward the end of the section, after which he drops down very quickly by means of the whole tone scale in the first trumpet part. By contrast, the high point of "Lilacs" occurs near the opening of the B section, beginning a canon between the two violins and the second cello and contrabass that continues for four measures until the falling movement at the end of the section. This falling motion is no longer a straight descending scale line, but rather an undulating line that meanders leisurely downward toward its goal four and a half measures away. It is truly linear music, and Carl is demonstrating his knowledge of contrapuntal technique.

The third movement, "Marching Mountains," was the only one wholly new, and I think the least successful of the three—at least in this first version. Like the first movement, it is for the entire ensemble. It begins with the same opening motive of "Lilacs," a descending whole step; but here the motive is used majestically as a grand introduction and rises quickly to a climax, after which the march begins. The very nature of a march implies a steady repetitive rhythm, and that is the very opposite of the irregular and uneven rhythms with which Carl wanted to work. Part of Carl's problem with this movement is that there is no resolution of the tension between the two views.

The march figure is eight steady quarter notes presented twice in unison, with a slight variation in rhythm the second time (see example 19). Carl then introduces a more interesting melody loosely based on the march, which he alters and transforms in the course of the movement. Then the opening march figure returns, and the rest of the movement consists of a steady change of those eight notes from eighth notes to triplets to sixteenth notes, with ever-increasing dynamics until the final triple forte dissonant chord. This buildup, however, is too obvious and too flat-footed. We feel screamed at rather than uplifted by the final chord. The contours of the mountains are there, but the grandeur has still eluded Carl in this final movement.

Example 19. "Marching Mountains," mm. 6–7, from *Men and Mountains* (© 1971 by Theodore Presser Co. Used by permission of the publisher).

At the Guild performance, the audience response was, as usual, vociferous and mixed, and so was the reaction of the critics. Most were either snide or negative, but there were two rave reviews, and these are what mattered to Carl. Lawrence Gilman's review began, "By far the most original item on the program was Mr. Carl Ruggles's 'Men and Mountains.'" Further on, he wrote: "He is the first unicorn to enter American music. He is the master of a strange, torrential, and perturbing discourse.... His music seems to us to be utterly original. . . . This New Englander with a touch of Blake—of Blake's rhapsodic fantasy, Blake's piercing and swift simplicity—may not write music that we should call 'beautiful.' Yet tomorrow or the day after we may call it that."[4]

Another rave review came a few months later when Paul Rosenfeld wrote about the work in *The Dial*: "If the compositions of this Cape Cod American offered in other seasons by the Guild gave evidences of an energy struggling for expression, the new suite for small orchestra reveals a living powerful touch upon material."[5]

The most telling criticism came from his old friend and confidante, Charles Seeger, who, we must remember, had not worked with him on this composition. Shortly after the Guild concert, he wrote to Carl and tore the piece apart. Then he offered some advice: "You can . . . divide the melody among the instruments . . . and the trumpets could double on high notes. . . . Remember, also, just because an instrument *can* reach a high note that does not say that the sound fits a long sostenuto or declamatory melodic line." Then he concluded: "If you don't stop writing for theater orchestra I shall give you up. Lilacs is a work of art—the other two very interesting musically—but to hell with piccolos especially on high C in fits and starts. If you were not the only person in this country whose creative work I care anything about, I would not advance the points above mentioned—it would not be worthwhile. I want to see the piece get over."[6] Initially Carl may have been hurt by Seeger's criticism, but he learned from it and saved the letter.

Something else happened that evening of the premiere of *Men and Mountains* that was to have a profound effect on both Carl and Charlotte. When the concert was over, Kent invited them to go with him to meet a friend. Many years later Carl spoke about it: "He said she was a very wealthy woman who was a generous patron of the arts." So they all went to her place on Park Avenue, and he remembered that she had a "big place, many rooms. And her name was Mrs. Harry Payne Bingham."[7]

Kent was right about Mrs. Bingham. She was an artist herself, a sculptor, and very active in support of the arts. The Ruggleses and Mrs. Bingham liked one another right away, and she was fascinated with Carl's looks. She saw immediately that with his bald pate he would be a wonderful subject for a piece of sculpture, and soon after they met, she asked if she could do a bust of him.[8] Mrs. Bingham, separated from her husband, had recently purchased a home in Vermont, just south of Arlington. She spent the winter months in New York and planned to spend summers in Vermont. In the coming year she saw the Ruggleses occasionally in New York, but it was during the summer months that they came to know each other better.

That winter Carl and Charlotte spent most of their time trying to keep warm in the schoolhouse. No matter how much coal they burned in the big stove, the cold blasts of air kept coming through the huge main room. Carl seemed to thrive on it, insisting that he could work just fine, but poor Charlotte suffered. She said she was never really warm again after going through that bone-chilling winter. But they stuck it out.

The big news was that Curwen had accepted "Angels" for publication and intended to bring it out by the time it was to be performed at the International Society for Contemporary Music Festival in Venice, scheduled for early September. Since Varèse and Salzedo were in London, Carl agreed to allow either of them to read the proofs, so the work could be published in time.

By this time Carl was hard at work on a new piece. He had taken Seeger's advice: no more compositions for just a few instruments and no more small pieces. This was to be a short symphony, and he had already announced the names of some of the movements: "Scherzo," "Finale," even "Coda for the Final Movements." But he knew there would be trouble with the Guild over it. In February, in a letter to Charlotte, Louise Varèse wrote that Carl's new work was supposed to be ready for the first concert of the next season, and that Varèse was worried about his expressed determination to write for a larger ensemble than the Guild could afford.

Undaunted, Carl continued working on the new piece. Then at the end of March he sent the projected instrumentation for the work to Schoen and asked him to forward the information to Varèse. He should, of course, have sent it directly to Varèse himself, but he knew he was asking for more instruments than he should, and he hoped that Schoen would try to persuade Varèse to make an exception for him. Perhaps, too, he hoped that Schoen would make a large contribution to the organization to pay for the additional instruments. Unfortunately that did not take place.

At the end of April Varèse wrote to Carl that the number of instruments he requested was completely out of the question. The absolute maximum, Varèse noted, was five woodwinds (flute, oboe, clarinet, bassoon, with one doubled) six brass (double horns, trumpets, and trombones) solo string quintet, piano, and harp. Then to further confirm his position, the entire board, at a meeting that Carl did not attend, stipulated that only chamber music ensembles were acceptable, and further, that no individual composer could hire extra players at his own expense.

The next move was up to Carl, and he simply did not know what to do. So he turned for advice to Seeger, who replied: "If I were you I would certainly not write any more for that movie orchestra just because Varèse likes it. Write for 20 strings if you can get them. Can't you make a row about the brass?"[9] It was easy for Seeger to offer the advice. He was not the composer who wanted to get his music performed. Carl was caught in the middle, and typically for the time being he did nothing.

Then suddenly there was an even more serious problem facing them. Charlotte had not been feeling quite right for some time, even visiting Dr. Bartlett when they were in New York for *Men and Mountains,* but there seemed to be nothing seriously wrong. Then in May Carl wrote to Schoen: "Two weeks ago Dr. Russell found a hard bunch in Charlotte's breast. He says it may be malignant, or it may only be a cyst. But it should be seen to *immediately.* Dr. Russell thinks Charlotte should go to New York where she can have expert advice, and examination. . . . Charlotte is greatly depressed, and the uncertainty of everything is having a bad effect upon her."[10]

It was a frightening time, but as always friends rallied around them with support and financial help. Dorothy offered to look after Micah, and Carl and Charlotte went to New York as soon as they could. On May 29 she was admitted to New York Hospital for an operation to remove the tumor. She remained in the hospital until June 10, while Carl stayed with the Robinsons. A collection was taken up among their friends to cover the cost of the hospital bill, and as soon as she was discharged and able to travel, they returned to Arlington.

Slowly but surely Charlotte began to feel better, and gradually they resumed their normal activities. In their worry and haste, Carl forgot to make the annual mortgage payment on the house, and when he received a second notice, he turned for help to Schoen, who responded generously, and the payment was made. Charlotte was not one to stay down for long, and by mid-July she was working with the Arlington Community Chorus again. They had made her honorary chairman of the society while she was in the hospital, and she felt a great loyalty to all the members.

Meanwhile Olive Fremstad, the famous Swedish soprano who had sung at the Metropolitan Opera Company, was staying at the Brick House for the summer. A friend of Dorothy's, Mme Fremstad met Carl often during that time, and while they sometimes quarrelled, they also enjoyed each other's company. Carl remembered that he would walk up to the Brick House to visit with her and even play some of his music for her. The first time he did that, she told him, "You're a terrible pianist — but that music is great!"

One time he and Charlotte decided to have a dinner party for her, and she insisted on bringing the main course, chicken, to be sure it was properly cooked, she said. After dinner Carl quite naturally took out a cigar. Fremstad demanded, "What are you going to do with that?" "Smoke it," he replied. "You just put that right out!" she ordered, and he did.[11]

One acquaintance who was to become a close and valued friend was the painter, Henry Schnakenberg, whose parents lived in Manchester, Vermont, just a few miles north of Arlington. They often invited friends to afternoon teas, especially "strawberry teas" — vanilla wafers loaded with fresh strawberries and whipped cream, served with tea. Carl and Charlotte were frequently invited, and if they could not catch the local bus, Henry drove down to Arlington to pick them up.

When Mrs. Harriette Bingham arrived in Arlington for the summer, she contacted Carl and began work on the sculpture, for which he had promised to model. Soon they were on a first name basis, and Harriette liked Charlotte every bit as much as she liked Carl. Often she would visit them at the schoolhouse, and sometimes the three of them would go for a drive in her black Buick. She gave some of her clothes to Charlotte, and some of her son's clothes to Micah, which Charlotte altered to fit him. One time Micah remembered that he wore a cap with Harriette's son's name sewn in it. By chance one of the neighborhood boys grabbed it from him and seeing the different name, a group of them began to taunt Micah about it. He had to fight each one of them, he said, to stop their teasing.[12]

On September 8 "Angels" was performed at the International Society for Contemporary Music Festival concert in Venice. Arturo Toscanini attended, and after Carl's piece, he stamped out, calling it a piece for "six muted strumpets," adding, according to Carl: "this place should be fumigated!" His comments rapidly spread throughout the musical world, and Carl recalled with delight that "Larry Gilman called me up and said I was famous all over the world after that remark."[13]

Curwen had brought out the score, which interestingly carried the note that it "was conceived for six Muted Trumpets (five Trumpets and Bass Trumpet), but it may be played by any six instruments of equal timbre." Some years later, Carl revised it for four muted trumpets in C and two muted trombones, and he made it clear that this was the only group for which the work was written.

All through the summer Carl had been working on the new piece, which he had proudly named "Portals." It was for strings only (he had given in to the Guild), and soon he would have to go to New York for the premiere. Since it simply was not possible to spend the winter in Arlington again, they agreed that Charlotte and Micah would spend the winter months with her parents, who had retired and purchased a modest home in St. Petersburg, Florida. Carl would have a room at Mrs. Blanche Wetherill Walton's in Bronxville.

Carl had met Blanche Walton through Cowell and Seeger. She was a patron saint to artists, opening her home in Bronxville to them for as long as they liked, and later, when she moved into the city, taking her artists with her. Mrs. Walton was born into a wealthy family in Philadelphia. She married a businessman in New York, and when he died, leaving her a young widow, she gave over part of her house to those artists whom she liked and admired, and felt deserving of support. Luckily for Carl, he was one of them.

By mid-October they were mutually settled in their winter quarters, but with quite a difference. Carl wrote to Charlotte that he was able to work not only in the morning but again in the afternoon. Seeger was coming out to visit and stay for the night, and one day he and Blanche had driven over "to Larchmont in her Ford. The sea was fine."[14]

Meanwhile, Charlotte and Micah were in cramped quarters in exceedingly hot weather with no air conditioning, and Mrs. Snell was not at all well. Charlotte complained to Carl, who responded sympathetically, even suggesting that he would try to work something out for them at Blanche's. The letter made Charlotte feel better, but she knew very well that she and Micah could not move to New York. Moreover, as had happened from the very beginning of their marriage, Carl had left the house and gone off whenever he wanted to, leaving her to handle the chores and business. He hadn't changed over the years, and she and Micah would only be in the way if they came north. So they stayed in Florida.

During this period Carl continued to depend on the stipend from Mrs. Whitney for their support. But he never knew when the money would arrive, and it seemed to be given in a haphazard way, as if Mrs. Force sent the check only when she remembered. Charlotte worried about this, and so did Carl, who wrote: "Yes I'm somewhat worried about Mrs. Force. . . . If she doesn't come across pretty soon, don't you think I'd better have a talk with her, or have some one else do it."[15]

Carl wrote that letter on a Friday, and the next day he and Kent went up to Arlington to visit with Harriette. On the way Carl told him of their financial problems, and once more Kent acted on Carl's behalf—with stunning results.

"Wonderful!" Carl wrote exultantly to Charlotte the next Tuesday, and underlined it with the five lines of the treble clef. "Harriette is giving $170 a month taking the place of the Whitney-Force outfit. And as she said in her note it *will* be sent. Here is Harriette's note," he continued:

Carl darling—
From now on I want you to let me take the place of the Studio Club—So, a check of this amount will be sent every month. (And it *will* be sent.) There is only one thing I ask and that is—no thanks in words. All and more you have told me in Portals—and will tell me in the future works that are deep down in that soul of yours.

Rockell [*sic*] had a hand in it. He took the matter up with H—I'm sure, because I told him about things in the train. At least I think this is so, because he knew all about it. and asked me to write Mrs. Force and Mrs. W- [Whitney] telling them *not to send* any more money.

Harriette wants me to break with that crowd, and write them a 'nice' letter to that effect.[16]

That was such good news that both Carl and Charlotte continued to write about it to each other for several days. Finally Carl wrote Mrs. Force that she need not send him any more money. He had shown the letter to Blanche and to Kent before sending it, and then he enclosed a copy for Charlotte:

Circumstances have arisen which make it unnecessary for Mrs. Whitney and you to further continue your kind assistance to me. It is needless to say how deeply I appreciate all you have done for me in the past. And I further wish to say that I hope the time is not far distant when I can return that which you generously contributed to the furtherence [*sic*] of my art.

Don't you think that a nice letter? I had to write it right off, as H- asked me to, but I knew you would approve.[17]

Harriette had already given Carl his first check; he immediately deposited it in the bank, and of course had no intention of returning any money to Mrs. Whitney or Mrs. Force—nor did they expect him to. In a previous letter to Charlotte he had written that Harriette was "grand" and loved them both, and that was true.

Her marriage to Bingham was breaking up. They had been separated for some time, and soon she would divorce him. The Ruggleses appeared in her life at just the right time, and, as it turned out, they all needed one another. Harriette was true to her word about the stipend. She arranged with a New York bank to send the money directly to Carl every month without fail, and that continued for as long as she lived.

Carl showed his appreciation by dedicating "Portals" to her, the first of several works to be so inscribed. In the Bennington Museum there is the large and beautiful first page of the score that Carl had copied out for her. "To Harriette Bingham with deepest affection," reads the inscription. Harriette's bust of Carl is there, too, signed on the back: "Harriette G. Bingham 1925." For Carl and Charlotte it was the beginning of a new and happy sense of security in their lives, and they were truly grateful.

On the other hand, $170 a month was certainly not a lot of money, and they would have to live very carefully if they were to be limited solely to that amount. Carl and Charlotte could live cheaply; they had been forced to. But they both loved nice things, and they liked to circulate with their rich friends, enjoying that way of life and the largesse those friends bestowed on them. Carl, especially, never stopped expecting gifts and bounty from them, and more often than not, they did not disappoint him. Still, Harriette's stipend was the only income they could count on.

Henry Cowell had come out to Bronxville to stay at Mrs. Walton's during the holidays, much to Carl's delight. He wrote that he was not seeing anyone "until Portals is finished" but Henry was right there. Four days later he went out to Forest Hills to dinner with the Schoens, and the day before he had had tea with Harriette, who was now at her home in New York.

Carl's new piece was to be given on January 24, 1926, and typically it still was not ready, though the day of the concert was fast approaching. However, with Henry nearby as well as Seeger, who often came out to Bronxville to visit, Carl had the support and the criticism that he needed to prod his creative efforts. He wrote to Charlotte from Harriette's, where he had gone for tea: "This morning I wrote a *new* slow movement for cello solo and strings coming in. Really the best thing I've done. Has a sublime sound, and is made up of the *1st* movement. It's a new scheme of composition and eminates [*sic*] from not repeating any note until the 10th. Seeger says it's the right track."[18]

This is Carl's first statement of his composition method, and one of the few he ever put into writing. It is clear, as he always admitted, that Seeger was its godfather, if not its source. The letter also shows that he still thought of the new piece as a multi-movement work. But he never did get beyond that first movement in any real way. Finally, just twelve days before the concert, he sent a postcard to Charlotte: "*2 p.m.* The child is born. The copyist has 'Portals,' Thursday I correct the parts, Friday rehearsal at 2. I feel as though I had been through a long illness."[19]

After Eugene Goosens, who would be the conductor for the new work, saw the score, Carl wrote that he thought it was "*wonderful.*" The first rehearsal took place on January 15, at the Hotel Majestic, and the next day he wrote to Charlotte about it: "Goosens was magnificent. He took his coat off, and went at it. The rehearsal was all for my work. Nothing else: from 2 to 4:30. After the rehearsal Goosens and I went to bed in his rooms, and Mrs. G. tucked us in."[20]

The performance was scheduled for Sunday evening, but on Saturday a near tragedy occurred. Carl, Seeger, and Cowell were together, celebrating in advance perhaps, after looking over the parts to "Portals," which they had with them. When they returned to Mrs. Waltons, to their horror they realized that these were missing, left somewhere, but no one recalled where. Both Seeger and Carl remembered it all quite clearly, though neither had any idea how they could have been lost. What later remained very clear in their minds was sitting up all night long copying out a new set, in a frenzy of activity, for they had to be ready for the final rehearsal in the afternoon as well as for the performance in the evening. Seeger remembered all three of them writing as quickly as they could, asking sometimes, "What note is this? I can't read the score." And Carl replying hastily, "I can't read it either. What do you think it should be?"

They did succeed. The parts were ready on time, and the performance took place at Aeolian Hall. The applause that followed was so enthusiastic that Goosens repeated the work, but the reaction from the critics was, as always, mixed. For Carl the review that counted was the one written by Gilman, and as usual it was the most thoughtful and perceptive. Here, in part, is what he wrote: "some new alchemy appears to have been at work in the case of 'Portals.' The network of melodic strands is softer and smoother in texture than of yore. We preferred Mr. Ruggles in his more astringent manner: in his 'Men and Mountains' of last year, for example, there was a sternness and severity, a tonic harshness, that was peculiarly personal to the music of Ruggles."[21]

Carl was not totally pleased with Gilman's review. The comments about being more melodious continued to rankle until he finally talked with the critic. To his delight, Gilman told him that "on second thought" he agreed with Carl (and Seeger) that it was the instrumentation that had made "Portals" sound less stern, and that if it had been scored for full orchestra, including brass, it would have sounded "hard," as Carl put it in a letter to Charlotte, explaining that the sound of strings gives to the dissonances a sweeter sonority, a fact that is generally true.

Let us now consider the piece. The title, "Portals," comes from Whitman, and has this quotation from the Whitman poem: "What are those of the known but to ascend and enter the Unknown?" It is scored for four violins, three violas, three cellos, and two double basses—twelve instruments in all. In a program note for a later performance, Carl wrote: "It is a prose poem in the form of Rhapsodic Variations based on a theme of 7 measures announced at the beginning by the cellos and basses in octaves."

Carl's description is accurate as far as it goes, but Henry Cowell provided more information about "Portals" in the program notes for that first performance. Carl's procedure in composing, according to Cowell, has three elements: (1) a long melodic line, each string part with its own melody; (2) never doubling the same note of the melody in the supporting harmony; and (3) never repeating a note or its octave until there are at least seven to nine different notes in between (not ten, as Carl had written).

If we look at the rhapsodic opening theme, we can see two of the above characteristics—the long line and the nonrepetition (see example 20). The first twelve notes, like a tone row, contain all the pitches of

Example 20. Opening theme of "Portals" (© 1930 by Theodore Presser Co. Used by permission of the publisher).

the chromatic scale, up to the D in the treble clef, the high point of the melody. The receding wave, or second part of the theme, uses only ten different notes, with the last two, B flat and A flat, a repetition of the first two notes of the second part.

Now it is misleading to think that Carl would keep this procedure throughout the work. He does not. In fact, immediately following the opening statement, the theme is broken into smaller segments that are repeated and modified. The long line of nonrepeating notes is used whenever the work approaches the major climactic moments. Then there is the grand sweep up to the high points, and the long falling away — much like the opening theme. At the *Largando,* from measure sixty through sixty-four, for example, which is the stretching out of the climax of the piece, Carl has the violins move from a twelve note figure to a nine note one, and then to a five note ascending scale that moves broadly and slowly in parallel dissonances to the cadence.

After that, there is a brief coda, and when the notes of the final chord at last come together, all twelve notes of the chromatic scale are sounded — this time vertically, in contrast to the beginning, where they were presented melodically and horizontally. Carl begins building the final chord two bars before the end, slowly adding one note against another until all are sounded; and because they are not sounded suddenly and simultaneously, and because they span five octaves, our ear does not find it jarring but rather an ascending ladder into that "Unknown." This building of dissonances with wide spaces in between is an important characteristic of Carl's music and one that permits it to be dissonant without being harsh.

It is also true, as Cowell points out, that the notes of the harmony are not any of the melodic notes. But this was not a new procedure. While Carl often doubled his melodic lines in an octave or even two octaves, he almost always thought about the music in terms of counterpoint and rarely if ever harmonically. Thus the notes that supported the melody would naturally be different ones.

What the listener hears in "Portals" is the sweep of the long non-repetitive lines alternating with the shorter motives that do repeat themselves. Slowly these shorter motives combine to build another long melodic wave — quite like the waves that Carl must have heard as a child growing up in Marion. Example 21 contains the important motives derived from the main theme. This was new, and a real advance for Carl.

Look again at the opening line (example 20), and notice the range of it, over two octaves from the bass clef up into the treble. Note, too, the undulating quality of the line, and finally the large variety of rhythmic figures. The only regularity occurs at measure three with the three eighth notes, and they foreshadow the end of the line with the four quarter notes. Dissonances abound, but the intensity is gained perhaps less by these than by the extreme ranges that Carl requires of the instruments. All of them must play in their upper limits, especially the violins.

Example 21. Motives from "Portals" (© 1930 by Theodore Presser Co. Used by permission of the publisher).

If we compare "Portals" with "Lilacs," the second movement of *Men and Mountains,* also written for strings, we can see how far he has advanced. "Lilacs" is only thirty measures, "Portals" is seventy, over twice as long. While the former had dissonances and rhythmic variety, "Portals" by comparison is far more varied, full of *sturm und drang,* and much more dramatic. Nonetheless both works carry Carl's musical signature, the major sevenths, the minor ninths, and the undulating lines.

"Portals" also differs from "Lilacs" structurally, and this, too, is evidence of Carl's growing ability as a composer. For in contrast to the drama of the work, the form is one of symmetry and strength. Essentially it is composed of two large sections, with similar material in each, and a coda. Note the diagram in example 22. Measures thirty-eight through forty-four are an exact repetition of measures six through twelve, while measures thirty-three to thirty-eight are reminiscent of the opening (measures one through five) in the use of the opening two notes and a similar final three measures that end with exactly the same regular quarter notes. This is not something esoteric. Our ear can hear

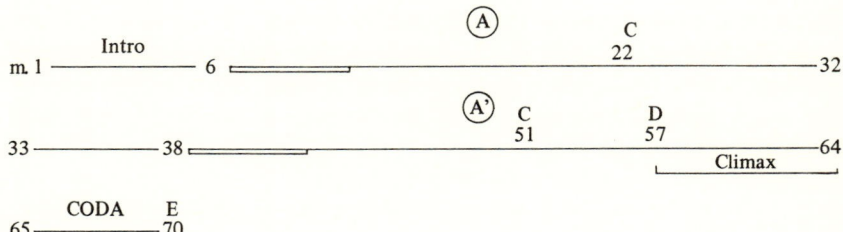

Example 22. Structure of "Portals."

these repetitions and likenesses, and as we hear them, the piece begins to have meaning for us.

Moreover, Carl has bound the entire piece together by means of those extremely high climactic notes. As the diagram shows, at measure twenty-two in the first A section, the first violins arrive at high C. In the second A section, the high C is confirmed at measure fifty-one, and then the violins add to the intensity by moving one step higher to high D in measure fifty-seven. In the final chord of the entire piece the first violin completes the line with the high E. Whether these connections were instinctual or conscious on Carl's part is not of great importance. In either case they demonstrate his developing sense of musical form and his increasing ability to handle larger canvases. Everyone expected that Carl would complete "Portals" as a multi-movement work. It never happened. He did rescore the work for a larger string orchestra, but that is as far as he went.

Poor Charlotte, who longed to be there to share in Carl's triumph, had to be satisfied with the news of it from Carl and his friends. Blanche Walton understood how she felt and sent her a long letter about the wonderful new piece, telling her how hard Carl had worked to make it just right. Blanche added that she fully realized the sacrifice and the courage required of wives of artists, and she regretted that Charlotte had not been with them for the triumphant evening.

Carl remained in New York for a concert of Cowell's music, then joined the family at Charlotte's parents' house, which was really too small for two families. There was little room for privacy, and work was out of the question. Whenever they could, the three of them went for outings to be by themselves. Sometimes they would go fishing, or perhaps Micah fished while Carl sketched, and often he and Carl went to watch the big league baseball teams at their spring training camps. It was a sport father and son both dearly loved, and they had many happy memories of those days. Whenever possible, all three of them went to the movies, for Charlotte was an avid movie fan, and her excitement over the films was contagious.

While Carl was in Florida, Harriette went to Paris as she generally did for part of each year. One of her first acts on arriving this time in Paris was to get her divorce. Then to the surprise of everyone, within a few months, on May 6, she remarried. Her new husband was G. Harlan Miller, the second secretary of the American Embassy in Paris, whom she had met only recently, on the European-bound ship. The *New York Times* carried the story, noting that "The marriage was a complete surprise to all except a few intimate friends of the couple."[22] Carl and Charlotte were concerned, for they knew that Harriette had broken off her friendship with Kent, and they wondered if the new marriage would affect their stipend. It did not. Harriette's personal life never interfered with that nor with the deep and abiding friendship that she felt for both of them.

When Micah's semester was over, they returned to Arlington and their active social life. Carl worked at his music and paintings, and soon they were both busily engaged with the Arlington Choral Society. That summer they presented Purcell's *Dido and Aeneas* with Charlotte as soloist and Carl conducting. It was a stunning success. Carl had put together a little orchestra for the production, and one of the players may have been Count Franz Lorenz, who was to become another close and trusted musical friend. Lorenz, a fine musician and an excellent cellist, lived in Manchester, Vermont, where he tried to earn his living by teaching and conducting a small orchestra for the Equinox Hotel. Carl soon came to depend on his advice and judgment, just as he depended on Cowell's and Seeger's.

The summer was marred by growing storm clouds over Carl's relationship to the International Composers Guild (in the person of Varèse), for Carl was determined to make "Portals" into a large work with fuller instrumentation than just strings, and Varèse, speaking for the Guild, warned Carl that it would then be impossible for them to perform it. But they did want a new work from Carl for the coming season, and Varèse was determined to schedule it for the opening concert in November.

In July Varèse wrote in desperation to Charlotte, pleading with her to persuade Carl to commit himself to a work within their limits. He said that if Carl did not answer him within two weeks and agree to work within their limitations, the Guild would not perform a Ruggles work the next season, and, further, that their musical relationship would cease.

Carl *had* written. In fact, their letters crossed, but what he had suggested for his piece did not make Varèse any happier. In addition to strings, Carl requested three trumpets and three trombones—in short, a small orchestra. Varèse responded that this would be impossible for the Guild, and he pleaded with Carl to rethink his demands, adding that Goosens was to conduct his new work on November 28.

But Carl was not ready to give up. He wrote to Varèse on July 25 and suggested that he could raise enough money from his friends (he was doubtless thinking of Gene Schoen) so that the cost of the extra brass players he was requesting would not have to come from the Guild's treasury. On August 1 Varèse angrily replied that such a proposal was against Guild policy, and that this was the final note he would write on the matter.

Nonetheless Carl pursued the dispute into the late fall. Varèse was determined to program Carl's new piece on the first Guild concert of the season, now scheduled for November 20, and of course, since it was still incomplete, Carl could not possibly send it to him. Nor could he tell him much about it, for Carl himself was not sure in what direction it was going. So Varèse wrote another angry letter, accusing him of being lazy and using subterfuge in his dealings with the Guild. This stung Carl, who replied:

> I'm not 'selfish,' nor 'lazy,' and neither have I tried to camoflage [*sic*]. And I've not had a year in which to write my work. . . . I have been perfectly frank with you, and sought to let you know in time, rather than stall. And when I tell you it is absolutely impossible to finish my work by the 20th it's the truth. I do think, however, that if you were so disposed you could easily shift one of the works on the other programs to the first concert in place of mine and let mine come later. Indeed, your letter—reading between the lines—shows that.
>
> Now I have promised you the work, and you shall have it, but it will have to be on one of the other programs, and if you're my friend, you will not quibble.[23]

It was obvious that the two men were squaring off for a showdown. Clearly Carl's piece was not going to be ready; the only question was whether Varèse would back down. In the meantime Carl wrote Gene Schoen to give his side of the dispute. Schoen answered quickly, offering to speak with Varèse if Carl wanted him to, but he warned that he probably would not be able to do anything. More important, he encouraged Carl to continue with the new work, saying that Carl no longer needed the Guild. Encouraged by Schoen's letter, and doubtless sustained by Charlotte, Carl sent in his letter of resignation. His action was almost inevitable, given the situation, but it hurt both men deeply. In spite of everything, they had valued each other's friendship enormously.

One of the reasons that Carl felt strong enough to cut his ties to the Guild is that he believed there were now other possibilities for performances of his music. Henry Cowell, for example, with his New Music Society in Los Angeles had already requested the score of "Lilacs" for performance at their concert on November 20. After the program Cowell wrote that it had been "the sensation of the concert." He added that he had heard about the trouble with Varèse, and, if Carl's new piece would be ready this season, he asked for "the honour of the first performance."[24]

As Carl worked on the new music he came to realize that he was really working on a wholly new work and not additional movements to "Portals." Typically the name came well before the work was finished. It was the title from the earlier third movement of the old *Men and Angels* that he had never used — *Sun-Treader*. The first mention of it was in a postcard to Schoen written in early November: "My new composition I'm calling Sun-Treader. It's a wonder."[25] But it was not to be ready for performance that season, nor would it be for several years. Perhaps the one good thing that resulted from Carl's break with Varèse and the Guild was that it freed him from the constraints of writing for small chamber groups. Now he could write for a group of any size. On the other hand, since there was little if any pressure on him to finish the work, he could procrastinate as long as he wanted over every single note. This lack of pressure brought back all the old insecurities, which he had to surmount over and over again.

They agreed to spend the winter with Charlotte's parents again, who had built a tiny wing onto their house to provide privacy and enough room for a rented piano. On December 29 they left Arlington and spent the night in New York at Blanche Walton's new home. Then Charlotte and Micah left for Florida, while Carl stayed on for a few days to visit with old friends. That short stay in the city proved eventful, for by a happy coincidence he met Varèse, and the two made up on the spot. Carl remembered that they were at a concert in Carnegie Hall. He was going up the steps while Varèse was coming down. "We rushed together with our arms around each other. I said, 'You know I'm no longer a member of the Guild' — and he said, 'Don't you know I never accepted your resignation?' "[26]

In late March Varèse wrote encouragingly about the next season. He would issue a new manifesto for the organization, and they would perform only American music, mainly that of Ruggles, Varèse, and possibly one or two others. It sounded like a fine idea, but it was not to be. At the end of the 1925–26 season the organization was six hundred dollars in debt and it was clear that the principal backers would not be forthcoming. So Carlos Salzedo paid the debt out of his own pocket, and that ended the Guild.[27]

NOTES

1. Carl Ruggles to Eugene Schoen, 30 Sept. 1924. The Blake quotation is: "Great things are done when men and mountains meet; These are not done by jostling in the street."
2. Interview with author, 25 Nov. 1966.
3. Ibid.
4. *New York Herald Tribune,* 8 Dec. 1924.
5. *The Dial* (Feb. 1925): 171–72.
6. Charles Seeger to Carl Ruggles, [Dec. 1924].
7. Interview with author, 31 Jan. 1967.
8. *Arts and Decoration* 14:4 (Feb. 1921): 296. Underneath a picture of Mrs. Bingham are the following comments: "Mrs. Harry Payne Bingham of New York and Westbury, L.I. who, before her marriage was Miss Harriette Gowen of Cleveland, Ohio, is one of the younger women of social prominence who are doing so much to raise the standard of American art."
9. Charles Seeger to Carl Ruggles, Miami, Florida, 20 May 1925.
10. Carl Ruggles to Eugene Schoen, 25 May 1925.
11. Interview with author, 20 Oct. 1966.
12. Interview with Micah Ruggles, 31 Jan. 1976.
13. Interview with author, 19 Jan. 1967.
14. Carl Ruggles to Charlotte Ruggles, 19 Oct. 1925.
15. Carl Ruggles to Charlotte Ruggles, 20 Nov. 1925.
16. Ibid.
17. Carl Ruggles to Charlotte Ruggles, 30 Nov. 1925.
18. Carl Ruggles to Charlotte Ruggles, [postmarked Dec. 1925].
19. Carl Ruggles to Charlotte Ruggles, 17 Jan. 1926.
20. Carl Ruggles to Charlotte Ruggles, 16 Jan. 1926.
21. *New York Herald Tribune,* 25 Jan. 1926.
22. *New York Times,* 7 May 1926.
23. Carl Ruggles to Edgard Varèse, [fall 1926].
24. Henry Cowell to Carl Ruggles, 28 Nov. 1926.
25. Carl Ruggles to Eugene Schoen, 5 Nov. 1926.
26. John Kirkpatrick, "The Evolution of Carl Ruggles," *Perspectives of New Music* 6:2 (Spring-Summer 1968): 156.
27. See Louise Varèse, *A Looking-Glass Diary* (New York: W. W. Norton & Co., Inc., 1972), 259.

9

Sun-Treader
1927–34

Happily for Carl there was the indefatigable Henry Cowell on whom he could rely as his champion and advocate, for in the spring of 1927 no one else seemed available. "Dear Henry," Carl wrote in May of that year, "I am deeply touched and honored that the New Music Society wishes to publish 'Lilacs.' But I feel that its [*sic*] unwise to take it out of its context, and publish it separately, and I'm sure you will agree with me."

He went on to say that the score was ready for publication, and that if Cowell and the New Music Society would pay for publishing "Lilacs," he would raise the money for the publication of the other two movements. "I'm sure I can get Schoen to give the balance. What do you say?" he concluded.[1]

When Cowell moved to San Francisco that spring to reorganize the New Music Society, he also started *New Music Quarterly,* a publication of contemporary music, and he wanted "Lilacs" from *Men and Mountains* in the first issue. It was a much needed enterprise, for none of the established publishing firms would have anything to do with the ultramodern music of Cowell, Ruggles, or the others.

For the new publication Cowell appointed an advisory board and solicited subscriptions—from Charles Ives among others, who responded favorably. Carl may have known of Ives before this time, but quite possibly it was this publication that resulted in their meeting and the beginning of another important friendship. Once again, as he had done with Carl and Seeger, it was Cowell who either knowingly or unwittingly brought the two older New Englanders together.

It is easy to see why the established publishing houses were not interested in publishing this new music. When Carl received his yearly account from Curwen for the year ending May 31, 1927, the account read as follows: "Stock last year—79, Present stock—76, Reviews and Spoilt Copies—3." Not a single copy had been sold in the entire year. In fact the total sales from the time of publication in 1925 consisted of only seventy-eight copies, and as the statement noted: "Copies to be sold before Royalty starts 250."

Cowell answered Carl that, while he would very much like to publish the entire *Men and Mountains,* he could raise only enough money for eight pages. So Carl immediately wrote to Schoen about the project and asked for his support. He explained that there had to be a guarantee of fifteen dollars per page, and he was confident that he could lay it out for the engraver with only six additional pages beyond the original eight. "So all you will have to pay is *$90,*" he wrote.[2] Carl had to write two letters to Schoen to persuade him, but the financial support was eventually forthcoming.

By this time the Ruggleses were back home in Arlington and summer was in full swing, with strawberry teas at the Schnakenbergs and parties with the summer people and the artists. At the local ball games Carl often served as umpire, and his loud voice and colorful language made him as much a star as any member of the teams. In addition, nearly every day he made several trips to the post office or the general store, to spend hours swapping stories with his neighbors and to make an occasional purchase.

Each morning, after a hearty breakfast, he worked on the new composition or fussed with his other ones. In the afternoon he occasionally sketched or painted. One project that summer was arranging "Lilacs" for wind instruments to perform at Cowell's opening concert in San Francisco. It was to take place shortly after the *New Music Quarterly* would be available, so he could announce the publication. One wonders how Carl felt about re-scoring the work, though he had certainly allowed it for "Angels."

Once he wrote to Schoen and asked to have his son, Leon, purchase some pencils for him, adding: "Also he might step into Schirmer 43st. near GCT [Grand Central Terminal] and get me a quire of music paper, 12 staffs."[3] The high-handed tone of this missive with its assumption that his friends would simply do his bidding was typical of Carl throughout his life. What is interesting is the fact that most of the time that is exactly what happened. He had the ability to make people feel they should fulfill his requests, and often it seemed to be the only way to treat him in order to continue to be his friend.

On October 15 *New Music* made its appearance with the full score of *Men and Mountains.* Cowell had been able to get 594 subscriptions from all over the world, and among the subscribers were composers, performers, critics, and conductors. Along with the score he had printed the glowing review by Lawrence Gilman, written at the time of its premiere. Carl was thrilled.

In November Cowell returned East, and, along with Varèse and Carlos Chavez, the Mexican composer and conductor, helped to found the Pan American Association of Composers, Inc. Since Varèse would be in Europe much of the time, Cowell was put in charge, serving as director of the North American section. Carl and Emerson Whithorne became vice-presidents along with Chavez. The organization covered a larger spectrum of composers than the old Guild and was more explicitly interested in national and international programs. When Charles Ives joined he became one of the most generous of its supporters.

Though Carl was listed as one of the vice-presidents, he was not really active in the founding of the organization, for the Ruggleses had gone to St. Petersburg in October. Since Charlotte's mother was not well, she wanted to be with her as much as possible; and Charlotte herself, in poor health during the summer, did not want to stay in Arlington to suffer any of the cold weather.

On their way to Florida they stopped for a few days with Blanche Walton, and during their visit Carl talked to her about his finances. It was clear that he was not going to make any money as a composer, and in spite of the monthly stipend from Harriette and the occasional gifts from their affluent friends, they often felt the lack of funds. Micah was growing up and needed more things, and Charlotte was not teaching regularly to help with their income. Carl was fifty-one years old, and he wanted to have more for himself and his family. He proposed that Blanche, with the help of other rich friends, create a sort of endowment fund out of which he would be paid several thousand dollars for each new composition that he wrote. He assured her that it would be a stimulus for him to write more quickly. The idea was not unlike a fund that Kent had actually managed to start for his paintings some years before, and Carl may have remembered that.

Blanche promised to think it over, and he did not have to wait long for her reply. She wrote that she feared Harriette would not approve, and advised him to talk with her, suggesting that he ask her to give him a special additional fee for each new work completed, perhaps two thousand dollars a composition. Carl felt he could not do this, and the project was dropped. This was one of several money-making schemes that Carl attempted throughout his life. None was ever successful, and invariably he had to fall back on additional support from friends, who were always forthcoming, including Harriette.

Shortly after he and Charlotte had left Mrs. Walton's, a note arrived for him in New York from the librarian for the Boston Symphony. Koussevitzky had received his copy of *Men and Mountains* and found it interesting enough to ask for the parts. Friends in New York took care of duplicating and forwarding them to the conductor, and all Carl had to do was wait and hope that a performance might eventually take place. He needed a performance, for there had not been any in New York since "Portals" in January 1926, and very few in other places. It was a difficult time, but Charlotte would not let him give up.

In early January 1928 Carl wrote glumly to Cowell that they were having a hard time, and, to make matters worse, were enduring ice and cold weather. And he wondered if Koussevitzky would respond and really do *Men and Mountains*. In addition, Charlotte was still not feeling well, though she continued to care for her mother, who was getting weaker and ever more infirm.

One reason for their gloomy winter was a lack of interesting friends, and they were thrilled when Henry Schnakenberg came for the opening of an exhibition and stayed to visit them. Schnakenberg wrote to his mother that Carl had found a "house-keeping apartment" for him for twenty dollars a week right along the park on the shore of Tampa Bay.[4] In another letter, he wrote that his time was filled with small things like painting watercolors, suppers with Carl and Charlotte, and trips to the beaches looking for shells. Collecting shells was a great hobby of Charlotte's; when she died, she left a number of tiny specimens that she had collected over the years. Oftentimes she would glue them on boxes of varying sizes, making lovely homemade gifts. Carl probably sketched or painted a bit with Schnakenberg while they traded stories and gossiped or talked about art.

Soon after their return to Vermont in May, Dorothy sent them a welcoming letter full of encouragement and enclosed a homecoming check. In Carl's thank you note, he wrote: "Now I'm going to lay my soul bare. Never do I start to write 3 measures before I'm confronted with a labyrinth of obstacles. Black despair—Sometimes one would rather do almost anything than write—And then, out of it all comes something fresh, and beautiful, and young. Just one line, Dorothy, just one line that makes it all worth while."[5]

The only one missing from the summer reunions was Kent. He and his new wife, Frances, had moved to a farm in Ausable Forks, New York. Kent wrote cordially inviting Carl to the new place, but Carl declined. He wrote that his work prevented him from making the visit and assured Kent that he would try to get over soon. But he never went, and though the two men remained friends, from this time on their lives took separate turns and gradually their correspondence ceased.

Carl hoped not to go to Florida again, for he really didn't want to be that far away from New York, and then fate stepped in to settle the matter. Charlotte's mother died. In late August when she took a turn for the worse, Charlotte wrote in desperation to Dorothy: "I hate to come to you at this time with your illness, but I am desperate—a telegram has just come that my mother is apt to pass away at any moment—She was taken to the hospital last Thursday. They have the smallest income and nothing to meet illness and death with—I am asking you for a loan of $500.00 so that she may be taken care of in a seemly way."[6]

The money was promptly given, and her mother's body was returned to Lawrence, Massachusetts, for burial, with Charlotte in attendance. Her brother had died some years before while a student at McGill University. Carl did not attend the funeral or offer much help; he did not like his in-laws, nor, in truth, did they like him. Charlotte did not have much time for grief. She had her own family to care for, and she quickly returned to Arlington.

It is interesting that they did not turn to Harriette for help with Charlotte's mother, and one reason was that they had already talked to her about another financial matter: paying off the note on their house. Carl may not have been able to find additional income, but he was able to make Harriette understand about the schoolhouse. On October 1, 1928, he gave $813.24 to G. M. Vaughan and A. H. Smith, and the mortgage deed was fully discharged. The schoolhouse was theirs. Years later when he was reminiscing about how kind and generous Harriette had been, he exclaimed: "Why, she bought the house and gave it to us!"[7]

Carl was never shy about discussing financial problems with his friends, and now that they would not be going to Florida, the question was how and where they should spend the winter, since they could not remain in the schoolhouse. One of their wealthier friends once told me that over the years they all came to feel that the Ruggleses were like special children who needed to be taken care of, and this was true, especially of Carl, who fostered this response.

Most of their rich friends did not stay all year in Vermont, and during the fall there was much discussion among them on what to do about the Ruggleses. Mary Powers, a painter and one of the founders of the Southern Vermont Art Association, finally came up with a solution. She had a winter home in Jamaica, and she invited them to be her guests for the season. It was an overwhelming offer, but not one that Carl could accept immediately, for once again he would be away from New York. On the other hand they certainly would live very well and it would be a good experience. Over and over he and Charlotte discussed it, and typically they vacillated. Not until mid-October did they finally accept the kind offer. Schnakenberg wrote tellingly about their indecisiveness to his mother: "Saw the Ruggles yesterday. They finally *think* they've decided to go with Mary Powers to Jamaica but there are so many objections on the part of Carl that there's no telling whether this decision is final or not. If any plan is ever broached to Carl he immediately starts crabbing about it."[8]

Carl still had not heard from Koussevitzky, and he had so hoped for such a performance with the Boston Symphony Orchestra that it gnawed at him. Finally he wrote about it to Schoen, who in turn spoke to the symphony's concertmaster to see if he could help Carl. The concertmaster told him that he had no idea why Koussevitzky had not yet performed Carl's music. Carl was so frustrated and angry that he asked Schoen to write directly to Koussevitzky about the music. And Schoen did that, too, receiving a prompt response that he sent on to Carl. It was not a happy reply, for Koussevitzky explained that he had already programmed so many "novelties" in the season that he could not use *Men and Mountains*. Carl was furious, but still unwilling to give up. He sent a copy of Gilman's rave review to Schoen and asked him to forward it to Koussevitzky, hoping to show the conductor that his piece was more than a mere novelty.

But it was not to be. The Boston Symphony Orchestra did not perform any of Carl's music until 1966, when they gave the first American performance of *Sun-Treader* in Portland, Maine, under the direction of Jean Martinon. By that time Carl was too old and infirm to attend, and too hard of hearing to really hear the tape that was made for him.

Meanwhile, Jamaica was a wonderful experience for all of them. Mary Powers, who had been a teacher before her marriage, had recently been widowed, and she was grateful for their company. She and Charlotte found a place for Carl to work on his music, and she herself tutored Micah so he would not get behind in his schoolwork. Most of the time, though, she painted, and it was contagious—there was so much to look at, so many vivid and exotic colors and objects that they had never seen before. Soon Carl, who admitted that he borrowed her watercolors, was painting along with her, and Micah, too. Almost daily they went on painting excursions.

Then it was the first of May, and they left the island to return to Vermont, stopping first in New York for Carl to catch up on musical contacts and old friends. One of the people with whom he visited was Adolph Weiss, a friend from the International Composers Guild. Weiss was now an active member of the Conductorless Symphony Orchestra in New York, serving with the "Committee on Interpretation," and he had a voice in choosing the repertoire. Carl and he talked about the possibility of doing some Ruggles in the next season, and Weiss was encouraging. Before they parted, he promised that he would try to get "Portals" accepted for the 1929–30 season. "Portals" had been Carl's last New York performance, but that had been for only thirteen strings; this time it would be performed by a full string orchestra.

During the summer he continued to work on the new piece at his usual snail's pace. In addition he went over the parts to "Portals" to ready them for the possible performance. He also umpired for some of the town baseball games and kept up with his painting and sketching.

This year when it came time to organize the annual Southern Vermont Artists show, Mary Powers, who had charge of the executive details, invited Carl to submit his Jamaican pictures. She invited Micah to submit his, too, for there was to be a special exhibit of works by children from five to fifteen. The members of the jury included two good friends: Herbert Meyer and Henry Schnakenberg, and both Carl and Micah had their works accepted.

Edward Alden Jewell, the art critic, viewed the show and devoted his Sunday column to it, noting especially the superb Jamaican scenes of Mary Powers. He added: "Here is Carl Ruggles, a young modern composer [Carl was fifty-three at the time]; and he paints you music, because it is the thing he knows best."[9] We don't know which paintings Carl exhibited, but from the above statement, it would seem that he saw even the exotic sights of Jamaica filtered through the rhythms of music. Furthermore, this may have been the origin of Carl's oft-quoted remark, always proudly proclaimed, "I paint music!"

While this was the first time Carl showed his artwork in the company of professional artists, it is important to remember that this was not the beginning of his painting. As we have seen, that dated all the way back to Winona days, and though he might pretend that this art was unimportant, he took it very seriously — even asking Anne Ahern, Charlotte's pupil and friend, to send to him in New York a special package of his sketches that he had left behind in Winona.

On the other hand, it was probably the first time that he realized he might make some extra money from his artwork, for several of his paintings in the exhibit were sold. They were not expensive, only twenty-five or fifty dollars, but it was a new and interesting opportunity, and he took advantage of it from that time forward. Micah, too, sold his paintings. The Schnakenbergs, Henry's parents, bought them.

In mid-September Weiss wrote to confirm that the Conductorless Symphony Orchestra would do "Portals" on their opening concert on Saturday, October 26, 1929, at Carnegie Hall. He asked Carl to send the parts and some publicity on himself and the work. Carl responded by asking Dorothy Canfield Fisher to write it, as she had done with *Men and Mountains*. She agreed, and sent a long, flowery article full of praise for Carl and his music. The concert was a huge success for Carl. He was surrounded by friends, and the audience was so enthusiastic that the piece was repeated.

Winter was fast approaching, and once more the question of where to spend it needed to be answered. As before, the question also concerned their friends. This time Rowland Hazard, a wealthy Rhode Islander, invited them to winter at his new ranch in Alamogordo, New Mexico. There were several houses on the property, and the Ruggleses would have one all to themselves, but as usual Carl grumbled and vacillated, complaining that it was such a long trip and so far from New York.

While they considered Hazard's invitation, Carl received several pieces of good news. Martha Graham wanted to dance to "Portals" at her performance in January at the Forest Theater. He did not know her then, but in the future they would meet on several occasions. Cowell wrote, too, that he was going to publish "Portals" in the *New Music Quarterly* and wanted the score at once. He was also interested in the new piece, *Sun-Treader*. Both Blanche Walton and Seeger had been pushing Cowell to publish "Portals" — even offering to put up some of the funds needed for the project. And all three of these old friends wanted Carl to get on with *Sun-Treader*.

Cowell had even written to Blanche, "If you can give the 'Sun Treader' some rehearsals, I expect Carl will finish it, and perfect it."[10] Carl, typically, was making slow progress, for this was to be his biggest work to date, and he felt he must go even more carefully. But Cowell was quite right. Since there was no specific prospect for a performance, there seemed no rush to complete it. So he progressed even more slowly than usual.

In the meantime Carl and Charlotte were being pressed for a definite answer about the winter. Carl was persuaded finally to accept Hazard's kind invitation when Schnakenberg promised to visit them at the ranch. Hazard, who had already gone West to check on the building progress, was quickly notified, and he immediately responded with delight, assuring them that everything would be ready for their arrival, including horses for Micah to ride. Then he wired the train fare, which was $136.57 for the three of them, and all the books, scores, and painting materials that they were taking along.

Hazard's ranch, just outside of Alamogordo on one of the nearby mountains, consisted of the main house, where he lived, and several smaller guest houses. When Schnakenberg, true to his word, visited in March, he wrote to his family that "the place is high up on a mountain looking for miles into the distance."[11] Carl remembered that everyone spoke Spanish, and that the cowboys taught Micah to ride horseback.

Carl spent much of those months in New Mexico helping to get "Portals" in print. In addition to the score itself, there was the question of some sort of introduction or notes, and this time Carl himself would have to write it. Meanwhile the engraver sent him the first set of proofs, and they were so full of errors that Carl simply rejected the whole collection, sending specific directions on how the piece should be set. It took until the end of March for him to accept the proofs. Of course the introduction remained for him to finish, and finally he turned to Seeger for help, sending him whatever he had managed to put down. Seeger quickly returned it, with some excellent advice: "As a rule, the less composers write about their work the safer (not to say the more dignified) they are."[12]

Carl took Seeger's advice, and "Portals" was printed without Carl's introduction. Cowell meanwhile was championing Carl's cause in other ways. He had proposed "Portals" to the International Society for Contemporary Music, and it had been unanimously accepted for submission to the international jury for performance in Liège. He had also proposed it for the ISCM catalog, which was soon to be printed. What would Carl have done without Henry Cowell?

Life in Alamogordo was not all work. Often there were dinners at the ranch house with their host, who arranged sight-seeing trips for them where Carl could paint or sketch. When Henry Schnakenberg arrived, there were even more festivities, and he, too, had his own little house near the Ruggleses. Hazard arranged for all of them to go on a three-day day trip to the Carlsbad Caverns, guided by his overseer, the state geologist of New Mexico. After the excursion into the caverns, Schnakenberg reported that they lunched in a "cafeteria 750 feet below the ground." He added that he worried about Charlotte's "walking out because of the climb — but she did it gradually."[13]

The Ruggleses stayed at the ranch through the month of April, then returned to their beloved schoolhouse. Carl was still working at *Sun-Treader,* and after a visit during the summer, Schnakenberg wrote perceptively to his mother: "Last evening we went to the Ruggles [*sic*]. Carl played some of the recent stuff that he has been working on and it certainly is extremely beautiful. I do wish that he had some *outlet* in the way of a performance or two. He needs it desperately for his own satisfaction."[14]

Often Carl had Franz Lorenz come to listen to what he had written.

Lorenz seemed to understand that Carl, as he himself stated, was trying to write soaring dissonant melodic lines. He wanted to reach new heights of tension and grandeur. When they got together, Lorenz would ask Carl to sing a line, then he would tell him, "That's not what you've written," and they would wrestle over the problem of notating the uneven rhythms that Carl wanted. Sometimes they would work at the schoolhouse; sometimes Carl would go up to Manchester to see Lorenz at his house, which he had named "Walhalla."[15]

But Carl missed Seeger's advice. He sent him numerous invitations to visit, until Seeger finally accepted. He and Ruth Crawford drove up in August for a few days of intense talk and "grand fun," as Carl put it. They went over the new piece, note by note, pounding it out on the piano and singing and shouting other parts. Then they put the music on the floor and got down on their hands and knees to study it. Carl used extra large sheets of music paper, often homemade from brown wrapping paper; he chose them partly to save money, partly because his eyesight was not very good, and partly because he loved to have the pages spread across the floor. Moreover, in the sketching stages he would write all over the large sheets, which gave him much more space than the regular printed music paper.

Perhaps it was on this visit, when they were driving back from Manchester in Seeger's car, that a police officer stopped them and started to give Seeger a speeding ticket for driving five miles above the speed limit. Carl leaned out of the rear window and said, "Oh John, let him off this time." When the officer recognized Carl, he did just that, to Seeger's relief and amusement.

August in Vermont provides halcyon days, and on one they had tea out on the lawn in back of the schoolhouse. They sat in the warm sunlight and looked out over the cleared land to a meadow below, where cows were grazing contentedly. With a wink at Seeger, Carl said slyly to Ruth, "There, Ruth, that's what an ideal woman should be like. A cow." Then Seeger said, "He sat back and waited for the fury. And he got it!"[16]

When the leaves began to turn in early fall, Carl and Charlotte invited Seeger to make a return visit. Ruth was in Europe on a Guggenheim Fellowship, so they invited Blanche Walton to come with him. Their invitation was so heartfelt that it was gladly accepted.

When their guests returned to New York, Seeger wrote to Carl that he simply had to finish *Sun-Treader* soon. Cowell wanted to take it to Europe, and Seeger was sure that if Carl worked very hard (although he wondered if Carl could) he would complete it in time. Meanwhile in October Cowell programmed "Portals" on his New Music Society concert in San Francisco. The conductor was a young man from Havana, Cuba, Pedro Sanjuán. It was Sanjuán's first contact with Carl's music, and he became an ardent champion.

The problem of money and where to spend the winter continued to nag at Carl and Charlotte. The latter problem was solved when, with the advice, urgings, and doubtless financial help from friends, they agreed to spend the cold months boarding at a house next door to the Schnakenbergs on West Road in Manchester. It was owned by Mrs. Binkerd, who thought it would be fine to have the Ruggleses live with her. The money problem, however, was not so easily resolved.

Dorothy was called upon for advice, and she suggested a possibility that appealed to them in every way. The president of Bennington College was beginning his search for the first faculty for the new institution, and since Dorothy was on the board of trustees, she would write to President Robert Devore Leigh, recommending Carl for a position, and Charlotte, too, for that matter.

Dorothy was true to her word, and soon after their conversation, she sent a rough draft of the letter for their approval. Her letter to President Leigh was full of praise for Carl and Charlotte, and, rather than suggest that Carl wanted the job, she took the position that he allowed her to recommend him because he was interested in supporting the college. She went on to recount Carl's international reputation, and finally, she suggested that he drive up to Arlington to meet the Ruggleses. Two weeks later President Leigh responded, and not unfavorably. He explained that it was still too early for him to make a commitment, but he promised to consider Carl first. And he hoped that soon he would be able to talk with him.[17]

At about the same time that Carl received this encouraging news he also received a letter from a young conductor named Nicolas Slonimsky, director of the Chamber Orchestra of Boston. Carl had not even heard of Slonimsky, who was dedicated to bringing modern music to staid Boston. Slonimsky sent some of his programs, which included his own program notes, and a sample program to show that he planned to perform *Men and Mountains* on his New York Town Hall concert scheduled for January 10, 1931. He hoped that Carl would approve, and he invited him down for the rehearsal on January 9. Carl was jubilant and answered quickly: "Your annotations are about the best I've seen for many a year. Indeed, your analysis of 'Men and Mountains' is masterly. Your style is both fresh and original. I'm fed up with the stale junk these critics write. In fact I'm fed up with critics generally."[18]

With much anticipation, Carl went to New York for the rehearsal and performance of *Men and Mountains*. He and Slonimsky got along well, and the interesting program included works by Ives, Riegger, Cowell, Robin Milford, and Mozart. The "Relevant Notes," as Slonimsky dubbed the program notes, were his own, and though he got Carl's birthdate wrong (1883), he wrote tellingly and with a light touch: "There is little affinity between Ruggles's personal idiom and that of the various European schools. Ruggles is scaling heights, plumbing depths, proclaiming polysyllabical millenia. This immensity of design is utterly un-European. Since Ruggles's music cannot be Asian, African or Australian, it must be American."[19]

Slonimsky's modern American music programs were receiving wide acclaim, and, with the support of Ives and under the auspices of the Pan American Association of Composers, he arranged to conduct two programs of American music in Paris in June 1931. For these concerts he would have a full orchestra, and once again he planned to include *Men and Mountains*.

In a letter to Carl he asked for the parts for the full orchestra, since Cowell had told him that they were available. Carl answered that he had indeed made parts for a full orchestra, but he thought they were still in New York, though he really wasn't sure they could be found at all. He would make new ones, and he promised Slonimsky that they would be ready within a week. Of course they were not, but they were, however, ready more quickly than usual by Carl's standards, and soon Slonimsky had them.

The concerts were to take place on June 6 and 11, and Adolph Weiss and the Vareses were on hand for the events. The latter's "Intégrales" was scheduled for the program on the eleventh. Since Varèse was native born and knew many of the French musicians, he attended all the rehearsals, helping to smooth over any rough spots that arose over this modern music.[20] Carl's piece was on the June 6 concert with other works by Weiss, Ives, Cowell, and Amadeo Roldan, a Cuban composer. In addition to writing the more extensive program notes, Slonimsky put a one-line summation under each work on the program page. For Carl's he wrote: "A brobdingnagian vision inspired by Blake."

Carl deeply regretted not being at the concert, especially since it was the first time that *Men and Mountains* had been performed with a full orchestra. It hurt him that he and Charlotte could not afford the trip; and over and over again he wondered if there was some way he could make more money. There was still the possibility of teaching at Bennington, and President Leigh had written again to Dorothy that he had not forgotten the Ruggleses. That certainly seemed their best hope, but there was nothing to do except wait. And waiting was much easier since it was summer again, and they were back in the schoolhouse.

In July the Colonial Theater in Manchester installed talking motion pictures, and whenever they could, the Ruggleses went to the movies. In August there were ground breaking ceremonies for Bennington College, but still no word from President Leigh. Carl was now a regular exhibitor with the Southern Vermont Artists, and he spent a good part of the summer getting ready for the show. It was a way to make some extra money, for he always sold at least a few of his works.

When September came, Micah enrolled in nearby Burr and Burton Seminary. He was old enough to drive, so they bought their first car, a Chevrolet with a rumble seat. The old shed became the garage, though, since it was a little too short, the car's rear end extended out. Now they could go to the movies whenever they wished. All three would sit in the front with Micah driving, Carl in the middle, and Charlotte on the outside. Micah could drive himself to school, too, and that was the real reason for the car.[21]

By mid-October Slonimsky had been engaged to conduct the Orchestre Symphonique de Paris in two concerts on February 21 and 25, 1932. He would feature Varèse's *Arcana* in the programs, and he also wanted to include Carl's new work, *Sun-Treader*, except that it was still incomplete. Carl had finally begun the full score, in pencil on his birthday, March 11, 1931, but in spite of the persistent pushing by Cowell and Seeger during the past year, he had as always moved slowly.

Cowell, Carl's "affectionate worker" as he signed one letter, decided to push even harder. First he arranged for a performance of "Portals" to be conducted by Sanjuán in Madrid on November 23. Then he wrote Carl that he wanted to publish *Sun-Treader* right away, and that he had already lined up Edition Adler in Berlin to print it.

Typically Carl delayed, responding that he only had his first pencil copy of the full score, and the need to make a fair copy would take some time. Cowell, however, was not to be put off. He notified Charles Ives about Carl's copying needs, and Ives generously offered to have Emil Hanke, his copyist, his best according to John Kirkpatrick, do the work at Ives's expense. Then Cowell wrote to Carl from Berlin: "Do hurry the copying of the Sun Treader! We just MUST have it! And instead of spending the money to have the score photographed, which costs a good deal, will you not let me have it printed right away, and give me the photography money towards the cost? . . . As you get part of the score done, you might send it to save time, registered, to the Edition Adler. . . . They will print it for me, and I will leave word there to rush it along. Then we can make parts at once from the finished score!"

He added more good news. He had persuaded the Berlin Rundfunk

Orchestra to accept *Men and Mountains* for performance in January. In addition Ernst Ansermet was planning to do "Portals" on his next concert for the International Society for Contemporary Music, which had been arranged by Copland, whom Carl had met in New York in 1930.[22]

Carl and Charlotte were excited and overwhelmed by the news, but before Carl could reply, Cowell wrote again. "Portals" would be done in December, *Men and Mountains* in January; and he pleaded with Carl to have *Sun-Treader* ready for a March concert that he was arranging. He urged him to send the material quickly to Hanke, the copyist, and Cowell told him that he was having a new edition of "Portals" (score and parts) brought out there in Berlin.

The Ansermet concert took place on December 9, and two days later Cowell reported that the concert had been well attended, and that "Portals" had sounded well. But Cowell explained that there had not been enough rehearsals, and he felt that the melodic lines were blurred in the performance. Then he added that he was coming back to New York by December 20, and he hoped Carl would be able to meet him there. They would stay at Blanche Walton's and work on getting *Sun-Treader* ready for print. The year was ending on a high note for Carl, but after this letter about the performance of "Portals," he never liked Ansermet. Whenever the conductor's name came up in his hearing, he would sneer, "Ass of Progress!"[23]

After the holidays Carl went to New York, and he and Cowell worked on *Sun-Treader;* Carl was still making changes and arguing with Cowell about each addition or deletion. Meanwhile Slonimsky, who was to conduct the work in Paris, kept after both of them. He was very anxious to have the score to study and he needed to take it all with him.

Work went on for a whole month, with Charlotte and Micah back in Arlington trying to keep warm without exceeding their far too tight budget. She wrote: "It will cheer you to know that we are burning only 2 scuttles of coal a day and the most devoted efficient service from the whole Cullinan family for $2.00 a week. All hail the Depression also fresh eggs have dropped to 20 cts a dozen."[24]

They were lucky in early January, for the weather was "warm and rainy," she wrote. But when the full force of winter struck, she had to order several tons of coal. "Bad news—I had to order another ton of coal. . . . Dunlap looked terribly sad this morning when he told me we owed him for 3 tons. This damn money—If we only had 50.00 more a month what a difference it would make."[25]

Finally Carl was able to write that the work was finished: "Yesterday

I didn't have a minute to write. A dreadful day. Copyists, *Nicolas,* a new score phostated [*sic*] for him—he sails tonight for Europe with the Sun-treader. You see we have to have a score for him, also two scores, one for the Brass and one for the strings, and I'm doing the work. Oh, it's a big job. Blanche will write you about it all. . . . You never saw anything so fine as the way the front page came out. Wonderful."[26] Then he drew a picture of a sparkling sun with the dedication to his patroness, "Harriette Miller," above it.

Slonimsky conducted the premiere of *Sun-Treader* with the Orchestre Symphonique de Paris at the Salle Playel on Thursday, February 25. It had not been an easy time for him. Many of the players found the music not only extremely difficult but unmusical. At rehearsals some refused even to try to learn their parts. There was shouting and stamping. Then Varèse, a fellow Parisian and not therefore a crazy American, stepped in to help. He went to each man and pleaded with him, soothing him, and making him feel how important he was to the entire undertaking. Reluctantly the men agreed to work and to perform the music; but soon it became all too evident that more rehearsals would be necessary, which meant paying the musicians extra money. Slonimsky notified Ives, who once again came to the rescue, cabling funds for the extra rehearsals. At last the performance took place, and as usual the reviews were mixed. But the Varèses, writing from Paris, assured Carl that the piece had been warmly received. In the coming weeks Slonimsky performed it in Berlin and Prague.

The sad part of the *Sun-Treader* story is that Carl and Charlotte were not in attendance at any one of these performances. Though the piece, on which he had labored for six years, would be performed again in Europe, it was not given in the United States until 1966. By then Charlotte was dead and, as noted above, Carl was too old to attend, and too deaf to really hear the tape of the concert. A recording of it was made in 1965, but even that was blurred for him. So the work that is his major undertaking, and regarded by some as his masterpiece, remained alive and crystal clear to him only in his inner hearing.

The title of *Sun-Treader* (the hyphen was added when the piece was properly copied) is from Browning's description of Shelley from the poem, *Pauline:* "Sun-Treader, light and life be thine forever." As we know, Carl had used the title before for the third movement of his earlier incomplete work, *Men and Angels.* It fit his vision of what he hoped this new much bigger work would be, and Charlotte, who may have found it for him in the first place, encouraged him to use it.

Though *Sun-Treader* only lasts about sixteen and one-half minutes, it is larger in every way than anything Carl had attempted so far, except the opera. But it harkens back to that earlier *Men and Angels* in another way, for that early work was supposed to be for large orchestra as well, and there are other interesting similarities.

Both pieces call for piccolo as well as flutes, English horn, oboes, bass clarinet in addition to B flat clarinets, and contrabassoon plus three regular bassoons. In the brass section, both call for six French horns instead of the usual four, and both employ two harps and the same percussion, namely timpani and cymbals. But the new *Sun-Treader* asks for even more instruments. It is almost as if Carl had decided to outdo his earlier unfinished effort and to prove, as much to himself as to the world, that he could write for such large forces. A decade ago he would not have been able to do this.

The complete instrumentation for *Sun-Treader* is: *Woodwinds:* two piccolos (interchangeable with flutes), three flutes, three oboes, two English horns, one E flat clarinet, three clarinets in C, one bass clarinet, three bassoons, one contrabassoon; *Brass:* six horns in F, five trumpets in C, five trombones, one tenor tuba in C, one bass tuba. Carl has even stipulated the number of players for the string section: eighteen to twenty first violins, eighteen to twenty second violins, twelve to fourteen violas, ten to twelve cellos, eight to ten double basses; then two harps, timpani, and cymbals (high and low). The minimum number of players called for is 107, a far cry from the chamber ensembles for which he had previously written. Yet those chamber ensembles were his training ground for this big work. "Angels" was written for brass alone, "Portals" only for strings, and *Men and Mountains,* though for a small ensemble, combined woodwinds and strings. Carl had learned with each work, and *Sun-Treader* was the culmination.

Despite the large forces, in the main the writing is for no more than three lines at once, so there is much doubling of parts, either in unison or at the octave. The upper woodwinds — flute, oboes, and B flat clarinets — double the violins; the English horn and lower woodwinds tend to double the trombones, tubas, and lower strings; while the trumpets, French horns, and E flat clarinet may form the third grouping. This instrumental distribution naturally varies throughout the 241 measures of the piece, but the maximum number of simultaneous lines is kept at three or less.

Whether Carl created sublime music, as he hoped, is open to question, but there can be no doubt about the enormous intensity of the work. The soprano instruments often play at their upper limits, while at the same time the bass instruments are playing at their lowest range.

And these two outer lines, the ones, incidentally, most clearly heard by the listener, are almost always sharply dissonant with one another. Since they are very far apart, there is room for the third strand of music to fill in the middle space, and it, too, is often dissonant to the other two. So in addition to the extreme ranges, there are the almost constant dissonances that also serve to heighten the intensity.

Another source of tension is Carl's remarkable use of rhythm. Each strand of music has its own rhythm, and, at the same time, within each line there is enormous variety. See, for example, the rhythm of one of the longest lines at the climax of the piece (examples 23 and 24). Note that example 23 shows the complete line with pitch and rhythm, while example 24 shows the same line with the rhythm alone. Note how each measure differs from the others.

Also, in these examples we see that, with four exceptions, each of the measures is tied to the previous one, thus inhibiting the downbeat and further enhancing the irregularity of the rhythm. The four exceptions are measure 174, the beginning of the line (see example 23); measure 175, the first crest; measure 180, the beginning of a downward movement and, significantly, the very center of the line that gradually ascends again; and measure 185, the high point of the line. Clearly Carl was trying to notate *tempo rubato,* his lifelong challenge. Perhaps here in *Sun-Treader* he was most successful.

Measures 172 and 173 are really only the jumping-off point for this line, which begins on beat three of measure 173 and climbs in undulating waves until it reaches its highest point at measure 185. At that point it drops down to return to earlier material that will bring the piece to its conclusion. One can tell the crests of the waves by the length of the notes: thus the first peak is at 175, then 177, then 178, and finally at 185. Each crest is higher than the others, and they lead to the final chord at measure 241 (see example 25). Example 25 also shows the dynamic level of each of the crests and indicates the entire line that stretches from the F in measure 177 to the G in measure 241. There are of course moments of gentle lyrical song in *Sun-Treader*—short moments for the listener to catch a breath, as it were, before the next undulating wave of music begins.

Sun-Treader is a difficult piece to perform. The lines must be carefully balanced, and correct intonation is essential. Moreover, to play at the extreme range of an instrument very softly, as Carl has indicated in measure 185, for example, is nearly impossible. It is a worthy challenge to any orchestra and its conductor.

By means of repetition and return of material, Carl achieved a structure somewhat like the traditional sonata form; but *Sun-Treader*

Example 23. *Sun-Treader*, mm. 172–88 (© 1934 by Theodore Presser Co. Used by permission of the publisher).

is not really in this form, for there are no contrasting tonalities to provide the drama and tension. He was primarily interested in developing linear, not harmonic, techniques, hence the emphasis on lines and contrapuntal devices.

What cost Carl the most effort and surely pleased him the most in *Sun-Treader* was his use of retrograde—a unifying contrapuntal device whereby a theme or portions of it returns played backwards. This was

Example 24. *Sun-Treader,* mm. 172–88, rhythm only (© 1934 by Theodore Presser Co. Used by permission of the publisher).

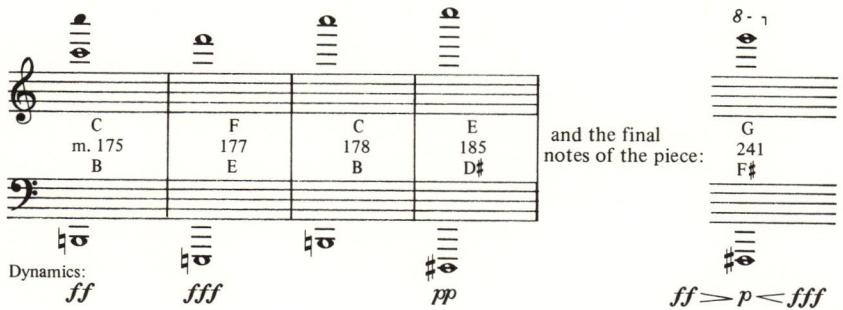

Example 25. Crests and final chord of *Sun-Treader* (© 1934 by Theodore Presser Co. Used by permission of the publisher).

the first time he had used it successfully, and he was very proud of it, though the listener may not even be aware of it. The measures involved are measures 52 through 62, and measures 124 through 133 (see examples 26 and 27). If one starts at the end of measure 133 and compares it with the beginning of measure 52, it is easy to follow the examples—one forward, the other backward. The spelling is sometimes changed enharmonically, notably D flat and C sharp, and there are slight variations in rhythm, but the pitches are exactly repeated. This is one more example of Carl's increased command of compositional techniques.

Example 26. *Sun-Treader,* mm. 52–62 (© 1934 by Theodore Presser Co. Used by permission of the publisher).

One final example of his greater sophistication as a composer might be the very opening motif that, pillar-like, recurs throughout the piece to mark off structural points (see example 28). Against the pounding, steady beats of the timpani and a long held note in the basses, this motif opens *Sun-Treader.* Note the regular diminution of the main

Example 27. *Sun-Treader,* mm. 124–33 (© 1934 by Theodore Presser Co. Used by permission of the publisher).

Example 28. Opening motif of *Sun-Treader,* (© 1934 by Theodore Presser Co. Used by permission of the publisher).

note values from dotted half notes, to half notes, to quarter notes. But notice, too, how Carl has balanced each measure by dividing the uneven beats into two equal parts so that each note of the measure is sustained for the same amount of time, and each measure is divided into two equal parts with the second part occurring on the offbeat. This provides syncopation against the steady timpani beats and at the same time makes for balance. The skips within each measure are the same distance, a diminished octave, even though they are of different pitches—more similarity and diversity at the same time.

While these are some of the devices that Carl used, we need to realize that much of this goes unheeded by the listener, at least until one has heard the work many times and listened both intellectually and emotionally. What one gets on early hearings is an enormous sense of tension and an awareness of the seriousness and depth of the work. Only later do the small details and snatches of lyricism emerge. But this is his masterpiece, on which he worked for all those years, and it is wholly worth the effort.

Carl loved to talk about *Sun-Treader*. He knew he had written a fine work. "I'm proud of those last three pages," he said once. Then he thought about the final chord. "Jesus, that was a great chord!" he exclaimed.[27] And indeed it is. With the chord based on a low strong F sharp, he then has the other instruments play C, E, F natural, A flat, and G at the very top—all as loudly as possible. It is dense and dissonant, just what he wanted. He was most proud of the retrograde section. "It took me six months to round the turn in the *Sun-Treader*, but it was worth it."[28]

Charles Ives had now come to occupy an important place in Carl's list of musical friends, especially since he had been so helpful and generous about *Sun-Treader*. Ives was two years older than Carl, much more worldly and better educated, in addition to their vast differences in financial situations. But they also had much in common. Both were New Englanders from the same generation and the same kind of America, and they shared many of the same values. In later years, when Carl would catalog composers in order of their importance, always with himself at the top, Ives was the only one he would admit to be his equal.

Cowell was continuing to send out Carl's scores for possible performances, and also planning to publish a symposium on American composers. He asked Seeger to write the article on Carl, and Seeger agreed. He wrote, as he said to Carl, "a fairly elaborate sketch of you," which was published separately in *Musical Quarterly*. Most of the article is a technical discussion of Carl's music, with comments comparing European and American music, but Carl was most proud of the first part, which is a loving portrait of the man: "He can tell stories to a mixed party that few dare tell in the proverbial smoking-room full of commercial travellers. . . . It is very difficult when with Carl not to be two gods legislating for the universe that lies tremblingly awaiting verdict after verdict. Later, when the universe gets in its say, one is likely to become a bit ashamed of oneself, of the legislative activity, and even of Carl. But at the next meeting, Olympus looms and compunctions vanish."[29]

In the summer Micah learned to his regret that there were disadvantages as well as advantages to being able to drive. More often than he liked he was called on to chauffeur his parents to their parties away from home. He hated those times, but he loved it when the three of them would go for rides. Unfortunately the car roof leaked, so when it rained, Charlotte would carry an umbrella for use inside the car as well as outside.[30]

This year at the Southern Vermont Artists exhibition a preview was held on the day before the opening, just for the artists and their friends. Mary Powers entertained with a buffet luncheon before the preview so that they could meet the distinguished guests from New York, who included Antoinette Kraushaar from the Kraushaar Gallery, and Juliana Force. After the preview there was another party in Peru, Vermont, and then dinner at the Russell Inn, followed by another social hosted by Herbert Meyer and his wife. It is easy to imagine Carl acting most courtly and at the same time loudly telling his uproarious and salacious stories, with drink in hand (bourbon) and a cigar not far away. Charlotte didn't mind one bit, and one suspects he slept on the way home. The show was a great success, and once again a few of Carl's paintings were sold.

With Micah still at Burr and Burton and with the depression in full swing, Carl and Charlotte decided to stay in Arlington for the whole year. They bought a kerosene stove that they put in the back hall to warm the bedrooms and braved it through, but the winter was especially hard on Charlotte, who suffered a great deal from the cold.

These were slow times for Carl. He had spent himself on *Sun-Treader;* now he had to refuel. He kept up a correspondence with his friends and talked about his work, but the truth was there wasn't any new work. He painted some, did odd jobs around the schoolhouse, and tinkered with his music. Nothing was ever completely finished in his mind, and he looked long and hard at *Men and Mountains,* especially the last movement.

He also had to deal with a disappointment. Bennington College opened its doors to the first class of students in September 1932, and Carl had been ignored completely. Instead, Kurt Schindler was selected as the first director of music. Carl never quite got over it. Even years later he spoke scornfully of "that gang down there," though he made close friendships with some of the faculty members. Eventually he did attend some of the college events and was honored by the institution.

Carl remained on the board of the Pan American Association of

Composers, though he hardly took an active part, since he was in Arlington. But that spring the organization was considering enlarging its membership base, and he foresaw trouble. More composers would minimize his influence, he felt, and since a few of the prospective members were Jews, he was even more opposed to the idea. He wrote to Cowell: "Another matter, I agree with Adolph [Weiss] and Salzedo that it is a great mistake to have that filthy bunch of Juillard [*sic*] Jews in the Pan American. They are cheap, without dignity, and with little or no talent. . . . They will double cross you Henry — I'm sure — in every way. My advice is to promptly kick them out before it is too late."[31]

This anti-Semitism was surely one of Carl's worst traits. Even though he knew that some of his closest friends and supporters, like the Schoens, were Jewish, he continued with this mindless prejudice. Unfortunately he was not alone.

In that same letter he asked about the score of *Sun-Treader,* which still had not been published. He demanded his fair copy of the score in a six-page letter full of concern and outrage. Where was the clean score that he himself had seen Cowell put into his suitcase when he left New York for Berlin? That clean score, he howled, had all the bowings and extra pages, and it was his only complete score. Adler had written that he had seen only one score, and Carl wanted to know which one. Carl was furious, for it looked as if he would have to make a new copy, and since there was no record of the changes he and Lorenz had made, they would have to do it all over again.

Cowell's response did not help matters. He had to tell Carl that it would be impossible to get the good score because the National Socialist party in Germany, the Nazis, had forced Adler, a Jew, out of business and destroyed his plates. Carl was not at all sympathetic, insisting that he had had to give up important new work to ready another score of *Sun-Treader* for publication — never mind the unfortunate Adler — and it wasn't true that Carl was giving up "new work" to prepare a new score. There wasn't any new work. But it did mean a delay in the publication of *Sun-Treader,* which he very much wanted to see in print. It took Cowell several months to soothe Carl, but finally he wrote that arrangements had been made to have the score printed in California.

For the 1933 art show, in addition to the regular exhibition, there was a New Collectors' Gallery in which no work was priced over twenty-five dollars, and Carl had works in both sections. Among the guests at the preview luncheon was Frederick Clay Bartlett, Jr., of Chicago, who soon became both a good friend and an important collector of Carl's paintings. In a publicity story about the show there is a paragraph on Carl, which states that "His 'Composition in One Part Counterpart,' would be first played in San Francisco this coming season."[32] There was no such composition, of course, and Carl must surely have enjoyed thinking up that title!

Winter was fast approaching, and in spite of the hardships of the previous year, Carl and Charlotte decided that they would try to stay in the schoolhouse again. This year, however, the winter was even more severe. By the end of January 1934 it was clear they could not continue in the house, and Henry Schnakenberg came to the rescue, arranging for them to move to an inn, the Colburn House, in Manchester Center. "We like it here," Carl wrote to him. "It's warm and the food is good. . . . Well Henry I'm not going to try to tell you what it means to us our being here. Words are inadequate."[33] They stayed at the inn until April.

In the late fall of 1933, the board of the Pan American Association decided to present two concerts in the spring at Town Hall, and Carl wanted to be represented. Cowell obligingly saw to it that he was, even though he had to exert his influence all the way from California. Slonimsky would conduct, and "Portals" was on the first program, along with "Equatorial" by Varèse, "In the Night" by Ives, and a work by Carlos Salzedo.

Carl went to New York for the final rehearsals and the concert itself on Sunday, April 15, 1934, and, as far as he was concerned, it was a total disaster. He exploded with frustration and anger and gave vent to it all in a letter to Cowell. He accused Varèse and Salzedo of using the organization for their own means, and said he thought Varèse's piece had "no real musical impulse back of it." Further, "Portals" had been "massacred." There had been inadequate rehearsal time, and Slonimsky "had no idea of the score." Carl declared that he was "through with him as a conductor." On the other hand, he thought the Ives work "one of the finest in all modern music," and he went on to tell Cowell that when he visited with Ives the next day, Ives had suggested a recording of their music — on one side Ives's "In the Night" and on the other, Carl's "Lilacs." He was to send Ives the score and parts the very next day.[34]

While Carl may have been furious at Slonimsky, Ives was not, and he wanted Slonimsky as conductor for the recording. Fortunately Carl's explosions, though huge, were soon over, and he did not let his disappointment with Slonimsky stand in the way. As it turned out, each composer was represented by two compositions. The Ives pieces were "Barn Dance" from *Washington's Birthday,* and "In the Night"; the

Ruggles pieces were "Lilacs" and "Toys." By mid-May the recording was completed as the third issue of Cowell's *New Music Quarterly Recordings*. This was Carl's first record.

That summer they traded in their old leaky car for a 1934 Chevrolet, pleasing Micah, who continued to serve as chauffeur. Among their summer visitors were Thomas Hart Benton and his wife, Rita, a special treat for Carl because he got to paint alongside Benton. At the same time Benton was making sketches of Carl for what would become one of his important paintings.

To keep himself busy with music, Carl returned to *Men and Mountains* and enlarged the orchestration of the two outer movements. Then he submitted it to Hans Lange, the assistant conductor of the New York Philharmonic. It was a brave act, since Toscanini, hardly a champion of Carl's music, was the permanent conductor. However, Lange was known to be friendly to modern composers, and Carl decided to take the gamble.

It was probably at the summer art exhibit that he began to meet a few of the faculty members from "that place down there," Bennington College. For example, there was Tom Brockway, who taught political science, and fellow artist, Simon Moselsio, and his wife, who were active in the art association. In September Otto Luening became the new acting director of music at the college, and he soon sought out Carl and paid him court, thus easing somewhat the pain of his disappointment at not being selected for a position. Luening also introduced Carl to the young Julian DeGray, a fine pianist, who also taught at the college. Over the years DeGray and his wife, Margaret, whose apple pie was one of Carl's favorites, were often together, either in Vermont or in New York, where DeGray kept a studio.

Shortly after the first of the year, Carl and Franz Lorenz, on whom he greatly depended, had finally completed a new score of *Sun-Treader* and sent it to the engraver, Golden West Music Press of San Francisco. To save money, Cowell wanted to use regular size plates for the engraving despite the large number of instruments that Carl wrote for. This was possible, but it required tight layouts; and Langinger, the engraver, had numerous disagreements with Carl over how it might be done. They were still working with the proofs in August, and, unbelievably, still making slight changes in the music. Finally, on August 27, Carl returned the third set of corrected proofs, in which he admitted to Cowell that he had made "a few *important changes,* and some minor ones. . . . *I* will *pay for these final corrections* which is only fair."[35] Those changes cost him thirty-five dollars.

At last the score was ready, and now Carl wanted it distributed as widely as possible, and as quickly. He hounded Cowell about getting it in the mail until finally, in October 1934, it was out. The next month Cowell delivered a lecture at Bennington College, and Carl and Charlotte accepted an invitation to attend. It was probably their first visit.

NOTES

1. Carl Ruggles to Henry Cowell, 13 May 1927.
2. Carl Ruggles to Eugene Schoen, 6 June 1927.
3. Carl Ruggles to Eugene Schoen, 1 Sept. 1927.
4. Henry Schnakenberg to Mrs. Schnakenberg, 27 Oct. 1928.
5. Carl Ruggles to Dorothy Canfield Fisher, 19 May 1928.
6. Charlotte Ruggles to Dorothy Canfield Fisher, [late Aug. 1928].
7. Interview with author, 9 Mar. 1967.
8. Henry Schnakenberg to Mrs. Schnakenberg, 27 Oct. 1928.
9. *New York Times*, 8 Sept. 1929, sec. 9, p. 7.
10. Henry Cowell to Blanche Walton, 14 Dec. 1929.
11. Henry Schnakenberg to Mrs. Schnakenberg, 21 Mar. 1930.
12. Charles Seeger to Carl Ruggles, 3 Mar. 1930.
13. Henry Schnakenberg to Mrs. Schnakenberg, 28 Mar. 1930.
14. Henry Schnakenberg to Mrs. Schnakenberg, [summer 1930].
15. Interview with author, 22 Sept. 1966.
16. Interview with Charles Seeger, Bridgewater, Connecticut, 20 Nov. 1974.
17. For more on the founding of Bennington College, see Thomas P. Brockway, *Bennington College: In the Beginning* (Bennington, Vt.: Bennington College Press, 1981).
18. Carl Ruggles to Nicolas Slonimsky, 29 Dec. 1930.
19. Concert program of the Chamber Orchestra of Boston, Town Hall, New York, 10 Jan. 1931. For more information on Slonimsky's conducting, see his autobiography: Nicolas Slonimsky, *Perfect Pitch* (New York: Oxford University Press, 1988).
20. See Nicolas Slonimsky, *Music since 1900*, 4th ed. (New York: Charles Scribner's Sons, 1971), 532.
21. Interview with Micah Ruggles, Miami, Florida, 19 Feb. 1975.
22. Henry Cowell to Carl Ruggles, 5 Dec. 1931. Also, see Copland and Perlis, *Copland: 1900 through 1942* (New York: St. Martins/Marek, 1984), 190.
23. Interview with Charles Seeger.
24. Charlotte Ruggles to Carl Ruggles, [Jan. 1932].
25. Ibid.
26. Carl Ruggles to Charlotte Ruggles, 29 Jan. 1932.
27. Interview with author, 28 Jan. 1967.
28. Interview with author, 30 Sept. 1967.
29. Charles Seeger, "Carl Ruggles," *Musical Quarterly* 18 (1932): 578-92.
30. Interview with Micah Ruggles.

31. Carl Ruggles to Henry Cowell, 21 June 1933.
32. *Manchester Journal,* 24 Aug. 1933.
33. Carl Ruggles to Henry Schnakenberg, 12 Mar. 1934.
34. Carl Ruggles to Henry Cowell, 19 Apr. 1934.
35. Carl Ruggles to Henry Cowell, 27 Aug. 1934.

10

The University of Miami
and *Evocations*
1935–43

December of 1934 was an exciting month for the Ruggleses. Micah graduated from Burr and Burton Seminary and was about to begin the winter term at the University of Miami in Coral Gables, Florida, on an athletic scholarship and with Harriette's additional assistance. Carl and Charlotte, persuaded by Schnakenberg and others that they, too, must leave their cold schoolhouse, were going to New York to stay at the Hotel Holley on Washington Square West. Their quarters were on the eighth floor—a "perfectly lovely suite sitting room, bedroom and bath looking out over the park." And being in the city meant being almost constantly on the move.

They went to concerts at Carnegie Hall and Town Hall, and the Schoens invited them to their home in Forest Hills. They attended a Stravinsky reception (no comments about how the two composers got along) and the following night dined at the Bentons'. One afternoon they went to "four different exhibitions" and decided that they liked best Guy Pène Du Bois's. Henry Schnakenberg took them to dinner, and Felicia Meyer, Herbert Meyer's daughter, and her husband, Reginald Marsh, entertained them.

The Iveses invited them to their apartment several times, and Carl especially enjoyed those visits. If Ives was feeling well, he and Carl would start to sing the old marches they remembered from their youth; then in a burst of enthusiasm they would get up and march around the dining table singing and pretending they were playing the trumpet or the trombone. Charlotte and Harmony would look on fondly at the "two boys." But Carl remembered that if Ives was not feeling well they had to speak softly and gently, and not stay too long.

Isabel Bartlett sent them two tickets to the Metropolitan Opera's production of Wagner's *Tristan und Isolde,* and as Charlotte reported to Micah: "Of course Dad groaned and fidgeted and swore and wiggled, you know how he acts. I looked straight ahead with a simpering smile, you know that expression too—He really enjoyed the Wagner part. It is great music, but the opera part is so absurd—all the critics were there, Lawrence Gilman, Olin Downes, Pitts Sanborn, Paul Rosenfeld and in between acts we had a nice little chat—."[1]

There was no piano and very little music work for Carl, but he did get a performance. Quinto Maganini, who had conducted "Lilacs" in 1932, programmed it again for his Town Hall concert on February 17. To celebrate, Blanche planned a big reception for Carl and Charlotte the next day. Before that, on Valentine's Day, they went to dinner at the Varèses', and "Goofy" (Edgard's nickname) cooked. Then everything caught up with Carl, and he came down with bronchitis. He was too ill to attend the concert, and Charlotte went with the Varèses as his representative.

He recovered sufficiently to attend Blanche's reception, and they did not get home until 2:00 A.M., Charlotte wrote. There were "writers, painters, poets, pianists, singers, conductors, doctors, lawyers, newspaper men and just fine people. . . . I wore my black lace gown with no back and the boys all said, for 'an old gal' I looked pretty snappy." The Iveses, who had been invited, had not been able to attend, but they sent three "huge boxes of the most beautiful flowers."

When they weren't seeing people, Carl painted. "Dad made a quite lovely watercolor last night of the Square with all the lights shinning [sic] through the mist—as usual he made it on a lousy paper and I felt like spanking him."[2] Painting came easily to Carl, and he was relaxed about it, even a bit offhand. He would use any free piece of material available: paper, cardboard, wallboard—seldom canvas. He was equally careless about framing. Harriette often gave him her cast-off frames, and he would use whatever one fit the size of the work; never mind whether they looked well together. This was partly a simple lack of funds for materials; but it also indicated his attitude toward painting. There were exceptions, of course, when he was working on larger pieces that were important to him, but these were in the minority.

As Charlotte hoped, they decided to return to Arlington on March 1. The winter had not been too severe, and Carl was anxious to return to a piano. Up north, neighbors had cleaned the schoolhouse for them, and when they walked in, fires were going in the wood stove and the kerosene heater. It was a wonderful homecoming. For their first meal at home, Charlotte broiled a big steak and made "the first decent cup of coffee we've had since we left home."[3]

That spring Bennington College offered Carl his first one-man show. Jean and Tom Brockway had helped to bring it about, and they were in charge, along with other members of the art department. The show was scheduled for opening on April 12, and in the midst of all the activities in late March, Carl was suddenly working on a new composition, a set of short works for the piano. It would be a good number of years before their completion, but this was the beginning of *Evocations*.

One reason for his interest in doing a work for piano was his growing friendship with Julian DeGray, the handsome young concert pianist who was on the faculty at Bennington College. With Julian nearby and interested, Carl had someone with whom he could test his attempts at writing for the piano. He himself, for all his pounding and dependency on the instrument for his composing, could hardly be considered a pianist, and he knew it. There was, however, no rush for this music, no impending performance, so Carl worked at it slowly, as always.

Meanwhile there was the coming exhibition. He borrowed most of the paintings for the fifteen in the show, which ran for two weeks with great success. Carl began to think that Bennington College wasn't quite as awful as it could have been. While he was preparing for his show, Tom Benton was doing the same thing in New York, where his portrait of Carl would first be seen by the public. Benton himself was pleased with it, and just before the show opened, he wrote to Carl: "The portrait I made of you came off fairly well though Charlie [Seeger] says (in fun) that the piano looks like it's going to take flight. . . . The whole thing with the exception of the head is in violent foreshortening. Most people who have seen it and who know you like it very much. As a picture it is the best thing I've done this winter."

The main reason for this letter, however, was not the painting, but a harmonica duet that Carl had written and sent down for Benton to play. Benton was delighted with it, and asked Carl to write another one—this time a little longer—and not to use note values quicker than sixteenth notes, because "the old tongue won't work on 32nds."[4]

Carl obliged almost immediately and sent down an arrangement of the "Ave Verum Corpus" for four harmonicas. Benton was elated: "You are the best help we have yet had," he wrote. Then he went on:

> Now I must tell you about last night. A big public farewell party was given us at the [Ferargil] Gallery where my pictures are hung. . . . We stood out in front of your portrait, and played that first thing you wrote us with 4 harmonicas and we got such a hand that we swelled up as if we were regular performers. We had to play it four times before we could go on. The reception we got for that gave us enough confidence to play through our

other stuff without a slip. The boys were grand and you have no idea how curiously penetrating that thing of yours sounds on our instruments. It goes swell with their sharp tin-ny [*sic*] sound.[5]

During the summer Robert Manzer, music director of the International Society for Contemporary Music 1935 Festival, to be held at Carlsbad, wrote that they hoped to include *Sun-Treader* on the final orchestra concert. It was wonderful news for Carl, but unfortunately the entire festival was called off because of the increasing unrest in Germany. No one knew until later that this would happen, and the news lifted Carl's spirits for days.

In the mornings he worked on the piano pieces, and it was a struggle. They were to be a series of short works, each dedicated to a person important in his life. The characteristics of his style—long lines, uneven rhythms, dissonances, and notes held across each other—had somehow to be shaped into piano music. So he sat and pounded, tried out sounds, chewed his cigar, and struggled with the same old problem: how to notate the fluid sounds of *tempo rubato* in this medium, new for him. He asked Julian to come to the schoolhouse and then plied him with questions about notation and sound possibilities.

Suddenly, at the end of August, just before the annual art show, Carl fell ill and had to be taken to the Bennington hospital. They hoped it would be only a brief stay, but for a long while his condition did not improve. In desperation Charlotte notified Dr. Bartlett in New York, who contacted the hospital and attending physicians, and shortly thereafter went to Bennington with another colleague, Dr. Farr, for a consultation. Dr. Bartlett also notified Cowell, who immediately wrote to Ives, in the hope that he might help out in case the Ruggleses needed some financial assistance. Fortunately they did not. Harriette was taking care of that.

Soon after the New York doctors' visit, Carl began to improve, but it was a slow recovery. He had first been admitted to the Putnam Memorial Hospital on August 27, 1935, discharged on September 11, and readmitted three days later. This time he stayed in the hospital until October 28. The diagnosis was prostatitis, but no operation took place, and slowly, under Charlotte's watchful eye, he recovered.

While he was recuperating, he received word that Hans Lange had accepted *Men and Mountains* for performance with the New York Philharmonic on March 19 and 20, 1936. That news made Carl feel one hundred percent better almost immediately. Once again friends helped with winter plans, and after the holidays Carl and Charlotte moved to an apartment at 1 Christopher Street in New York.

Carl was sixty years old on March 11, and eight days later Lange led the Philharmonic in the newly orchestrated version of *Men and Mountains* at Carnegie Hall. Only the first and third movements of the piece had the new orchestration, which called for piccolo, flute, oboe, English horn, B flat clarinet, bassoon, two French horns (playing mostly in unison or octaves), two trumpets, trombone, piano, cymbal, tenor drum, and the usual strings. The musical content of these two movements was not changed, but with the addition of these instruments the coloring was altered and enriched. "Lilacs" remained for strings alone.

The reviewers were divided in their opinions, but his old friend, Lawrence Gilman, remained a staunch champion: "His music is the pure virgin gold of dissonant speech," he wrote. He thought the music "far more effective in its enlarged orchestral form; and certain of the unison and octave passages in the last movement came into their own . . . in their new scoring for the full orchestral strings."[6]

Sometime during the winter Carl took his sketch for the piano piece to Julian. They met at his studio in the city, and Margaret DeGray remembered that Charlotte had brought along food for a light supper after the work session. Carl wanted help with the notation for "Statements for Piano," his first title. DeGray said he acted as midwife to the first *Evocation,* for on that occasion he himself put down on score paper the music to the first piece. It was the barest of outlines, but the lines were there along with the overlapping held notes that marked Carl's music. From the fragments that Carl had brought along, from his singing and playing, and then from Julian's playing and asking "Is this what you mean?" they very slowly and haltingly managed to get a musical score, the first of the *Evocations.*[7]

During that winter there was another evening of music making at the home of Geoffrey Parsons of the *New York Herald Tribune,* where a young concert pianist named John Kirkpatrick played portions of the "Concord" Sonata by Charles Ives. Carl was overwhelmed not only by the music but also by Kirkpatrick's stunning performance. He liked the sensitive young man very much—so much that ultimately John Kirkpatrick became another one of those musical friends on whom Carl leaned heavily for advice and consultation. Before Carl died, he named John as his music executor, as Ives had done before him.

That spring Bennington College gave Carl a second show, with Edwin Avery Park, the director of art at the college, responsible for the exhibition this time. Then on April 22, 1936, at the fourteenth Festival of the International Society for Contemporary Music in Barcelona, Spain, *Sun-Treader* was performed with the Philharmonic Orchestra of

Madrid, under the direction of Pedro Sanjuán, who had already conducted Carl's earlier works in Cuba and California. It opened the second orchestral concert of the festival, and station WABC in New York announced that they would broadcast the concert live from Barcelona. Since the Ruggleses did not own a radio, they telephoned friends, who brought them to their house to hear the broadcast, but the reception was so poor that the only thing they could make out was the announcement of the work given in English from Barcelona. As Carl wrote to his son: "I couldn't hear a thing but a roaring. We were dreadfully disappointed."[8]

There was one dark cloud that summer, the news that Henry Cowell had been arrested in California for homosexual practices. It was a shock to all his friends, some of whom stood by him. Carl remained loyal to Cowell, and when the latter was found guilty and sent to prison for several years, Carl corresponded with him through the entire period. Eventually Cowell was released, and in 1942 he was pardoned by the governor of California.

Meanwhile during that summer of 1936 the Ruggleses met Constance and Edward P. Richardson, who were summer visitors. It was another of those fortunate friendships; Richardson was assistant director of the Detroit Institute of Arts and shortly would be appointed its director. He and Constance, a painter, admired Carl's paintings, and when the art show was held, they bought several small ones for their own collection.

When autumn arrived, Micah returned to the University of Miami, and after some thought, Charlotte and Carl decided to spend the winter in Florida to be near him. They arrived in Florida in time for the holidays, and Carl lost no time in seeking out the musicians, especially those attached to the university, where there was at least one person who had heard of Carl Ruggles and wanted to meet him. That person was Bertha Foster, the dynamic dean of the School of Music. She was one of the original members of the board of regents, and when the school opened its doors in the fall of 1926, her Miami Conservatory became the university School of Music.

In 1928 she was officially named dean of the School of Music, and in her role of director she was able to hire whom she wished for her staff, including some remarkable people. Among them was Arnold Volpé, who had conducted the first series of summer concerts at Lewisohn Stadium in New York, and who conducted the university symphony orchestra, composed of students and members of the community. Walter E. Sheaffer was conductor of the university band. He had been solo clarinetist with the Sousa band on its world tour, and had first come to Miami as clarinetist and assistant conductor of Arthur Pryor's band. In addition President Bowman Foster Ashe brought his close friend, the colorful Franklin Harris, to the university to take charge of publicity.[9]

One must also note that because of the university's precarious financial situation during the early years and during the depression, the music staff was paid from the School of Music funds rather than from the university directly, and this continued until the fall of 1937. When Bertha Foster heard that Carl was in Coral Gables, she arranged for a meeting and explained that she had heard of his ultramodern music. She wondered if he would be interested in offering a seminar in modern music to advanced students during the spring term. Although Carl was thrilled with the offer, he probably growled his acceptance, because he didn't like the idea of having a woman hire him. The salary was small, but he would be attached to a university at last.

When the new seminar was hastily announced, there seem to have been only two students who enrolled, as one of them remembered. Classes were held in the Anastasia Building on University Drive. Designed originally as a hotel, it had been quickly and cheaply converted into a classroom building, whose walls, far from thick or soundproof, were in fact constructed of beaverboard or cardboard, and the students called it the "cardboard college."[10]

The seminar met twice weekly for fifty minutes, but if the bell rang announcing the end of class when Carl was still carrying on, he simply ignored it. So did the students, who were almost always caught up in his excitement. Carl was not intimidated in any way by the thin partitions and banged away with dissonant chords, shouting to his two students about the merits of ultramodern music, especially his own.

He had the students write short pieces in modern style, in which no note could be repeated until a minimum of five different intervening notes had been used. Sometimes he would bring in short motives and figures of his own on scraps of brown paper bags and demonstrate how one could expand from these seemingly insignificant beginnings.

The students' delighted approval of Carl was soon obvious to the rest of the staff, and he got along with them as well, especially with Walter Sheaffer. Their conversations were loud, colorful, and full of laughter—and Bertha was not daunted by any of it. She knew she had been right to hire Carl, and at the end of the term she asked him to return for the following spring in 1938. This time, she promised, there would be time to attract more students. Carl of course accepted.

That winter he painted, for the warm bright colors attracted him, and he reworked that first piano piece. Instead of bare, stark lines, the music became more elaborate. The original ideas were enriched and made more truly pianistic. According to Kirkpatrick, Carl was able to date the completed new version, "May 1937," shortly before they left for home.

This year for the annual art exhibition a Purchase Fund was set up by the association itself, which was supported by a group of wealthy sponsors. Gallery directors could make their own selections, and the paintings would be purchased through the fund. It was a way of assisting the artists and the museums during the lean depression years, and Carl was one of the artists to benefit. The Addison Gallery at Phillips Academy in Andover, Massachusetts, purchased two of his works: "Green River" and "Polyphonic Stanza." Edward P. Richardson, now the director of the Detroit Art Institute, bought a small one for himself, "New Mexico," and then purchased a larger one for the institute, titled "From 1 Christopher St." In total Carl netted $533.50 from sales at the exhibition.

When it was time for Micah to return to the university in September, Carl and Charlotte went with him. Since rents were so reasonable (around four hundred dollars for the entire season), they took a house in Coral Gables, and Micah lived at home. "There are *three* bedrooms, a nice living room with fireplace, dining room, bath, and a large porch, and kitchen, with all modern improvements," Carl wrote to Schnakenberg. He invited him to visit and wrote that the Boardman Robinsons expected to visit after Christmas.[11]

At the beginning of the winter term, *The Miami Hurricane,* the weekly university newspaper, carried a long story on the front page about Carl and his forthcoming seminar. As a result ten students enrolled in the two credit course, and Carl's official title was part-time lecturer. His salary was approximately $450, which still came from the music department.

There were some bright students in the group, and all of them were interested in Carl, if not in the work. The class began at 4:00 P.M., and if Carl felt especially enthusiastic it might continue until 8:00 P.M. Carl criticized nearly every composer, living or dead, and one story has it that a student who was an admirer of Sibelius tried to defend him after Carl had said that Sibelius was not much of a composer. " 'But surely, Dr. Ruggles, you think the "Swan of Tuonela" is a good work?' Carl chewed on his cigar, scowled, and finally said: 'That's no swan; it's a goddamn duck!' "

Then at the end of February, Carl's old problem, prostatitis, reappeared without warning and with severe pain. Charlotte rushed him to the doctor, who immediately put him in St. Francis Hospital in

Miami and operated within a few days. He was in the hospital for over six weeks, and this time Harriette was not there to help with the added expenses.

Once Carl was out of danger, Charlotte wrote to several of their affluent friends and quite frankly asked for assistance. One such letter went to the Iveses: "I am in desperate need of money to meet the hospital expenses and am asking my friends to help me through this most difficult time—I seem so alone and so far away from everyone that we know and that knows us. . . . My expense at the hospital this last week was $335.56 not counting the surgeon—It just doesn't seem right—and you can see the plight I am in."[12]

She sent a similar letter to Frederick Clay Bartlett, Sr., and both he and Ives quickly responded generously, along with Henry Schnakenberg and Dorothy Canfield Fisher. By mid-April Carl was home but still convalescing, and there were no more classes at the university or any music work of his own. As he regained his strength, however, he began painting, and he was able to bring back to Arlington a good number of newly finished pictures. He and Charlotte stayed in Florida until Micah's graduation at the end of May.

The art show was again successful for Carl. The Brooklyn museum purchased a small piece, "Southern Pine Florida"; and a particularly fine painting, "Fishing Boat," was sold to a private collector. In all, seven of his paintings were sold, netting him $432.

During the summer he resumed working on the piano pieces. The first was presumably finished but typically he was still tinkering with it. The second was somewhere midway, still not complete. What he really needed was someone to push him, someone like Seeger, who could encourage, criticize, advise, perhaps even edit a bit. But in Carl's mind, that person had to be someone special, with impeccable credentials. He was lucky. There was such a person, both available and interested.

In mid-September John Kirkpatrick stopped for a brief visit on his way to perform at Yaddo. He and Carl went over the piano pieces and the various versions of the first one. When he left, Carl gave him a copy of the first piece in its latest version, and John promised to learn it. This was the beginning of their long and fruitful relationship.

When the Ruggleses returned to Coral Gables in the fall of 1938, they took a different residence, not wanting to be in the place where Carl had become ill, and Carl was more than ready to resume his seminar and participate in the university life. At the end of October, John Kirkpatrick wrote the first of many letters to Carl on *Evocations*. Carl was thrilled with it: "The piece is a constant joy, and I am more and more impatient to see the others. . . . Perhaps it is just as well I didn't write you sooner, because I have been going through various stages of wanting to make various suggestions. Mostly with reference to the earlier versions, but in all of them I ended up by liking it best just as is. I guess you know your stuff all right."[13]

Because Carl knew that the hardest part of doing the pieces would be making them fit the piano, to have John respond so generously and with such praise gave him real confidence. It also served to make John even more important to him, for anyone who genuinely praised Carl became not only his good friend but also the best in his own field. The fact that John was close to Ives settled matters in Carl's mind: John was immediately ranked among the finest concert pianists in the nation. DeGray remained a good friend, but from this time on, Carl turned to John for musical help and advice.

Beginning with the 1938–39 academic year, the university completely absorbed the School of Music, and Carl was officially on the staff as part-time lecturer. His two-credit seminar was again offered for the winter term, and his salary remained the same. In the fall, before he began teaching, he and some of the other members of the music faculty organized Sunday readings of modern music. Sometimes he would arrange the music, sometimes others would take charge, and there were always a few interested faculty members and students who attended. In Carl's Christmas greeting to Ives, he wrote about those Sunday readings and asked if Ives had any music that they might play. "Not too difficult. We have to lead them along gently," he cautioned. He told Ives that they had three cellos, a horn, clarinet, bassoon, at least three good violins, and a flute. He also asked for a copy of Ives's song, "General William Booth Enters into Heaven."[14]

The Sunday musicales stimulated Carl, too, who desperately wanted a performance. Since Volpé, the conductor of the orchestra, was not at all interested, he turned to the symphonic band under the direction of Sheaffer, by now a good friend. There were excellent musicians in the organization, and Sheaffer thought it a fine idea to perform a Ruggles work during the spring. Carl immediately turned to "Angels" and worked it over into a new and more playable edition. The entire piece was transposed down a minor third (three half-steps), and it was re-scored for four trumpets and three trombones. The middle part was extended a few measures to make a more leisurely descent from the high point of the piece, a change that also made the last section more musically satisfying.

"Angels" was scheduled for performance on Monday, April 24, the fourth and final concert of the spring series. Carl had also arranged the "Prelude" and the "Siciliana" from Mascagni's *Cavalleria Rusticana* for band, and along with "Angels," he was to conduct these works. Joseph Barclay, a faculty member, would be the baritone soloist.

As the concert date approached, everyone grew more nervous and excited. Carl held the rehearsals for "Angels" at his house, and they were lengthy, often much too long, as he drilled his student ensemble over and over again. The problem was not so much with the notes, but with balance and intonation, and with getting the students used to hearing the close dissonant harmony. He admitted in a letter to Ives: "We had *14 rehearsals* of two and a half hours each. It took 10 rehearsals before it became flexible. After that we went to town."[15]

The program took place in the auditorium of the Miami Senior High School, and Carl's part in the program came just after intermission, when he directed the selections from *Cavalleria* and then "Angels." Any negative reactions to his music were drowned out in the wildly enthusiastic applause, and the shouting and stamping of his adherents — of whom part were the entire athletic department, sitting in the balcony, whom Micah had corralled into attending, and part the members of the local fraternity, Delta Sigma, who had made Carl an honorary member.

Both Micah and Carl remembered the evening well. Delighted with the tumult, Carl came before the audience with a grin and said: "Thank you for that wonderful applause. And now we'll play it again." Years later, in the nursing home, he reminisced about that time and the "wonderful applause." When they had finished playing the second time, there was even more tumult. "There all those fellows were clapping wildly," he laughed, remembering, "and they didn't have any idea what it was all about."[16]

Shortly afterward, perhaps because he had overworked himself preparing for the concert, Carl became ill. He canceled the seminar for the last few weeks, and by the end of May he and Charlotte were ready to return to Arlington.

Norman Rockwell moved to Arlington that year, and Carl quickly got to know him, along with the other artists from the *Saturday Evening Post* who visited Rockwell and eventually came to live there as well. They would get together to discuss their work, and Carl would join in, amusing them with his endless stories and limericks. Meanwhile he worked on the music and the painting, the latter in preparation for the annual exhibition.

In July Cowell wrote and asked Carl about "those five piano pieces," adding that they should be recorded by a fine pianist and published by *New Music*. But the piano pieces were far from completion, and there never were five. Carl was still working on the second one and consulting with John. In addition, he was now enthusiastic about writing for concert band. He wrote to Ives: "What have you for Band? I'm going to conduct another concert this winter—if I feel strong enough—and I should love to do a work of yours. The Symphonic Band has a great future I'm convinced of that. The orchestra of today is a stuffed shirt proposition. Of course the music must be conceived for the Band, not arranged from an orchestration. Our band at the U- is a good one, 87 pieces. And some really fine players."[17] But for all that, Carl never did get around to writing an original work for band. And Mrs. Ives, responding for Charlie, said he only had very early marches and nothing important.

John continued to prod him gently about the piano pieces. He wanted to see the second piece and to copy it so that he could make his own notations for their discussion. He told Carl that he would be near Arlington in September and suggested a visit. When they met, he and Carl looked over the second piece, but Carl still was not ready to give him a copy of it, though he did allow him to take notes. And he listened carefully to John's suggestions.

The art exhibit continued to be profitable for Carl. He netted $669.37 from the show, and Ted Richardson purchased four paintings for the Detroit Institute of Art. Three others went to private collectors.

By the end of September, Carl and Charlotte were back in Coral Gables, and Micah was in nearby Miami, teaching and coaching. Since Carl's seminar was such a special class, it did not follow the school calendar precisely. He did not begin it until the winter months and spent the fall painting, socializing, and working on his music. That autumn, while the band played for the football games under a student director, Sheaffer, who had been ill for several months, called on Arthur Pryor and Carl for assistance with the spring concert series. Pryor agreed to direct the first concert, and Carl consented to do the second.

He immediately set to work arranging music for the organization. This was his chance to prove that the symphonic band could play fine classical music if it was properly scored, and he was certain he could do the scoring. One senses a certain competitiveness with the university symphony, which under the direction of Volpé had so far snubbed him.

The first band concert under Pryor took place in February. Then it was Carl's turn. The concert was scheduled for the middle of March, just a month away, but it was postponed twice "because of Dr. Ruggles' illness" according to the university newspaper. This was nothing serious and probably nothing more than an excuse to get in a few more rehearsals. Finally it was announced for Monday evening, April 8, 1940, in the Miami Senior High School. Arturo de Fillipi would be the tenor soloist.

The program opened with Sheaffer conducting a march, after which Carl took over, beginning with the "Canon" from the *95th Psalm* by Mendelssohn. A duet for cello and clarinet, "Under the Lindens" by Massenet followed. Then came the Prelude to *Cavalleria Rusticana* by Mascagni, along with a selection from the opera sung by the soloist. The second half of the program opened with a march, "Vienna Forever," followed by Gounod's Prelude to *Faust*. Mr. de Fillipi then sang the air, "La fleur que tu m'avais jetée" from *Carmen,* and the band closed the program with the church scene from *Cavalleria Rusticana*.

There was a full house, and the audience was enthusiastic in its response. Carl certainly knew the music. He had first used these pieces in the original orchestral versions as far back as Winona days, and they had served him at the Rand School, too. Unfortunately his band arrangements have been lost.

That summer in Arlington was an especially busy one for Carl, for in addition to all the other activities, John Kirkpatrick and his bride, Hope Miller, spent the season in nearby South Shaftsbury. About every two weeks they would have dinner at one or the other's home, and in between John would drive up to Arlington to work with Carl. With John so close to spur him on, Carl worked even harder at finishing the second work, but there were distractions. For one thing, with the help of the WPA and other sponsors, Carl's old friend, Franz Lorenz, had established the Bennington County Musical Society for young musicians from nine to seventeen years of age, and arranged for a concert with the group in mid-September. He planned to include the string version of "Angels," and Carl was very much involved with that.

Then there was the annual art exhibit, and he needed to see that his entries were framed and ready to be hung. As we have seen, he didn't much care about matching oil paintings to frames, using whatever hand-me-downs and discards came his way. But about his watercolors he was more particular. He wanted these matted, and one of his neighbors in Arlington used to help him with that, as she helped Harriette. Carl liked to use a double mat—first a small narrow one, then a wide one—especially for the small paintings that went to the Collectors' Gallery.

On September 12, Lorenz and his Bennington County Musical Society presented an "All Star" concert. It was a gala event with the Honorable George Aiken, then governor of Vermont, addressing the audience before the program. Carl and Charlotte attended, of course, and "Angels," though it was performed with some difficulty by the young musicians, was enthusiastically received by the audience.

It had been a wonderful experience working with John during the summer, and more and more Carl came to rely on him for musical criticism and advice on all of his music, not just the new piano pieces. For example, Carl decided to prepare another score of "Angels" for publication, using the version he had made for the performance at the university. John offered his editing and copying services, and Carl accepted with pleasure. So in fact it was John who made the new copy, leaving it for Carl to proofread. The only disagreement they had over the piece came when John tried to score it for trumpets in B flat; Carl insisted that it be printed for trumpets in C with an explanatory footnote, and John graciously agreed.

When they left for Florida, Carl finally gave him a copy of the second piano piece for his suggestions and corrections. Neither of them was satisfied with the climax of the work, and all through the autumn they struggled with the problem through the mails. Their correspondence gives a clear picture of how closely they worked together and how the music finally evolved.

John had copies of the completed first piece and the unfinished second. He was to go over both carefully, edit them, and make fair copies. Carl had composed opening snippets for several of the other proposed pieces, and talked even more about these, so John, in his first letter, boldly suggested an order for the five pieces: "1, 3, 5 would be essentially religious expression (religious, not churchly) 2, more purely imaginative and 4 more active or dynamic. I think that whatever order or choice be decided, your most touchy problem will be to keep their several characters perfectly distinct—never to let any one poach on the phraseology of another." Then he added: "I'll be patiently (or impatiently) awaiting the patch for the hiatus."[18] The order of the pieces continued to be problematic for several more years. At the moment, they were calling this second piece number three; and the "hiatus" to which John referred was the climax, measures nineteen through twenty-four.

Within a few weeks Carl responded by sending off two versions of those measures, though there were very few differences between them, and asked John for "suggestions as to the *spelling* or criticisms rhythmically and harmonically" (see example 29). He added: "After thinking it over, it seems to me that your original title is best."[19] And to make it official he drew an illustration of the title page, including the expected date of completion, 1940. He was considerably premature on the date,

Example 29. Two versions of mm. 19–24 of *Evocations* (© 1945 and 1956 by Theodore Presser Co. Used by permission of the publisher).

and in the end there were only four, but John's title, *Evocations,* remained.

John hastened to reply, sending off a detailed letter in just four days. He was not satisfied with Carl's working out of the climax, and said so:

> To my ear the patch is unnecessarily dissonant—to a degree that (to me) doesn't fit very well with the rest of the piece. . . . I feel no such consistent richness of inter-relation in the patch—[He had been discussing the measures just preceding the climax.]— to me the dissonances get a little too multiplied and bring into the mood a certain bitterness that makes something quite different, after which the return seems a little weak, when it should seem transcendently clear. . . . Then, too, the melodic line throughout is so really simple and distinct (like a good side of Puccini) that it seems to me a pity to seem to transform its clear octaves sometimes into 7th and 9ths, which (in this piece) seem more in place in the accompanying elements.

Turning to the final chord of the climax, John suggested different bass notes: low C up to D flat, rather than the G sharp up to A that Carl had proposed. "Sorry to be so fussy," he concluded. "I suspect my first reactions are perhaps truer than my 'judgment' (if any)."[20] Surprisingly Carl accepted the criticisms gladly and gracefully. Clearly John's role was more than just a performer; he had become like a coach or even a teacher to Carl, who responded almost as would a highly gifted student.

"Thank you very much for your criticisms," he wrote. "I have weighed them carefully, and I think they are all *sound*. No pun intended, by the way." He accepted all of John's suggestions, including changing the final left hand chord to the low C up to D flat. Then he changed his mind and sent a different version ending with a low E up to an F natural (see example 30), but instead of mailing the letter, he kept it for several days and added a long postscript. He was concerned about the ending of the piece and the proper time signatures throughout the work, as well as how to strengthen the sound of some of the important notes.

John was tremendously enthusiastic over Carl's new version of the climax, though he had some further ideas about notation: "The patch is perfectly beautiful—but perfectly beeootiful!" Then he went on to suggest that the final chord of the climax in the left hand be dropped one octave so that the low E would not interfere with the return of the theme and so that the F would sound stronger. And he liked the

Example 30. A third version of the climax of *Evocations,* beginning with the third measure of example 29 (© 1945 and 1956 by Theodore Presser Co. Used by permission of the publisher).

progression of ever larger intervals in the left hand as it moved down the keyboard. He also suggested not holding over the C in the right hand beyond beat one, referring to the C that Carl had held throughout the measure. Instead John suggested that perhaps the high G on beat one might be held over through the second beat.[21] John also opted for keeping the time signatures simple, just plain 4/4, and using descriptive words to help the performers play with the rubato that Carl wanted.

Carl responded quickly, naturally delighted with John's praise. In an overconfident vein he assured him that the other three pieces would soon be on their way for his perusal. And he sent yet another copy of the climax because he felt there were too many barlines in the previous example and that they cluttered the score. He wanted to find out what John thought,[22] and in example 31 we can see that, except for the final two measures, which are now 5/4 and 6/4 respectively, he has changed the time signature to 4/4 as John had suggested.

John's reply came within a few days, and he agreed with Carl. The new notation was "clearer," he said, but the C natural in the right hand in the penultimate measure could not be held over, as Carl wanted.

Example 31. A fourth version of the climax of *Evocations* (© 1945 and 1956 by Theodore Presser Co. Used by permission of the publisher.

It "really sounds bad," he wrote. The last two chords could be blurred, however, as Carl wanted and as he had written them. Then John went on to discuss other sections of the piece and told Carl that he could almost play it. "It feels very wonderful," he wrote, adding that he needed to play it from memory and for an audience before he could really know if all his suggestions were correct.[23]

He assumed that the piece was now finished, but he underestimated Carl, who a few days later sent another version of the climax in which he changed the rhythm of the third from the last measure. "I feel that the passage should be stressed and notated thus: Otherwise they will play it in a gutless way. I like the delayed beat which gives it added stress. And it comes fine and logical at *," he wrote (see example 32).[24]

Carl was right about that, for beginning in the right hand in the fourth measure from the end of the example, a chromatic scale pattern is made clear, namely: B-C-then up an octave to D flat-down to D natural-up to E flat-down to E natural-up to F-down to F sharp-and finally up to the high G. It does clarify the line, and the "delayed beat" gives stress and tension to it as well.

Presumably this *Evocation* was now finished, but it would be revised

Example 32. A fifth version of the climax of *Evocations* (© 1945 and 1956 by Theodore Presser Co. Used by permission of the publisher).

before publication by *New Music,* and revised again for a later edition. One thing the exchange of letters shows is that Carl never thought in terms of chords or a harmonic system. While John might write of a "series of bi-modal chords" [major and minor first inversions], as he did about a different section of the piece, Carl wrote about individual notes. Even when they were to be played simultaneously, forming chords, he viewed them as discrete notes and discussed only how they would sound together.

A comparison of the four examples shows that the biggest changes occurred between the first two versions, examples 29 and 30, after Carl had received John's lengthy criticisms. Example 29 has a convoluted melody and almost constant dissonances. It is not pianistic and shows Carl attempting to pack more and more bite and harshness into the music without much regard for clarity and organization.

The second version has been much simplified, reduced to its *urline,* or basic skeleton. Note that the chromatic line described in version 4 is already there, though not as prominently as Carl wished it. Note, too, that the dissonant ninths and sevenths have been for the most part moved to the left hand, as John had suggested. But the right hand still has the dissonant octaves across the bar lines, as the last note of one bar is held over while the first note of the new measure is sounded. This was surely one of Carl's favorite devices for achieving dissonances, and one which is heard in all of his pieces.

Example 31 is much like its predecessor, except that there are more of the held notes that Carl simply could not resist. He loved the piling up of sounds. But he had taken John's suggestions: the time signature is mostly 4/4, and he has dropped the final chord to the lower octave.

Example 32 remains very similar, but there are two changes. There are fewer held notes, because of John, and more important, there is the shift in rhythm to prevent "gutless" playing, as Carl wrote. These are significant changes, but not nearly so striking as the ones that occurred between examples 29 and 30.

And how did that passage finally turn out? Here, in example 33, is the latest version published in 1956 by American Music Edition. It has become more complicated. One finds Carl's love of piling up dissonances, of tones held on top of other tones. By this time John had discovered through his many performances of the piece that such overlapping was possible through careful fingering and use of the pedals.

Other important changes have also taken place. The melodic line in the right hand is in octaves, and the rhythm is simpler. Moreover, while the chromatic line from B up to G now extended to G sharp remains, there is a secondary scale passage also in the right hand—a symmetrical scale of two half-steps: beginning E to F, then F sharp (the middle note of the triplet); then three whole steps: G sharp, A sharp, and C; and from C another two half-steps: C to C sharp, and finally D in the last chord.

At the same time the left hand has been changed three measures before the end. Now it, too, has a chromatic scale passage like the main melody: B flat-B natural-C-C sharp-D-E flat to E natural and F sounding simultaneously, and on the penultimate chord in the left hand to G flat and G natural, also sounding together. When this left hand scale begins, it goes with the right hand on beats one and three in measures twenty-two and twenty-three in consonant intervals of the third. Carl often used these intervals to sweeten his dissonances, as he does here. So the final version turns out to be more complex than the earlier ones with the exception of the first. But this last edition shows its evolution from example 30. The *urline* has not changed, and the additions follow logically from that. One could not say that about the complexities of example 29.

We shall not deal with each of the pieces in as great detail as we have done here, but these examples show clearly how much Carl

Example 33. The final version of the climax of *Evocations* (© 1945 and 1956 by Theodore Presser Co. Used by permission of the publisher).

depended on someone else to make final judgments about his own music. First there had been Seeger, and in a lesser way Varèse and Cowell, then Franz Lorenz, later Julian DeGray, and now John. As time went on, there would be many examples of this partnership between Carl and John, for a partnership is what it was. Henceforth in every future composition John's criticisms would be Carl's touchstone.

Now at last it was time for John to try out the two *Evocations* in public. He performed them at a private concert in Greenwich, Connecticut, on November 18, 1940, and soon after wrote to Carl that they were well received and felt good in his fingers. He had some other good news, too: Pro Musica, a musical organization in Detroit, had booked him to give a program of American music in January 1941. The concert would take place at the Detroit Institute of Arts, where Carl's friend, Ted Richardson, was the director. Naturally John intended to play the two *Evocations*. Within days after Carl had heard the good news from John, Richardson himself wrote that he wanted to have a small show of Carl's paintings in the museum at the time of the recital, and he asked Carl for the names of collectors from whom he could borrow the works. This was very exciting news, and soon nearly everyone at the university knew about it.

What he really wanted was to have John perform more of his music than just the two *Evocations,* but he knew that he would not be finished with any of the other *Evocations* in time for the recital, which was scheduled for January 31. His solution was to make a piano arrangement of one of his orchestra pieces, and he settled on *Men and Mountains.* Interestingly, he started with the last movement, "Marching Mountains," believing that it would translate to the piano more easily than the others. By December 16 he was able to send John his new arrangement, and wrote that he thought it would sound "fine as a piano piece." John was generally pleased with it, but he did have a few suggestions, which Carl gladly accepted: "Your suggestions are fine. And if you feel like putting more of the score in—as you suggested at [measures] 13—18 go right ahead. You know the piano and how to make it *sound.* . . . I tried for a majestic quality when I made the theme."[25]

Carl still was not satisfied with his share of the program, but he had nothing else. John, however, had made a piano reduction of "Angels" when he had made the fair copy for the new edition, and he offered to perform that along with the other Ruggles pieces. "I'm amazed that you can make the Angels take wings," Carl wrote with delight and immediately approved its addition to his group.[26]

The concert officially opened Carl's exhibition, and both events were well received. There were twenty works in all; two were oil paintings, twelve were watercolors, and six were drawings. They came from friends and from other museums; Carl himself loaned only one work, a watercolor done in Florida, entitled "Orchids."

Once the Detroit exhibit and program were settled, Carl turned his attention back to the piano pieces and to his seminar, which was in full swing. The university had raised his salary to five hundred dollars, and he was very pleased about that. Meanwhile *New Music* was interested in publishing *Evocations,* and Ives was more than willing to assist financially. Harmony, who now often took care of Charlie's correspondence, wrote enthusiastically: "He says 'It is not only important to have the piano piece published but also important to have every note you have ever written published, whether you want it or not.' And he wants to say to Charlotte and Micah 'but not to you because if so he may hear a cuss word from Florida'—'The man to whom the world of music owes a great debt is Carl Ruggles—but it may not be fully paid 'til he and an old friend from Redding and "Uncle Deac" are walking up that New England mountain in the next world.' "

She added that they would send the score and parts of "In the Night" to Carl, as he had requested. There were "about 40 pieces of Chamber Music" by Charlie, and if Carl would let them know what the instrumentation of his class was, they would pick out some appropriate pieces to send to him.[27]

Carl was thrilled with the letter and soon responded, writing in more detail about his class, which this year numbered enough to become a class in orchestration and performance:

> Every Thursday evening I have a class of about 30 of the best players of the Symphony here. The class is for the study of New Music. I have had to prepare their ears—in a way—to the sound of 'strange intervals,' also the technique of playing them. Exercises like this: [see example 34]. They have a tough time with this rhythm [see example 35]. We tried over the "Cage" [by Ives]. I had to make the parts. It sounded beautiful. The harmony of chords founded on 4ths was a new experience for them. First the English Horn played the solo, then a young singer sang it very well. I wish you had been here Charles. They were all so happy about it. It is, I think, the way to make music.
>
> I shall be more than glad to have anything Charles thinks I can use. I think the short pieces would be best at first, as it takes many rehearsals to *ballance* [sic] *dissonances....* They all want to *let go of the tone.* If one plays C natural sharp and another C sharp sharp its [sic] just too bad, or if one plays louder than the other.

Then he listed the available instrumentation, which included "Flute

Example 34. Exercise with "strange intervals." (1 Feb. 1941 letter to Harmony and Charles E. Ives).

Example 35. Exercise with difficult rhythm. (1 Feb. 1941 letter to Harmony and Charles E. Ives).

Oboe E. Horn Cls. Bsns. Hrns. Trpts. Trombone Piano Bells lst Violins 5 parts, 2nd Violins 5 parts, Violas 3 parts, Cellos 3 parts, C. Bass 2 parts." He hoped to give a little concert in May, he wrote, "Just Ives and Ruggles. The New England Renaissance. I've always thought how wonderful it would be to have an *orchestral concert of Charles and my works*. It would knock them cold."[28]

This was Carl's best time at the university. With this class he experimented with orchestration, using Ives's pieces as well as his own. In addition to teaching, he, too, was learning, and all through the term he wrote with delight about the large class and his future projects. He had discovered a vocal composition, "Crucifixus," by Antonio Lotti (perhaps Charlotte had brought it to his attention), and as he wrote, he found it "amazingly beautiful. And extraordinary in its revelation of the dissonant counterpoint. Of that time." He orchestrated it for full orchestra, and they tried it out. "It sounded *wonderful*," he boasted.[29] In addition, John Bitter, the new conductor of the university symphony, seemed more sympathetic to contemporary music, and Carl felt sure that *Men and Mountains* and "Portals" would be performed at one of the orchestra concerts during the next year.

All through the spring and summer Carl continued working on *Evocations*. The third one, which would become number two, was nearing completion, and Carl decided to dedicate it to John. At one point in their correspondence, John caught a wrong note in the manuscript, and Carl responded: "Of course. What an ear! I must have copied it wrong. I never could have repeated the G sharp six notes away from A flat. My manuscript reads exactly as you have written it."[30]

The statement shows that in this piece, at least, he did consciously try to avoid repetition of pitches until at least eight or ten notes had been sounded. And in this new *Evocation* it was especially important, for the piece opens with a straightforward tone row that uses all twelve notes of the chromatic scale, which is then immediately repeated. Setting up the complete tone row at the beginning meant that Carl would try to use it in a variety of ways throughout the piece, and that would preclude the return of pitches before at least most, if not all, of the twelve tones had been used. Carl's statement also demonstrates once again that he was not interested in the spelling of the notes (G sharp or A flat); it was the sound that mattered.

At the end of August when John, who now lived in Connecticut, wrote that he and his wife would be in Bennington for a week and that he could visit Carl on September 3, Carl promised to have some music for him: "I think number two will be all ready for you. . . . *It is of some consequence.*"[31] They had a wonderful visit, but hearing John play the music made Carl realize that it still was not right. It would be several more months before John could get him to say that it was finished.

During that summer, like all parents of young men, Carl and Charlotte worried that Micah would have to serve in the armed forces. Micah, too, suspected that he might not be able to return to teaching, and he was right. On September 11, he was inducted into the army and reported to Camp Stark in Florida.

That fall Charlotte and Carl remained in Arlington, waiting to hear from Dr. Ashe about Carl's seminar. Things were so uncertain, with so many young men being called into service, that they feared his position might be in jeopardy. When they still had not heard in mid-October, Charlotte wrote that they probably would pass the winter in New York and wondered if Micah might be able to spend his Christmas leave with them. Then at the end of October, Carl received his official invitation from Dr. Ashe. Everything would be the same, including his salary. They were relieved and delighted, especially since they would be closer to Micah, now training in Georgia, and they decided to remain in Arlington until January.

By this time Carl had written that he was going to dedicate a new *Evocation* to Micah. It wasn't written yet, of course, but Micah was thrilled. Carl's idea was to have Micah's *Evocation* be number four, a march, and the fifth would be the one that contained the working out of his theory of fifths. As we shall see, neither of these developed, though there are various sketches for them.

Meanwhile John and Carl were still uncertain about number two, with John rejecting some of Carl's latest ideas: "the harmony is cruder— the dissonances aren't so beautifully tempered," he wrote. He planned to visit Carl on December 5, when they could go over the entire piece once more.[32] It was a good visit, and between them they settled the second *Evocation*. Now there were three finished pieces that John could perform on his forthcoming New York recital at Town Hall in January.

They braved the cold in Arlington by huddling around their huge wood stove, waiting until it was time to leave for Florida. And until their departure Carl worked on, fuming at the state of the musical world that seemed to ignore him and his friends, especially Varèse, to whom he wrote:

> I heard [Deems] Taylor say over the radio [at a friend's house] that there were over four thousand symphony orchestras in this country. Think of that, and not a damed [sic] one will play either your music or mine. . . . Think of all that shit Stokowski has been feeding the public, and that lousy youth stuff. And Symphonys [sic] by Diamond, that dirty little poop, and Barbar [sic] and that prick of a Harris. What the hell is music coming to? . . . This is an era of Shit in Art. The only thing for us to do is to go on making music as we feel it should be made, and to hell with them. . . . I certainly would like to have a long session with you. First, because you *know,* and second because I love you.[33]

He was putting it on a bit thick in this letter, though he believed what he wrote. It had become almost a tradition between him and Varèse to express themselves in as colorful a fashion as possible. In person he was justly famous for his scatological speech, but in reading his letters one rarely comes across one like the above—except to a few old and special friends. In a note, Carl assured John that he was hard at work on the fifth piano piece, and he sent best wishes for John's recital on January 14. The Varèses attended and reported that *Evocations* had been well received.

One of Charlotte's favorite Christmas presents that year was a brand-new sewing machine, for nearly all of her clothes were handmade, or at least hand-altered. Oftentimes they were hand-me-downs from Harriette, which she then trimmed and styled for herself. She had a real flair for this, and almost everyone described her as looking artistic and well dressed, even exotic, with her dark hair (which she later dyed) and dark eyes. With the new machine she was able to make clothes for Micah and Carl, too.

By early February they were settled in Coral Gables, and while John was now playing the three *Evocations* on his concert programs around the country, Carl was busy teaching. Though he loved to act the "great professor," he kept his classes open and easygoing, sitting with his feet up on the desk, smoking his cigar, while he talked informally to the students. Frequently he would go to the piano to illustrate, and while he was no pianist, he was able to make his points clear, mostly using the music of Bach, Beethoven, and especially Brahms, for demonstration. He encouraged the students to write in a modern vein, but he let them write in any style they chose, criticizing whatever they brought to him. For the seminar, Carl orchestrated the latest *Evocation*, number two. It opens with the piano and clarinet, then is followed by the oboe and flute, and in the middle there is a brief canon. But there was no performance with the orchestra.

Some friends photographed Charlotte and Carl, and they sent copies to Micah, who showed them to his friends. "All the boys said you both looked very young," he wrote, "and wouldn't believe it when I told them your ages."[34] Carl was sixty-six, and Charlotte, sixty-two.

Evocations number four was occupying Carl now, and periodically he sent sketches from it for John's perusal. He also had a new project. The war had not interrupted Franz Lorenz's work with the Bennington Music Society, since most of its players were too young for active service. When he told Carl that he was planning a string ensemble program for the end of the summer, Carl suggested he do the "Crucifixus" by Lotti, and he offered to arrange it for Lorenz's group. The latter accepted with pleasure. So along with his continuing work on *Evocations*, Carl worked at the string arrangement.

On Saturday evening, August 29, at the Dorset Playhouse, Lorenz opened the program with Carl's arrangement of the "Crucifixus." It was also the opening day of the annual Southern Vermont Artists exhibition, and as the newspaper reported, one could take in both events on "one ration of gasoline." Carl and Charlotte attended, of course, and sat in the front row, so he could take his bow, though Micah said he never learned to bow properly. According to one member of the audience, he was also the only one to stand up and shout "Bravo!" at the end of the program. But the audience did appreciate his arrangement, and it had to be repeated.

That year the art show was not successful. The war was having an effect, and Carl sold only one painting. None of the artists did well, and it was decided to cancel further exhibitions until after the war. They did not resume until 1946.

Meanwhile the university had hired another conductor for the symphony orchestra in late spring, and Carl fervently hoped that he would be more responsive to Ruggles music than the others had been. He knew there was pressure from his students and friends on the faculty to have a work of his performed, but so far he had been able to do just small bits of pieces in rehearsals. Only "Angels" had been performed with the concert band.

He turned once more to *Men and Mountains,* and with Lorenz helping him, they began to work on the ending of the third and last movement. Carl had never been quite satisfied with the way it closed at the very peak of the climax. Now he thought he could correct it. He added ten more measures to the piece as a retrograde of the opening measures of the movement, winding down the line in a snakelike way through three octaves to a quiet ending. It was the sort of thing he could do after *Sun-Treader.*

About this time Micah wrote that he was seeing a lovely girl from Tampa, Rosemary Lamb, and they wanted to marry. After a flurry of letters and phone calls, Carl and Charlotte wrote that they had complete confidence in his ability to make his own decision and gave him their blessing. The wedding took place in Tampa on Wednesday, October 7, with only a few people present, including Rosemary's parents, and the newlyweds had a four-day honeymoon. Carl and Charlotte were not able to attend, for they simply could not afford to make a special trip south, and they were not yet ready to leave for the university. Perhaps they remembered that when they got married in Winona, no one from either of their families was present.

One reason they had to remain in Arlington was that Carl was having another exhibition at Bennington College, beginning on October 15. In that same month Dr. Ashe wrote, inviting him to return to the university. They decided to go straight to Coral Gables and get settled, then visit Micah and his bride over Thanksgiving. When they met, both Carl and Charlotte were overjoyed with their daughter-in-law. The only flaw in the visit was that Charlotte stumbled on something sharp and cut her leg. Once she was home, it did not heal as quickly as she wished, so Carl took her to a doctor, who discovered in his examination that she had high blood pressure. The leg healed, but from then on, she was on medication.

Shortly after they had arrived in Coral Gables, Bertha Foster gave them a party, and that gave Carl a chance to renew his acquaintance with the new conductor, whom he had barely met the previous spring.

The two men liked each other, and Carl sized up the situation in a letter to John: "We have at last a magnificent conductor, with very poor orchestral material. He is Dr. Modeste Alloo, a Belgian, with a world of experience and a great ear. He is keen to do the new *Men and Mountains*."[35] Carl felt that finally he had an ally at the head of the orchestra. According to Kirkpatrick, it was Alloo who suggested the added drum parts to the introduction and coda of the final movement of *Men and Mountains*.

But the war was taking its toll. The entire enrollment at the university was down, especially the male segment. Total enrollment in 1941 was 1,504; by 1942 it had dropped to 1,122; and in 1943 it would go even further down to 1,047. Carl's title was changed to that of consultant, and his seminar dwindled to only a few students to whom he gave private lessons. One of those was a young freshman, seventeen years old, who would later become the distinguished poet, Donald Justice.

Justice had taken a music theory course at the university during the summer and decided that he would try to get into Carl's course, even though as a freshman he would get no credit for it, and Carl accepted him. Nearly always, he recalled, the lessons began with four-part harmony exercises, generally completing given phrases from Bach chorales. Then Carl would look at the student's original work and would scrutinize it carefully, sometimes writing in one or more notes as corrections, but, as Justice emphasized, Carl was not rigid. Afterwards he would demonstrate his own work. He would sit at the piano and play — holding down notes with his elbows sometimes to get the sonorities, and singing, too — with a cigar in his mouth or on the piano. When he came to a passage that especially pleased him, he would shout, "God, isn't that marvelous!" or "Now you're hearing something!"

Later in the school year, Carl occasionally invited the students for sessions at his house. That year Carl and Charlotte were staying in a little apartment that cost them only forty dollars a month. As Justice remembered it, there was a long living room and dining room at one end of the house, and an alcove where Carl set up his easel. They had brought paintings from Arlington, and these were displayed on the walls around the house. There was also a small upright piano on which he and the students worked.

Classes at their apartment took place in the late afternoon, and at the conclusion of the session Charlotte would serve sherry to everyone. She seemed very tall and elegant to the young freshman, and much younger than Carl. Interestingly, Justice recalled clearly that her hair was gray, though nearly everyone else thought of her as having jet-black hair, obviously dyed in her later years. Carl, it seems, wore mostly white suits in those days; while Alloo wore gray seersucker.[36]

The main activity for Carl during that season was overseeing the preparation of his three *Evocations* for publication. Henry Cowell wanted to publish them in the *New Music Quarterly,* and John had undertaken the tedious job of making the fair copies. Carl wanted them to be out in January when John planned to perform them again in New York, but that was impossible; and they did not appear in print until the April issue, which was all Ruggles, for Cowell also included "Angels" in its latest version for four trumpets and three trombones.

At the end of the term, Carl was notified that his seminar might be canceled, depending on future enrollment, and canceled it was. The news did not surprise or disturb him, however, for he had been expecting it. The teaching experience had been a very good one for him. He had been so proud of his position that he'd had stationery printed with the University of Miami as his address. More important, he had learned by taking advantage of his classes. Carl was never again attached to an institution, but he did occasionally accept a private student.

NOTES

1. Charlotte Ruggles to Micah Ruggles, 7 Feb. 1935.

2. Charlotte Ruggles to Micah Ruggles, 17 and 19 Feb. 1935.

3. Charlotte Ruggles to Micah Ruggles, 2 Mar. 1935.

4. Thomas Hart Benton to Carl Ruggles, [late Mar. or early Apr. 1935].

5. Thomas Hart Benton to Carl Ruggles, [early Apr. 1935].

6. *New York Herald Tribune,* 20 Mar. 1936.

7. Interview with Margaret and Julian DeGray, Warren, Connecticut, 21 Apr. 1975.

8. Carl Ruggles to Micah Ruggles, 27 Apr. 1936.

9. See Charlton Tebeau, *The University of Miami: A Golden Anniversary History, 1926–1976* (Coral Gables: University of Miami Press, 1976).

10. Much of this information was provided by Lawrence Tremblay, one of the students, via telephone and two letters dated Feb. 25 and Mar. 18, 1975. In addition, Nedra McNamara, former publicity director of the university, explained, in a letter to the author, that the university had no records on the music staff until 1937–38, since their salaries came from the School of Music.

11. Carl Ruggles to Henry Schnakenberg, 30 Sept. 1937.

12. Charlotte Ruggles to Mrs. Charles Ives, [Mar. 1938].

13. John Kirkpatrick to Carl Ruggles, [Oct. 1938].

14. Carl Ruggles to Charles Ives, [Dec. 1938].

15. Carl Ruggles to Charles Ives, 8 Sept. 1939.

16. Interview with author, 7 Nov. 1966.

17. Carl Ruggles to Mr. and Mrs. Charles Ives, 8 Sept. 1939.

18. John Kirkpatrick to Carl Ruggles, 28 Sept. 1940.

19. Carl Ruggles to John Kirkpatrick, 10 Oct. 1940.

20. John Kirkpatrick to Carl Ruggles, 14 Oct. 1940.

21. John Kirkpatrick to Carl Ruggles, 25 Oct. 1940.

22. Carl Ruggles to John Kirkpatrick, 28 Oct. 1940.

23. John Kirkpatrick to Carl Ruggles, [either 31 Oct. or 1 Nov. 1940].

24. Carl Ruggles to John Kirkpatrick, 3 Nov. 1940.

25. Carl Ruggles to John Kirkpatrick, 4 Jan. 1941.

26. Ibid.

27. Harmony T. Ives to Carl Ruggles, 6 Jan. 1941.

28. Carl Ruggles to Harmony and Charles E. Ives, 1 Feb. 1941.

29. Carl Ruggles to John Kirkpatrick, 2 June 1941.

30. Carl Ruggles to John Kirkpatrick, 15 July 1941.

31. Carl Ruggles to John Kirkpatrick, 26 Aug. 1941.

32. John Kirkpatrick to Carl Ruggles, 23 Nov. 1941.

33. Carl Ruggles to Edgard Varèse, 2 Jan. 1942.

34. Micah Ruggles to Charlotte and Carl Ruggles, 15 May 1942.

35. Quoted in John Kirkpatrick, "The Evolution of Carl Ruggles: A Chronicle Largely in His Own Words," *Perspectives of New Music* 6:2 (Spring-Summer 1968): 161.

36. Interview with Donald Justice, Iowa City, Iowa, 12 July 1977; and letter, 4 Nov. 1977.

11

Organum
1943–48

On July 23, 1943, Rosemary and Micah became the parents of a baby girl. The very next day Carl wrote to them: "When you were born, Micah, it was the most momentous event in our lives, and still is, and your little babys [*sic*] entrance into this world will, I'm sure, effect [*sic*] you in the same way. . . . A new kind of love will have come to you."[1]

Throughout the summer Carl continued working on *Evocations;* not on the march for Micah, but with new ideas. And slowly number four took shape. At the end of July, John visited them, and he and Carl spent two days carefully going over the piece. It was the ending that troubled them, and afterward Carl sent several "corrections" to John. None proved satisfactory, however. Then, in mid-August, he thought it was finished, for he'd tried it out with Franz Lorenz, his old friend, who had approved; and Carl was exuberant about it: "I've just *finished* the finest short composition damed [*sic*] if I don't think its [*sic*] the best of my career. It's Evocation *No. 4*. . . . It's very dramatic, and has a great impetuosity, and its *finished*. It is 28 measures long, and a fine contrast to the others."[2] This was partly bravado, for the piece was not quite finished. John had not completely stamped it with his approval, and Carl, too, had a few misgivings. There were two main problems, one the ever-present one of how to notate Carl's tempi, the other centered on the ending.

Early on, Carl knew he wanted a big ending, but at first the final chord came after a descending run and the big ending neither made sense, nor was really that big (see example 36). The music called for something more, as Carl realized, but it took a while before he found a solution. Carl sent that first ending to John on August 23. By December he had decided to give up the single note runs. Once that decision was made, the piece began to fall into place, and by the spring he had reached a solution, as we can see from the *New Music* edition of 1945 (see example 37).

It is interesting to compare the two versions, for the second is so

Example 36. *Evocation, No. 4* (© 1945 and 1956 by Theodore Presser Co. Used by permission of the publisher).

Example 37. *Evocation, No. 4,* New Music Edition 1945 (*No. 3,* New Music Edition 1954) (© 1945 and 1956 by Theodore Presser Co. Used by permission of the publisher).

much richer. Note that while the first series of chords is similar, in the final version Carl has moved the whole series up by one step. Note, too, that both are essentially the chromatic scale with octave displacements. Example 36 is from G up to C sharp in the soprano line, and example 37 from A up to E. In addition each chord of the series in both examples uses a dissonant interval, either an augmented fourth or a diminished fifth.

Example 36 then hints at the opening figure, which is followed by a descending run and the final chord. Example 37 is more sophisticated. It follows the implications of the preceding chords and starts another chromatic scale, but begins it with the exact rhythm of the opening motive. This time, instead of using the chromatic scale notes successively, Carl uses some of them simultaneously, thus logically building to the grand dissonances of the last chord. Note, then, that in the penultimate measure of example 37 the progression begins on G and goes to an A flat and an A natural at the same time, then to a B flat and a B natural simultaneously, then C alone, then C sharp and D simultaneously, to the final chord, which contains E, F, F sharp, G, and A flat all at the same time, leavened by a C. From the chromatic scale only the D sharp is omitted, which had been used in the previous measure, and over which in a later edition Carl put an accent mark.

Once again the chords in this series make use of the same dissonant intervals as before, while the final melodic leap from C sharp up to G is also a diminished fifth. Again, in the later edition of 1954, that C sharp is held over as a grace note to the final chord, adding one more dissonance to the pile. Carl dedicated this *Evocation* to Charlotte, and at the opening he marked it "Moderato, Appassionato, Plangently." The second ending may not be "Moderato," but it surely fulfills the two latter directions.

Occasionally Carl sold a painting to friends who visited; one such lucky person was Henry Schnakenberg's niece, Betty, who bought one of his big Florida paintings, "Storm at Coconut Grove." Carl and Charlotte had known her from the time she was a little girl, and they were delighted when she asked to purchase the work. Over the years she collected several of Carl's paintings, and continued the Schnakenberg tradition of befriending the Ruggleses.

Early in October Micah brought Rosemary to Vermont on a fourteen day furlough. While he was there, they discussed their winter plans. Without the income from the university, it was questionable whether Carl and Charlotte could afford to go anywhere, but Henry Schnakenberg and his mother offered to pay for their winter lodgings in Coral

Gables, and they agreed to drive back to Florida with Micah and
Rosemary.

Meanwhile the new version of *Men and Mountains* that Carl had
hoped would be done at the university had still not received a performance. Alloo had been interested, but the university symphony was
simply not up to it. So Carl sent Schoen a copy of the new version,
and Schoen (without consulting Carl but knowing full well he would
approve) sent it on to the New York Philharmonic, urging them to
consider it. Artur Rodzinski was the conductor, and Leonard Bernstein
his young assistant. Within a month Schoen was notified that they also
wanted the parts to the work for a rehearsal, and he quickly air-mailed
a letter to Carl in Florida with the good news.

"It begins to look promising," Carl wrote back. He explained that
he would have to make a set there, which he would do immediately —
copying one part for each of the instruments and duplicating the rest.
"*We can have the parts finished, and in N.Y. in 3 weeks,*" he promised
Schoen.[3] It took a bit more than three weeks, but on December 8 Carl
sent off the parts to Schoen by Railway Express.

Micah and his family drove down to Coral Gables to be with Carl
and Charlotte at Christmas, and since it was the first holiday with their
new granddaughter, they tried to make it a very special one. In addition
Henry Schnakenberg had sent them a Christmas check, and Charlotte
responded with charm and gratitude: "Your Christmas present to Carl
and Charlotte has taken the form of a new Dobbs hat for Carl and a
pair of very snappy shoes for me — and are we strutting!"[4]

This year their landlady was also staying in their rented house —
presumably in her own quarters, but it wasn't working out quite that
way. When Schnakenberg's niece, Betty, visited them, she remembered
very well that Mrs. Perpall hid behind doors and tried to hear their
conversations. In particular she remembered the last breakfast they had
before she returned to Palm Beach. Charlotte had served it to them
on a card table, and Betty was sitting facing the landlady's bedroom.
She noticed that at regular intervals Mrs. Perpall, her hair still rolled
in curlers, would open the door and peek out to hear their talk. In a
whisper Betty reported what was happening to Carl, whose back was
to the door, and they schemed together to get back at her. Whenever
she opened her door, Betty signaled Carl, who would launch very
loudly into one of his more lurid off-color stories. Thereupon Mrs.
Perpall, horrified, would quickly close the door, sometimes even forgetting to do it quietly — only to open it again when Carl's voice
dropped to a whisper. It was a hilarious breakfast, Betty remembered.[5]

Throughout the winter Carl painted and worked on the music. But there was no word from the Philharmonic. "Don't you think it's strange I've had no word from the Philharmonic?" he wrote to Schoen. "I should think they would like to perform a *new work,* instead of the crap they have been doing." And he asked Schoen to make some inquiries for him.[6] Schoen, ever the staunch friend and supporter, did just that, and then had the sad task of reporting that the Philharmonic had decided against his piece.

For his sixty-eighth birthday on March 11, Carl asked Micah to send him some of the best Tampa cigars from the Thompson Cigar Factory. It was no small request because of the war, but Micah tried. Finally he wrote to his father that the factory would not sell him any cigars because Carl's name was not on their list of pre-war customers. As a consolation Micah sent him four boxes of Tampa nuggets, which were the best cigars he could buy. And how Carl loved them. He smoked or chewed on them almost to the end of his life. When the doctors finally forbade him to smoke any longer, he would sit in his armchair in the nursing home and hold the cigar in his mouth without lighting it. Just having it seemed to comfort him.

In the spring Harmony Ives wrote to Charlotte that Charlie had decided to have a photostat made of his copy of *Sun-Treader,* "so there would be a duplicate." Then she added: "Charlie is blue and indignant you might say over his failing eyesight — He had some correspondence last summer with Lou Harrison who did some copying for him — in one letter Mr. Harrison says 'I consider you with Ruggles, the two most important composers of this century.' Charlie loves to be bracketted with Carl."[7] This is the first mention of Lou Harrison, who was soon to become important in Carl's life.

Five days later Carl sent a thank you letter, and promised that he would have someone in Arlington receive the package for him. "Charles," he continued, "for the past two months I've been experimenting with an *Invention for Orchestra.* Its [sic] the rhythmic physiognomy of the *2nd* part that intrigues me. Perhaps I'm stumbling on something new."[8] Then he enclosed a music example to show what he meant (see example 38).

This is the first mention of the new piece for orchestra that would eventually become *Organum.* Carl's comments to Ives and the accompanying music example give us a glimpse of this new work; for with certain significant changes these measures became measures five to twelve of the final score, and the first four notes of the example would form the opening motive of the piece. The significant changes were in rhythm, as we shall see, but the pitches remained the same as in the example.

Example 38. An early original example from *Organum* (© 1947 by Theodore Presser Co. Used by permission of the publisher).

Normally in a canon the lines are imitated either at the octave or at another fixed distance—and imitated exactly in terms of rhythm, intervals, direction, and pitch, as in "Row, Row, Row Your Boat," or "Three Blind Mice." Carl was aiming for imitation only in terms of pitch, mostly in terms of intervals, somewhat in direction, and not at all in rhythm. The result would not only give him a sense of unity because of the imitation of pitches, but would also offer variety, since we would hear those pitches in a different setting in their second appearance. That is what he meant by the "rhythmic physiognomy of the second part." It is almost like having sameness and difference simultaneously, which is of course impossible. I think when we listen to what he eventually named *Organum,* the differences take precedence, though one does have a sense of the lines following one another.

The example also indicates once again how little concerned Carl was with harmony or the verticality of music. He really did think in terms of lines, like the curved flowing lines of his paintings. The only vertical aspect that concerned him was to see that dissonances generally occurred at strong points, so that the music remained in motion, and unstable, and so was truly dissonant counterpoint.

If we look at example 38 in more detail, we can see other aspects of Carl's style. For one thing, the nonrepetition of notes is carried out about as far as Carl ever carried it. In the top line there is a series of ten notes before any note is repeated; next another series of ten; then, beginning with the D sharp in measure three, a complete twelve note series that ends with the B natural in beat four of the fourth measure. It is also noteworthy that the three accented notes in this latter series, C sharp-D-F natural, form a group consisting of a half step dissonant interval to a consonant one, D to F—a three note grouping that was one of Carl's favorites and that he often used as a melodic motive on which to build.

In music, the intervals between two notes are basic building blocks, and the consonant ones are thirds and sixths, the so-called perfect octaves, perfect fifths, and their inversion, the perfect fourths. If we analyze Carl's opening series, we find there are only two consonant intervals: A to C sharp, a major third, notes two and three; and B to D, a minor third, notes seven and eight. In the second series, starting on A flat of the second measure, there are three consonant intervals: notes one and two, A flat to E flat, a perfect fifth; notes six and seven, C down to F, another perfect fifth; and notes nine and ten, E down to B, a perfect fourth.

For the twelve note series starting on D sharp in measure three, there are four consonant intervals, if we allow for enharmonic spelling (and we know that Carl did) they are: notes one and two, D sharp to A flat (G sharp), a perfect fourth; notes five and six, B flat down to C sharp (D flat), a major sixth; notes eight and nine, F down to C, a perfect fourth; and eleven and twelve, E up to B, a perfect fifth. The point of all of this is that out of a possible thirty-two intervals, only nine are consonant; and this is how Carl built his melodic lines. He sat at the piano, sounding out combinations by trial and error, with a stubborn determination to avoid consonances as much as possible. And it was very difficult work for him.

One other point about this early original example from *Organum* (example 38) is that the canon is broken by having the second line hold the E in beat three of measure two, when to keep the canon going it should move to B flat and A flat before dropping to the E flat of measure three. Carl wanted the E held, because that would make a fine dissonance with the F natural and F sharp in the first line. On the other hand, the E also weakened the climactic high E on the downbeat of the next measure by foreshadowing it. As we will see, in the final printed version, measure seventy, or measure four of our example 39, the canon has been restored. The E is no longer held and that line does move to B flat and A flat.

Example 39. A final version of mm. 67–72 from *Organum* (© 1947 by Theodore Presser Co. Used by permission of the publisher).

And finally there is another interesting change from the original in the first line at this same point (see example 39). The F natural to F sharp has been reversed so that it now moves F sharp to F natural. This change first took place when he worked on the piano version, after which he altered the orchestral score to keep it the same. But it would be a long time before that happened.

On their way back to Vermont, they stopped in New York and Carl showed his new score to Varèse, who looked at it carefully. He suggested that Carl name the work *Organum,* since it was so concerned with canon, an early contrapuntal form, and used intervals of the fourth and fifth. Actually the music was a far cry from medieval organum, but Carl liked the name and adopted it.

By May 31 they were at Georgetown to visit with the Kirkpatricks, and the next afternoon they visited the Iveses. For Carl, that was the high point of the trip, and it was a grand reunion. Before the Ruggleses left Georgetown, John and Carl went over the *Evocation* number four. There were still a few changes that needed to be made, but these were quickly attended to when he was back in Arlington. He also left John and Hope one of his paintings, "Stormy Trees," which he had brought from Florida.

That summer Carl went back to the music of the old masters and tried to hammer them out in his own special way at the piano, looking at their music with an inquiring eye, and along the way rediscovering Bach. With great excitement he wrote to John: "I've just run across a perfectly amazing Preludio and Fuga by Bach, especially the Fuga." It was the B minor fugue from Book 1 of the *Well-Tempered Clavier*. The fugue theme, according to Carl, "is one of the greatest phrases in all music. How magnificently modern it is; and the . . . glorious way he has worked it out."[9]

Carl's mind was taken up with the new piece now, and he was probably looking at the Bach for hints and clues to enrich his own contrapuntal thinking. He was also sending snatches of the new work to John, for his wonderment as well as for his criticism. "Enclosed is a tentative sketch for the Coda of the Organum," he wrote. "The final measures should sound quite wonderful in the orchestra. I hope you like it."[10] Two weeks later, he sent another version of the coda, and then made the astonishing statement that he was "just finishing the orchestral score."[11]

That was a bit of an exaggeration. *Organum* would occupy his attention for many months yet, but the music example that he sent to John, the coda, demonstrates his continued use of imitation in his new way—using imitation only for pitches, but not in rhythm or necessarily in direction. This can be seen most clearly by comparing measures sixty-seven through seventy-one in the violins with measures sixty-nine through seventy-two in the celli and double basses (example 39). Note not only the differences in the rhythm of the two parts, but also the shift in direction in the lower instruments from the end of measure seventy. These are also the same pitches as at the beginning of the piece, measures five through ten. Note, too, how the music has been simplified from the original (in example 38) that he sent to Ives. The rhythm has been flattened out; it has less variety. And as we noted, now the canonic imitation in pitches has been completely carried out. Clearly the work was progressing, but it wasn't finished yet.

Carl was also concerned with getting the new *Evocation* published. John had made a fair copy of it for reproduction, and he was preparing to perform it in his annual New York recital. Carl sent one copy to the Iveses and one to Cowell, asking about publication. Cowell accepted with alacrity. Then Carl asked that it be done on an extra large sheet, 11 x 14 inches, since the piece took only one page. They went back and forth on that issue for several months, and eventually settled on a 10½ x 14 inch sheet for the publication.

John's New York recital was scheduled for November 13, and Carl and Charlotte hoped to attend by combining the trip to New York with their return to Coral Gables, thanks again to the largesse of Schnakenberg. Unfortunately train reservations were very hard to get. Charlotte even reported that she had heard a rumor that all civilian passenger trains to Florida had been canceled. That was not true, but since by November they still did not have their Florida reservations, they had to miss John's concert, to their great disappointment.

In the meantime Carl and Charlotte were having such difficulty in getting train reservations to Florida that they called upon Micah for help. Since he was in the service, they hoped he might be able to help, and they were correct. In late November, he wrote that they had reservations for December 20. They would go first to Tampa for a family reunion over the holidays, and then on to Coral Gables. There was a great sigh of relief when they finally got on the train and out of the cold, for they had already endured below-zero weather in Vermont.

They planned to spend two days in New York before going on to Florida, and Carl asked Cowell to meet them, so he could hand deliver the fair copy of the fourth *Evocation*. Cowell could not, but he sent in his place his young assistant, Lou Harrison, who was by now really running *New Music*. It was their first meeting, and Carl was especially delighted to find that Lou knew and admired all of his music. Afterward he wrote to Cowell about meeting Lou: "I found him a *very intelligent* and delightful person. We both liked him tremendously."[12]

With the one movement *Organum* finally finished, Carl was busy designing the cover for the forthcoming edition of *Evocation* number four. Lou Harrison was now officially acting editor of *New Music,* and he had to explain to Carl that because of the paper shortage the issue of *Evocation* would be appearing in small size—in fact, only a single sheet with cover. But he promised that "once peace has come, we will put out an edition in the size intended as a sort of festive occasion."[13]

Next Lou wanted to bring out a two-piano version of "Portals," and since Varèse had told him that Carl had a two-piano version of the new *Organum,* he asked for a copy of that as well. He concluded with a wonderful promise: "I am hoping I may be able to do a little toward bringing the more recondite and wonderful facts of your music into a broader public light. I suffer to realize how little the professional body of musicians knows of your achievement and its importance."[14] Unfortunately there was no two-piano version of *Organum,* at least not yet. Lou himself offered to make one of "Portals," and Carl quickly sent a score. He wondered how Lou would sustain the long melody notes on the piano, admitting that it remained a problem for him. But Lou was undaunted and promised to include all the changes.

Lou also wanted to honor the composers whose music was published by *New Music* by having a small reception for each of them with performances of their works. He decided to start with Carl, and planned the reception to coincide with their return to Vermont so that they would not have to make a special trip to the city. Carl, needless to say, thought it was a fine idea, and eventually it was set for Friday, May 25, the day following their arrival in New York.

Lou asked Harold Rugg, a distinguished educator at Columbia University, if they could use his studio on West 11th Street for the event, and Rugg readily agreed. Next he consulted with John about the music and the paintings, for he wished to show both of Carl's talents. Each guest was asked to contribute twenty-five cents to help defray the expense of refreshments, and Carl was asked to send his guest list, which numbered nearly fifty people, including all of his old New York and Vermont friends in music, art, and literature. The program began at 9:30 P.M. with introductory remarks by Lou, followed by reminiscences of Carl given by Henry Cowell. Then John presented the musical program, which included his arrangement of "Angels" and "Marching Mountains," and finally the *Evocations.* It was, as Carl would have said, a "grand" evening, and Charlotte was so proud of her "genius."

By this time, John and Carl had worked out the order of the four pieces, and it did not follow the order of composition. Number one remained first, but was followed by numbers three and four, with the *Evocation,* second in terms of composition, placed at the end. Since they both felt that numbers two and three were too similar in feeling and needed to be separated, they ended with the second. Each of the pieces is dedicated to people special in Carl's life. Following the printed order of the 1954 edition then, the first is to Harriette, the second to John, the third to Charlotte, and the last to Charles Ives.

Since Carl was not working on any music this summer, he spent more time on his paintings. Norman Rockwell attracted other painters from the *Saturday Evening Post* to the area, and that summer John Atherton, "Jack," moved to Arlington with his wife, Maxine. It wasn't long before they came to know Carl, and "Max," as his wife was called, remembered many visits during the summer with the Rockwells and the Ruggleses, where noisy discussions took place on art, mixed in with stories and limericks—the more hilarious the better.

Lou continued to play an important role as Carl's champion, and he had two more projects in mind: the first, a little book about Carl, and the second, a future performance of "Portals," which he himself would conduct, for he had given up the idea of arranging it for two pianos. Both projects delighted Carl. For the publication Lou asked Carl or Charlotte to write down some of Carl's personal history, though he knew it might be difficult to obtain because of Carl's habit of procrastination. But Carl replied that he would try. In the meantime Lou was able to report that the book was progressing quickly even without Carl's personal section: "A friend of Jack Heliker and Merton Brown in Yonkers, who is a bookseller, wanted me to do a little essay or something on you so he could put it out in small booklet form. . . . so I am getting into shape the fourth chapter of the large book. . . . It is the section dealing with the background to your music, historical and technical."[15]

Jack Heliker, painter, and Merton Brown, composer, were new young friends of the Ruggleses, too, and years later Lou remembered that Jack Heliker had told him of the bookseller in Yonkers who published little booklets by and about "far out" people of the time— the "beatniks" of that generation, Lou said. Oscar Baradinsky was his name, and he ran the Alicat Bookshop. Jack arranged an introduction, and when Baradinsky heard about Carl, he agreed to include him in his "Outcast" Series, which already included two works by Henry Miller in limited editions of 750 copies.[16] Carl arranged for a picture to be sent to Lou, saying that he preferred a profile view (which he got), and asked for a copy of the booklet so that he and Charlotte could proofread it. When it arrived, they both quickly read it and heartily approved.

They returned to Coral Gables for the winter, and Carl decided to orchestrate *Evocation* number four. Perhaps he thought there might be a chance for a performance there in Florida. This was the second piece that he had orchestrated. Number two had been done for his class in the spring of 1942, and now, instead of moving on to a new work, he chose to revise or rework the ones that already existed. Surely that

was, in part, because there was no demand for his music, no com-
missions for new works, and no outside pressures.

But there was the prospect of another performance of "Portals" to
look forward to. That was set, and Carl was especially delighted not
only because Lou would be the conductor, but also because the Ives
Symphony No. 3 was to be performed on the same program. "I see
that *we* are on Lou Harrison's program, which is as it should be," he
wrote in his Christmas card to the Iveses. "A *New England renaisence*
[*sic*] is long past due."[17]

By mid-March Lou's booklet was published. Entitled *About Carl
Ruggles* and dedicated to Merton Brown and John Heliker, Baradinsky
printed five hundred copies, which, like the others in the series, sold
for one dollar.[18] The essay is mainly about Carl's musical style, and
Lou attempted to show how his dissonant counterpoint was in the
ongoing tradition of Western polyphony. There is a broad survey of
that tradition, after which he points out how Carl's music continues
that vein but uses the material of his own age. It is a brief booklet,
only nineteen pages including Cowell's introduction. The subtitle is
"Section Four of a Book on Ruggles," and it is a pity that Lou never
got around to writing the complete book. However Carl and Charlotte
were thrilled with it, and they showed it at every opportunity, urging
their friends to purchase a copy.

Now they looked forward to the performance of "Portals" on April
5 at the Carnegie Recital Hall [since changed to the Weill Recital Hall].
The program, sponsored by the League of Composers, was presented
by the New York Little Symphony, whose conductor, Joseph Barone,
conducted half the program. Lou conducted the other half, which
consisted of three works: the first performance of Ives's Third Symphony, "Portals," and one of his own works, "Motet for the Day of
Ascension."

Immediately after the concert Lou sent a report to Carl: "Portals
was not done to my own satisfaction though many thought it quite
good. The piece, is, however, so elevated in expressive content and so
forceful in outline that it would survive almost any presentation I think,
and Friday nite it definitely stopped the show!" Lou went on to say
that he was putting himself on a five year plan to study the major
orchestral pieces of Ruggles, Ives, and Varèse, and "if no one else can
be coerced into playing them, I will find ways of doing them myself,"
he promised.[19]

In July, John wrote that since he had been invited to play at the
forthcoming Yaddo Festival in September, he would perform *Evocations,* adding that he hoped Carl would have a new fifth *Evocation*

ready for him. To his surprise Carl replied that he was working on yet another new piece, though none of the others had been finished. "I've been working for quite awhile on a composition for piano called 'Parvum Organum,' " he wrote. "I thought I'd be able to finish it in time for you to play it, but I'm rather dubious now. Some of it is [in] the form of a two part canon—with *Improvisations*."[20] Knowing full well that the new piece would not be ready, John replied that he would do *Evocations,* which had been suggested by Normand Lockwood, chairman of the festival.

A few weeks before John's performance, the Southern Vermont Artists held their first post-war exhibition at the Burr and Burton gymnasium where they had been held before the war. Carl, of course, had some paintings in the show, and he and Charlotte went to the opening. At one such occasion, perhaps this one, Carl took the arm of the wife of a friend, pointed to one of the paintings that had already been sold—not one of his—and remarked in disgust: "Jesus Christ, look at that! Some poor son of a bitch paid five hundred dollars for that piece of shit!" Carl himself sold only three paintings that year, and since the association now kept 12½ percent, he received only $428.75.

On Sunday, October 27, 1946, they left Arlington and met Lou in the main dining room at the Pennsylvania station for lunch, before boarding the train for Miami. During lunch most of the talk was about music, mainly Carl's, and especially *Organum,* which still awaited a performance. Lou returned again to the idea of arranging it for two pianos. He knew some pianists who might be interested, and Carl was persuaded. As soon as they were settled in Coral Gables, he started to work on the two-piano arrangement, putting aside his other composition projects. When John wrote in December asking about "Valse Lente" and "Parvum Organum," Carl replied that he was arranging the *Organum* for two pianos; and that is the last mention of "Parvum Organum."[21] The new two-piano arrangement now became the important piece, and Carl kept at it.

Shortly after the first of the year, Carl wrote to Frank Wigglesworth, who was now the editor of *New Music,* suggesting that he publish the two-piano arrangement of *Organum.* It was nearly ready, and Carl wanted a publication as well as a performance. Lou did not disappoint him on the latter score. He had talked with Cowell, who arranged for it to be done on one of the recitals of the New Music Society Series on April 20. The performers would be Maro Ajemian and William Masselos. By the middle of January, Carl had sent the score to Lou and with it a request that "you would see that they [the performers] understand my tempo rubato, and the emotion."[22]

In a letter to John, he wrote in more detail about the work: "I made the transcription, but as Beethoven once said in a letter, regarding a transcription he'd made from an orchestra work 'I had to make a new comp.' which of course I didn't do. It was a makeshift. I fell back on the naive scheme of giving to the 2nd piano the things the 1st piano couldn't manoeuvre. We tried it over here with a couple of ham piano players, and damed [sic] if it didn't sound. However, I think the whole work — with the exception of a few measures — the last two, could be made for *one* piano."[23]

At last the New York performance took place. It was a varied program of solo and choral works, and the only works for two pianos were by Carl and his young friend and occasional pupil, Merton Brown. In his review, Virgil Thomson preferred Brown's piece.[24]

But *Organum* still had not been performed with orchestra, so once more Carl turned to Modeste Alloo and the university symphony. Alloo agreed to try it out in rehearsal, saying that if it was not too difficult for the orchestra, perhaps they might give it a full performance. Carl was hopeful and spent a good part of the spring getting the parts ready. Near the end of their stay in Coral Gables, Alloo, true to his word, did perform it in rehearsal, or at least part of it. As Carl wrote to John: "Modeste Alloo, the conductor, read through it (just the coda). He thought if the orchestra could play the coda, it could do the rest of it. John, it sounded *wonderful.* Charlotte wept, and I guess I did, too. Modeste did a swell job. It's his plan to give both Organum and Men and Mountains."[25] Once again Carl was exaggerating, for it was more his plan than Alloo's, and, as in most such instances, the performances did not take place.

In the spring of 1947 Charles Ives was awarded the Pulitzer Prize, and after Carl and Charlotte had returned to Arlington, Carl sent a congratulatory letter. At first Ives was going to have his daughter, Edie, respond for him, and she did write out a letter to Carl. But apparently Ives felt it was not personal enough, so with great effort, since his hands were no longer steady and his eyesight not very good, he wrote to Carl: "Just a few snake tracks from an 'ole feller's' shaky paw, to tell you, that you are the best composer in Europe, Asia, Africa, and America — but if you should get a Pulitzer Prize swished on you, then that would mean that 'you ain't' —."[26] Carl realized how difficult it had been for Ives to write the letter, and he was so deeply moved by it that he framed the letter and hung it in the main room of the schoolhouse, where everyone who entered was invited to read and appreciate it.

Frank Wigglesworth finally accepted *Organum* for *New Music*. It was to be arranged for piano solo, not two pianos, and as always Carl turned to John for help. They worked throughout the summer getting the edition ready, and once again we can see John's influence. He made a draft of the piano version after visiting with Carl and playing over the two-piano arrangement that Carl had made. Then he sent the draft for Carl's approval with some thoughts on Carl's style:

> It seems to me that you have a kind of choice of range — that the more you limit yourself in the direction of dissonance the more your music dates itself as of the twenties and the smaller its real audience will be — or the more you simplify the harmony . . . the more the hearer will get a melodious effect and a timeless or undated impression and the more hearers will find it palatable. As far as I can see, the Organum is a tremendous step in just that direction (comparing it to Portals for instance), but sometimes it betrays the slightly embarrassed awkwardness of a transitional state, as for instance the way the two plain triads in [measure] 8 have so few similar effects in the piece to balance them (as if they were an experiment on probation). I would love to hear [measure] 70 the same way (I think it would make that whole passage much finer). I know you like the sound of 8, so why not take them off probation?[27]

John was suggesting that both measures eight and seventy, which are the same, make use of traditional triads. Measure eight was already leaning in that direction, and he wanted the ambiguities removed, so that the triads could sound directly. Finally, Carl agreed.

Let us look at measure eight. In response to John's letter, Carl sent him two versions of it: the original at the bottom of the example, and a new one at the top with *X*'s over the two chords in question (see example 40). In the original draft, because of the rhythm between the two hands (i.e., two eighth notes against a triplet) there are two triads and a non-triad: B flat-D flat (C sharp)-B flat-F natural; A flat-D flat-A flat-F natural; and A flat-D flat-A flat-F sharp (G flat). In addition the outside voices move in a contrary motion that provides the most clarity for each of the voices. In the upper new version, the rhythm has changed so that the two hands move together, and of the two chords in question only the first is a traditional triad: B flat-D flat (C sharp)-B flat-F natural; A flat-D flat-A flat-F sharp (G flat). Note that the contrary motion between the two outside voices remains.

Example 40. Two versions of m. 8 of *Organum* (© 1947 by Theodore Presser Co. Used by permission of the publisher).

Example 41. The final version of m. 8 of *Organum* (© 1947 by Theodore Presser Co. Used by permission of the publisher).

In early August John and Carl spent an entire day going over the piece note by note. We cannot know their conversation, of course, but the printed version is the result (example 41). Now there are clearly two triads: B flat-D flat (C sharp)-B flat-F sharp (G flat); and A flat-D flat-A flat-F natural. To achieve this, Carl gave up the contrary motion between the two outside voices by reversing the order and sounding the F sharp first. Now they both descend in similar motion, and the dissonances are delayed until the downbeat of the next measure, which remained as Carl had originally written it.

Admittedly this is a small detail, and perhaps even an improvement, but it is also an example of John's interpreting Carl's musical thoughts with Carl acquiescing. As John once explained to me, he used only one side of Carl. He meant, he said, that he smoothed out Carl's music, for he realized that Carl would have made it more "unstuck." He treated Carl's music in much the same way that he treated Ives's. He tried to do what they would have wanted to do "in their soul." Each man, he explained, had the kind of personality that would rather do something wrong than do it right. He added that he had heard both Ives and Carl say in effect that when people started to agree with them, they themselves were afraid that they were not doing things as they should be done. It was a part of their obstreperous personalities, John felt.[28]

It is certainly true that Carl had an obstreperous personality. But it is also true that he lacked the confidence and security to turn away from John's suggestions, or, in the early days, from Seeger's. He simply did not feel strong enough as a composer to hold strictly to his own dictates.

By the end of the summer *Organum* for piano had been sent to *New Music,* and Carl was involved in the annual art exhibition. After it was over, he was informed that one of his larger paintings, "The House in the Bayou," had been purchased by the Detroit Institute of Art. Carl was very proud of that, but in fact, that is not quite what took place. He received his money all right, and the painting did go to the Detroit museum, but Harriette Miller had purchased it and donated it to the museum—all unknown to Carl. It was another example of her generosity toward the Ruggleses.

This year they decided to try to find a winter place in the Tampa area closer to Micah, who was given the task of finding quarters for them before they got train reservations, something easier said than done. It took him well into November before he found an apartment in Clearwater for them. He wanted them to leave quickly, but train reservations were difficult to obtain, and finally in late November it was so cold that they had to leave the schoolhouse and move to the Arlington Inn while they waited for a reservation. Neither of them felt well, and it was a worrisome time.

They finally arrived in Clearwater in mid-December 1947, and within a few days Carl was feeling so ill that Charlotte insisted he see a doctor, who immediately put him in the Clearwater hospital. Micah remembered that his father had pneumonia and was a terrible patient. Fortunately he was released fairly soon, before the new year, and was able to write to John that he hoped to soon be able to "function." Shortly after the first of the year, Charlotte and then Carl came down with the flu. Soon the flu turned into a recurrence of the pneumonia from which Carl had really never recovered, and he went back to the hospital for another nine days.

It was a hard time. He was restless and irritable. The radio was their window to the musical world, and Charlotte encouraged him to listen whenever possible. She even suggested that he write down his thoughts about the music instead of sputtering and storming to her. "A long rambling letter and reflections" were the results that he sent to John. He headed the letter, "Reactions":

> *Stravinsky* I never cared much for his music. The *Sacre* has been tremendously overated [sic]. The opening phrase — Bassoon Solo is the best place in it, and that stems from the opening phrase of Apres Midi d'un Faun. The much vaunted last movement sounds like Hollywood junk. I listened to his 'Symphony' over the *radio* — for which I make allowances — but it was the same old Homophonic stuff. There were a few chords at the beginning which I liked. They had character and color. I thought he was really going to do something but no back to the same old monotonous routine. There is more Rhythmic Invention in one page of Charles' [Ives] Lincoln that all of S— put together. All Russian music is definitely 3rd rate, and that goes for the painting. . . .

> *Hindemith* His last three works are bores. The orchestra in Miami last year played one on a theme by Weber. I heard it 5 times, and each time it sounded worse. Too many damed [sic] notes, and dreary counterpoint. It made me think of Max Reger. . . . In my opinion De Pres is the only 1st rate composer France has produced, and this is not an opinion of the moment.[29]

When Carl received the program of John's recital at the University of Illinois, it prompted another mean outburst: "Never have I seen such an utter lack of discrimination and sense of values. Fancy giving Schoenberg 10 *lines* and me seven. Besides the wrong name. [Perhaps they wrote Charles instead of Carl.] Copeland [*sic*] with 27 and Finney [Ross Lee Finney] with 20, and Hindemith with 25, who can just about black Arnold's shoes. Seventeen lines for a dreary jerk like Piston; what an appropriate name."[30]

This lack of charity and unpleasant attitude toward his fellow composers, living and dead, was another aspect of Carl's personality. One wishes that these bad displays were due only to the hard time he was having that winter, but that would not be the truth. Such blustering was a characteristic of Carl's personality, and though sometimes it amused people, just as often it alienated them.

On May 8 they finally left Florida for Arlington. It was the last time they wintered in the South. That part of their lives was over.

NOTES

1. Carl Ruggles to Rosemary and Micah Ruggles, 24 July 1943.
2. Carl Ruggles to Henry Cowell, 16 Aug. 1943.
3. Carl Ruggles to Eugene Schoen, 13 Nov. 1943.
4. Charlotte Ruggles to Henry Schnakenberg, 11 Jan. 1944.
5. Interview with Betty Bartlett Madden, New York City, 21 Feb. 1974.
6. Carl Ruggles to Eugene Schoen, 24 Feb. 1944.
7. Harmony Ives to Charlotte Ruggles, 16 Mar. 1944.
8. Carl Ruggles to Harmony and Charles Ives, 21 Mar. 1944.
9. Carl Ruggles to John Kirkpatrick, 23 June 1944.
10. Carl Ruggles to John Kirkpatrick, 2 Aug. 1944.
11. Carl Ruggles to John Kirkpatrick, 18 Aug. 1944.
12. Carl Ruggles to Henry Cowell, 9 Jan. 1945.
13. Lou Harrison to Carl Ruggles, 1 Mar. 1945.
14. Ibid.
15. Lou Harrison to Carl Ruggles, [early Nov. 1945].
16. Interview with Lou Harrison, Aptos, California, 21 Mar. 1975.
17. Carl Ruggles to Harmony and Charles Ives, 17 Dec. 1945.
18. Unfortunately the booklet is out of print, but the material has been reprinted in: *Soundings: Ives, Ruggles, Varèse* (Spring 1974): 47–60.
19. Lou Harrison to Carl Ruggles, 5 Apr. 1946.
20. Carl Ruggles to John Kirkpatrick, 31 July 1946.
21. "Parvum Organum" remained in sketches, however, and after Carl died, John found them and put them together into an as yet unpublished work.
22. Carl Ruggles to Lou Harrison, 9 Jan. 1947.
23. Carl Ruggles to John Kirkpatrick, 15 Jan. 1947. The "ham piano players" were his good friend, Joseph Tarpley, and Mrs. Ellison, another piano teacher at the university. Carl's descriptive phrase was certainly not accurate.
24. *New York Herald Tribune,* 22 Apr. 1947.
25. Carl Ruggles to John Kirkpatrick, 8 July 1947.

26. Charles Ives to Carl Ruggles, [June 1947].

27. John Kirkpatrick to Carl Ruggles, 19 July 1947.

28. Conversation with John Kirkpatrick, New Haven, Connecticut, 16 Jan. 1974.

29. Carl Ruggles to John Kirkpatrick, 14 Mar. 1948. The Ives work referred to is his "Lincoln, the Great Commoner."

30. Carl Ruggles to John Kirkpatrick, 13 Mar. 1948.

12

The Good Years
1948–57

It was as usual a very social summer, once they had opened the schoolhouse and resumed their normal routine. But Carl, discouraged over his lack of recognition as a composer, spent more time working on his paintings than on music. He had some small works in the Arlington Street Fair and of course in the annual exhibition at the end of the summer.

Carl's disgust with the musical scene and his discouragement about his own music shows in the postscript of a letter to Varèse: "What a stinker K——[Koussevitsky] is, and the dirty little rats he surrounds himself with." In another letter a few weeks later Carl was still discouraged, "Everywhere there is an appalling cultural lag," he wrote.[1]

It wasn't a cultural lag that bothered Carl so much as the fact that orchestra conductors and soloists interested in contemporary music, always a small number, were turning their attention to the emigrés who had come to this country from Europe, such as Ernest Krenek, Hindemith, and Schoenberg. In addition, now there were younger American composers competing for performances. David Diamond and Samuel Barber, for example, had major performances with the Boston Symphony that year. No wonder Carl had harsh words for Koussevitsky. Carl was one of the older composers, and with his small output, his music could be, and often was, passed over.

Once the summer was ended, the issue of where to spend the winter had to be settled. Neither Carl nor Charlotte wanted to return to Florida, and in fact they both wished they could afford to stay in New York. That seemed impossible, until once again, as so many times in the past, friends, especially Schnakenberg, came forward with the extra financial help. So it was settled. They would winter in the city at the Chelsea Hotel on 23rd Street.

The Chelsea would seem to have been the perfect place for the Ruggleses. Built originally as a cooperative apartment house, by 1905 it had become a hotel and home to countless numbers of artists in all media. Edgar Lee Masters memorialized it in a poem entitled "The Hotel Chelsea," and such artists as O. Henry, John Sloan, and Dylan Thomas have lived there at one time or another. When Carl and Charlotte moved in, Virgil Thomson had already been there for a number of years.

In those days the lobby had a pineapple-shaped coal burning fireplace in the center, with red cushioned chairs around it. There were benches along the walls and a dark mahogany desk at the back. Just to the west of the lobby was the restaurant, which served "plain cooking," and only a few doors down the street was Cavanaugh's, a famous restaurant of the time.[2]

After they became part of the regulars, Carl and Charlotte usually had an apartment on the back overlooking the garden, either number 210 or 510. It included a living room with a small kitchen at one end, a bedroom and bath, and a southern exposure that caught the winter sunlight. It was altogether quite cheerful and homelike, especially after they hung some of Carl's paintings on the walls. And nothing delighted them more than to be in the city with the Varèses and Cowell and Lou Harrison, all of whom they immediately contacted.

At first Carl did not have a piano, but after about a month he rented an upright and began to work. He was making sketches for a composition for piano and brass. When he wasn't working, they would visit friends or go to museums, and often they would sit in the hotel lobby and visit with the other guests. Virgil Thomson invited them to his apartment several times, and Carl proudly wrote to John: "Been up to Virgil's three times. He's coming to like us."[3]

In January a memorial concert was held in honor of the disinguished critic, Paul Rosenfeld, and the Ruggleses attended. Rosenfeld had liked Carl's music, but although Carl felt some allegiance toward him, he wasn't at all pleased with the program. "Most of it was a dreadful bore," he wrote to John. "Then came Hyperprism by Varèse. . . . It's twenty years old, the same as Angels, and it sounded magnificent. Varèse and others were surprised that Angels wasn't played. Dirty work at the crossroads, they say."[4]

But Carl had some good news to relate, too. William Masselos was to play *Evocations* on February 17 at the T. L. Kaufman Auditorium, and the Ives First Sonata was also on the program. Carl also assured John that the work for piano and brass was going very well, though he felt strings would have to be added. Shortly after he learned of the Masselos performance, he found out that "Angels" was to be played on February 27 at a concert in Times Hall by the National Association of American Composers and Conductors. Lou was to conduct the work, which would be performed by students from Juilliard trained by Richard Franko Goldman. It was going to be a good February.

First came the Masselos performance, which Carl found disappointing in spite of the good reviews. Then came the February 27 concert. "Angels," conducted by Lou, was the final piece on the program, and for Virgil Thomson, it was the high point of the evening. He wrote a rave review. "Masterpiece Revived" was the heading, and he concluded: "Lou Harrison conducted Ruggles's 'Angels' reverently, admirably. It was a lovely concert, in every way out of the ordinary; and Ruggles's piece is great music."[5]

Surely Carl must have been elated by this recognition, yet when he wrote to John, once again he showed that mean contrary spirit: "Angels was like a jewel in a muck-heap. The performance was not good. Amateurs from Juilliard. They just played the notes, and Lou is no conductor. No sense of balance. . . . I thought the rest of the so-called music was pretty poor stuff. I loathe woodwind combinations, and I told Henry so. As for Carter, I fail to find the slightest indication of anything that would make me think it was music. . . . Yes, Virgil's criticism was grand. Nothing could be better." Then from his lofty stance he complained that most young composers write "too many notes," adding that "Portals" had been accepted for performance at the forthcoming Columbia University Festival on May 13.[6]

What Carl did not know about the performance was that because Richard Franko Goldman, who had trained the performers on "Angels," had refused to conduct it publicly because of Carl's anti-Semitism, Lou was called in to replace him. Lou, however, did not know why Goldman had not conducted until after the program. He remembered that when he was told the truth, he felt put upon, for he, too, objected to Carl's prejudices and to his loud and high-handed manner in restaurants and public places. From this time on their friendship became more distant, though Lou, like Carl's other friends, continued to champion his music.[7]

One important spin-off from Thomson's review was a note from Leopold Stokowski, then conductor of the New York Philharmonic, asking about *Sun-Treader.* He found it of interest and wanted to know the duration of the work, just in case they decided to broadcast it. And he asked where he could purchase a score, since Varèse had sent him his own *New Music* edition. By the time Stokowski's note reached them, the Ruggleses had returned to Arlington, and since there were no scores of *Sun-Treader* for sale, Carl decided to send him one of his own. He and Charlotte began a frantic search through his pile of scores, which were never in good order, but it was several weeks before they turned up one in good enough condition to send. Typically, Carl went over it to make some minor changes before finally sending it.

In the meantime the Columbia Festival was approaching, and Frederick Finnell, who was to conduct "Portals," wanted the score and parts, which Carl scrambled once again to find. When at last Finnell received the parts, which were old copies, he found them so marked up and illegible, that he objected, and at the last minute Carl had to have new ones reproduced under the aegis of *New Music,* with Cowell's consent. John attended the May 6 try-out in Rochester, where Finell also conducted "Angels." He was not very enthusiastic about the performances and in his letter added some personal criticism that must have given Carl a bit of a jolt: "Both Angels and Portals lacked breadth, and I told him so afterwards. . . . I must confess that for my ears Portals represents a degree of piled-up dissonance. It makes me wonder if it's all really essential to the communication of the inspiration involved."[8] The performance took place without Carl, who came down with the flu, and, regardless of John's criticism, the music was received with much enthusiasm.

Sometime during their previous stay in New York, Carl joined and deposited his orchestral scores with the American Music Center, an organization founded in 1940 to foster the performance of music by American composers. In 1948 Ray Green, himself a composer, had been made executive secretary of the center and he quickly set about enlarging the holdings by actively soliciting scores from a number of composers, among them, Carl, whom he had met through Varèse. For Carl, the association was simply with Ray Green, and he never tried to find out anything about the American Music Center.

Meanwhile Green began to act as his agent, writing to find out if he should send to Stokowski the corrected parts of *Sun-Treader,* which were on deposit. His concern was premature, however, for Carl had not yet heard from the conductor. At the end of June Stokowski finally wrote, requesting copies of other scores: "Angels," *Men and Mountains,* "Portals," and *Organum.* Carl quickly obliged, and during the last week in June, Stokowski finally made up his mind. It is quite possible that he was guided in his decision by Varèse, who had suggested Carl's music in the first place. At any rate, on July 1 he wrote that he planned to perform *Organum* on November 12, if that date was acceptable to Carl.

Carl could hardly contain his joy. It is true he still had not heard *Sun-Treader,* but at least it had been performed. This would be a first performance and with the New York Philharmonic in Carnegie Hall! But there were some sobering thoughts. Parts had not yet been made, nor was there a professional copy of the score, which Stokowski was already requesting. Carl stalled him by sending the piano score that John had made, with the assurance that the full score would soon be forthcoming. Then as usual he turned for help to his friends. Clearly he needed a good copyist, and Varèse suggested that he hire Mimi Wallner, who did copy work for him. She agreed to start work on the score and parts immediately, putting aside her other work.

That settled, Carl turned to John, for the Philharmonic wrote that they wanted a biographical sketch, a list of his works, and program notes on *Organum*. John had written out an analysis of the piece, and Carl was considering using that. Realizing that John was busy, he wrote that he would get all the material together and then send it along for criticism. He hoped that John would write and offer to take care of everything, but the latter was, in fact, far too busy, and much of the work concerned Carl. John was proofreading Mimi's work on *Organum* and preparing to perform *Evocations* at Woodstock, New York, on September 4.

It was a very exciting time for Carl and Charlotte, and by extension for all their friends. But there was a worry, too. Carl was seventy-three years old, and this summer, he did not feel well. When he came down with the flu, he was not able to shake it; he simply could not regain his strength. He remained under doctor's care for several weeks, with orders to rest and stay quiet. And how Carl hated going to the doctor! The office was just a few doors away, and Carl would slowly walk over to the house; then he would sit on the porch until someone inside noticed him there and went out to bring him in. But this summer he definitely needed the doctor's care.

All through this period Mimi was sending the copied parts of the score to *Organum* for either John or Carl to proofread. John made up the errata list on the score for her, and by mid-September she was working on the parts. Stokowski meanwhile was busy studying what was available, and in late September he wrote to Carl, requesting a copy of the score for his own personal library, so he could mark it up in any way he wished. Fortunately the score was ready, so Carl could send him one that had only recently been reproduced.

By the end of October score and parts were safely delivered to the Philharmonic, and in early November Carl and Charlotte returned to the Chelsea for the winter, in great anticipation of the forthcoming concerts. They both attended the rehearsals, and Carl was so thrilled with the music that it was hard for him to contain himself. At one rehearsal he appeared wearing a pair of overalls. To his surprise and delight, Stokowski said the overalls were just the thing for rehearsals and that he, too, would like to own a pair. Carl promised to see to it, and soon thereafter arranged for a pair to be sent to Stokowski from the Cullinan store in Arlington.[9]

The performances took place in Carnegie Hall on Thursday evening and Friday afternoon, November 24 and 25, and as many of Carl's friends who were able to attended one or the other. *Organum* opened the program, and the applause that followed was loud and long. Both Carl and Stokowski were called upon to take several bows, and Stokowski himself told Carl it was a great triumph.

Francis D. Perkins, who wrote the review for the *Tribune,* called *Organum* a "pungent and stimulating aperitif." The review that pleased Carl the most, however, was from Olin Downes in the *New York Times.* It was the best review Downes had ever given to Carl's music up to that time: "This 'Organum' was just the right opening . . . the matured and forceful expression of a composer who has been these many years a brave, original artist; one who never wrote music only to please and never hesitated to ride a conviction straight into the teeth of public disapproval or misunderstanding, . . . It is an admirably compact work."[10]

Carl called for a large orchestra in this piece: piccolo, two flutes, two oboes, English horn, E flat clarinet, three clarinets in C, bass clarinet, two bassoons and contrabassoon; four horns, three trumpets, three trombones, and tuba; piano, timpani, cymbal, and strings; and there is much color as a result. Unfortunately, many of the contrapuntal devices that Carl was so proud of are really not heard as such by the listener. Instead one is aware of the rise and fall and rise of the lines, the "large curves," as John described each section. There are three of them, with an interruption in the second one, before the return to the opening. The upward line of the solo piano marks the end of the third large curve, and at their peak one hears enormous tension.[11]

Carl's trademarks are there, too: the use of instruments at their extreme ranges, the undulating long lines, and the use of the consonant third to slightly sweeten the dissonances. One has a sense of integrity and purpose throughout the piece, but also perhaps a feeling that there may have been too much lunging, too much tension compressed into too short a period of time.

A friend made a private recording of the Friday afternoon performance, and Carl wrote to John that "We think it's the finest orchestral record we've ever heard." The performances had given him renewed vigor. "Now I have to go to work and finish that new composition for piano and orchestra. *Large orchestra.* To hell with chamber stuff."[12] He was referring to the piece that had started out as music for piano and brass. Then he had thought strings were necessary, and now it was to be for large orchestra. But in fact, as we shall see, it never came into being at all.

Charlotte, as always, was left to deal with such practical matters as how to afford a piano for Carl, something which so far, in spite of the performances, seemed not possible that winter in New York. Once again Henry Schnakenberg came to the rescue with a substantial Christmas check, and Charlotte wrote gratefully: "We have been turning and twisting, adding and subtracting our budget, but to fit in the renting of a piano, seemed impossible—now we can swing it and you know what that means."[13]

It was, alas, true that their financial situation had not measurably improved. For the Philharmonic performance of *Organum* Carl was paid a mere sixty dollars. Fortunately Harriette's stipend continued along with the generosity of their friends.

Carl and Charlotte began the new decade with high hopes; it really did seem that at last some of the major performers and organizations would pay attention to his work. Along with Ives, he was becoming the grand old man of American music. How much more new music there would be was a moot question, but he was determined to continue—albeit at his own snail's pace.

Then a few weeks before his seventy-fourth birthday on March 11, he became ill and had to see a doctor, who prescribed sulfa and penicillin. By his birthday, he felt well enough to visit with Ives's daughter, Edie, who had brought him a present from her father. Carl gratefully acknowledged it, a week later: "I really hate to smoke those fine cigars, I should like to keep them in remembrance. But the flesh is weaker than the spirit."[14]

They returned to Arlington on April 1, and shortly afterward George Szell, the conductor of the Cleveland Symphony Orchestra, requested a copy of the score to *Organum*. Meanwhile Julian DeGray performed the *Evocations* in mid-April at Bennington College, and the Ruggleses attended. It was their first reunion with old friends, and after the concert there was a jolly gathering to celebrate the concert and to welcome Charlotte and Carl back from New York. Within a few weeks, however, Charlotte became ill. Perhaps it was a bad cold or the flu, but she seemed unable to regain her strength. Carl was not much help in such a situation, but fortunately the neighbors brought in food and helped to keep the schoolhouse clean and orderly.

By the time she was feeling well again, there was more good news for Carl in a letter from Virgil Thomson, informing him that the Columbia Recording Corporation planned to record American chamber music on LP records. Each composer to be represented would have one side of a record, and the committee had chosen Carl as one of the composers. Thomson suggested that they record "Portals," "Lilacs," and "Angels" (in the string version) and possibly *Evocations*. He replied to Thomson quickly, saying that the news was almost too good to be true. Then he went on to discuss the project: "Angels," he wrote, was conceived for muted brass and that was the only way he would allow it to be recorded; "Lilacs" was fine, and so was "Portals," though the latter would require rehearsals and a "first rate conductor."[15]

Then Carl sent the good news to John and asked him about recording *Evocations,* too. Now that the pieces were to be recorded, Carl took the opportunity to have another look at them, and of course to make a few minor changes. John paid a visit in early August, and they went over *Evocations* again. There still was some discussion about the order of the four pieces. John preferred them with the one dedicated to Ives rather than the one to Charlotte at the end. But by the time John was ready to prepare them for the recording, Carl had made up his mind. He wanted the one with a loud ending, the one to Charlotte, as the final piece, and he wrote to John accordingly.

Although in the Columbia recording John followed Carl's wishes, that is not the end of the story, for he continued to press his point; and ultimately Carl changed his mind. In the 1954 printed edition of *Evocations,* the last one is the Ives, and in the later Columbia recording of all of Carl's music, when John again recorded the work, that order of *Evocations* is maintained.

There was still more good news that August. The manager of the Houston Symphony Orchestra wrote that Stokowski would be guest conductor during the next season and intended to perform *Organum.* They wanted program notes from Carl, who sent them along the following month. Interestingly, in his list of works, he chose to omit "Toys" and *Vox Clamans in Deserto.*[16]

In spite of all the good news, Carl was still not feeling well, and he complained to John that he was taking sulfa three times a day. Nonetheless he did complete some paintings in preparation for the annual exhibit of the Southern Vermont Artists Association. This year it was especially important, for the exhibit would take place for the first time in the new building that was to be their permanent home. The members' show was a gala event, and several of Carl's works were included. According to the center's accounting, he sold only two paintings: "Bird Island Light" to Henry Schnakenberg, and "Seascape" to a local resident.

When the nights grew cool in mid-September, Carl and Charlotte began to think about their winter season in New York. They decided to stay in Arlington as long as possible to save money, but as usual, Henry Schnakenberg was also thinking of their winter season; and once again, before the month of September was over, sent a substantial check.

Meanwhile John was to play *Evocations* in Baltimore on November 5 and on the following day make the recording. Columbia Records sent Carl the contract for the recording, which stipulated that he would receive 2½ percent of the retail list price of 90 percent of all the records sold if his music was on both sides. If it was on only one side, he would get one-half the amount of the royalty (1¼ percent) of 90 percent of the records sold. As it turned out, his music was only on one side. John wrote that *Evocations* had gone well, both at the performance in Baltimore and at the recording session. But the producer had expressed concern about the expenses of recording the other Ruggles works, and as a result, it would be several years before the record was finished.

The beautiful autumn weather held into early November in Arlington, and Carl wrote ecstatically about it to Ives, "The green grass, the trees and the mountains, all from our windows. No, we don't want to leave it all. It's our Home."[17] But of course it couldn't last. Shortly before they were ready to leave, winter arrived with fury. In addition to heavy snow, there was a powerful wind that knocked down tree branches and power lines. Arlington had no electricity for five days, and no train service. Somehow they managed, and as soon as service was restored, they left for New York, arriving at the Chelsea on December 1.

They were having a very good time in New York, seeing friends and visiting art galleries; it was especially pleasant, because Carl had two more performances scheduled for mid-February. On Sunday, February 11, *Evocations* was to be played by Irene Rosenberg at an International Society for Contemporary Music concert, and the very next day, *Men and Mountains* in its latest version was to be given by the symphony orchestra of the Manhattan School of Music, conducted by Harris Danziger. This latter program was part of the Twelfth Annual American Music Festival, sponsored by WNYC, which would broadcast the concert.

Carl particularly looked forward to the *Men and Mountains* performance, since it would be the first hearing of the new version with the retrograde at the end of the last movement. They notified as many friends as they could about the orchestra concert, and Carl wrote Schnakenberg that he was keeping his fingers crossed that the orchestra would be up to the piece. They needn't have worried. The piece went well, and since Danziger repeated it, the audience heard it twice. Carl reported to John: "The orchestra did very well, considering that it was a student O- and the tremendous difficulties of balance etc. Not enough violins, or violas. The conductor really did a good job. There was an ovation when it was *repeated*. . . . Varèse thought the music was 'magnificent,' and I agreed. *27 years old*."[18]

On March 8 and 9, *Organum* was performed by the Cleveland orchestra, and Carl was beginning to think he might have written a popular work — especially when he received a letter from Stokowski, just a day after his birthday, in which the conductor said he wanted to play *Organum* in Europe. Stokowski also requested that they borrow the parts directly from Carl, and he wrote that his manager, Andrew Schulhof, would contact him on this matter.

It is noteworthy that Stokowski chose to go directly to Carl for the parts rather than to Ray Green. For one thing it meant that Carl could keep the entire fee without having to pay Green the 20 percent commission charged for the other performances. It also appears that Carl did not have a signed contract with Green, for in that case the parts would have had to be obtained through Green, who was acting as Carl's publisher.

Though Green was still executive secretary of the American Music Center, he was preparing to found American Music Editions, which would indeed publish music, his own and that of other American composers, including Carl and many affiliated with the American Music Center. In Carl's case, even after Green's American Music Edition was established, it is unclear whether there was ever a signed contract. Carl was very sloppy about such things, and while Green may have drawn up a contract, Carl may not have signed it. In fact, I came across an unsigned contract among the Ruggles papers after his death. However, Green continued to operate as though he had provided a legal bond.

In May, Danziger conducted "Lilacs" at Columbia University, and Carl was pleased, but now his major interest was focused on Stokowski's tour in late April and May. There were two programs for the trip, and *Organum* was an alternate on the second program. The sponsor of the various concerts could choose between *Organum* and the "Roman Carnival Overture" by Berlioz. Five sponsors chose Carl's music, and they were all in England.[19] For those performances Stokowski himself sent a check to Carl for fifty dollars, ten dollars for each performance, and he added that he was sending it directly to avoid any inconvenience to Carl.

That fall Carl wrote to John about a wonderful discovery he had made: "Last night—over the radio—I heard a perfectly beautiful composition: A Suite for Strings by Corelli. Why, he is a great composer. I can't understand why he is so neglected. I think Handel and Bach must have been familiar with his music." Then he told him that they had gone to Bennington College to attend a concert and had heard a "magnificent sonata for cello and piano by Beethoven. Never heard it before." But he didn't like the Schubert piano sonata that was also on the program. And in a postscript, he added: "Robert Frost came down from Breadloaf and took us out to lunch. Another Grand Sun [sic]. What wit!"[20]

The distinguished poet was only two years older than Carl and was living in South Shaftsbury, Vermont, when Carl and Charlotte moved to Arlington. They soon met and probably were together fairly often at some of the summer social events during the twenties and thirties, when Frost lived in Vermont. However, they never became close friends. Rather they respected each other as two tough New Englanders, each remaining somewhat wary of the other. Perhaps they were both too prickly. When Carl referred to Frost in later times, he spoke with respect, aware of the other man's greater fame and wider culture, but he never showed a real sense of warmth or friendship.

The weather stayed warm enough for them to remain in Arlington until January 1, and once in the city, they looked up old friends and were soon entertaining and being entertained. Eileen and Joe Barber remembered going to the Chelsea for an evening with the Ruggleses when Charlotte prepared a lobster dinner for them. Charlotte was a fine cook, Eileen reported, and during the evening Carl drank bourbon, told his stories, and argued with Joe.[21]

They decided to wait until after May 6 to return to Arlington, for on that day there was a Martha Graham dance concert with May O'Donnell, Ray Green's wife, as guest soloist. She was dancing two solos: one to Carl's *Organum,* and the other to Ives's "Unanswered Question." While Carl was not very much interested in dance, he respected Martha Graham, and told me that he and Charlotte had once gone to see her at Bennington College. At intermission, he decided to go backstage to say hello. He found her dressing room and knocked. She said to come in, and when he did, there she was without a "stitch of clothing on! Not a rag on!" Carl backed out quickly, but in his confusion he left his glasses. When he got back to his seat, he told Charlotte, and she said, "Well, you go right back and retrieve them!" I laughed heartily and said that Charlotte must have enjoyed it all. "Well," he grinned, "she didn't have anything to worry about. You know Martha was all bones."[22]

In April of 1952 Carl had been nominated for membership in the National Institute of Arts and Letters for the following year. His three nominators were Ives, Cowell, and Otto Luening. Earlier Schnakenberg had been elected to the institute, and he, too, wrote in support of Carl's nomination. But it was not to be. Carl was passed over. He tried to appear nonchalant about the whole business, and even admitted to Schnakenberg that there were some good people in the organization, especially Ives and John Marin. Carl really wanted to be elected. He knew it was a great honor, and one that he hoped would eventually be his.

The big event of the summer was a one-man show of his paintings at the Southern Vermont Art Center from July 5 to 24. Harriette was in charge of the event, and for the opening there was to be a program of Carl's music, including the recording of *Organum* and a live performance of *Evocations* by John. The following week, on July 13, Robert Frost was coming to read "partly as a tribute to me," Carl wrote in a letter to Schnakenberg inviting him to the event. He added that Harriette had "framed all the paintings, and what frames."[23]

The excitement of the show kept Carl and Charlotte busy during the first part of the summer. Not that they had that much to do, with Harriette in charge, but Carl wanted to be consulted on everything. He watched over it all proudly, and in the end contributed some of his own paintings for the exhibition, though most were loaned from other sources. There were forty-nine items on display, including one page from his manuscript of *Organum,* Harriette's bust of him, and a group of portraits of Carl by Atherton, Benton, and Boardman Robinson. According to Dean Fausett, program chairman of the art center, Harriette not only took care of all the arrangements, but also paid the performers' fees.

On the day of the opening, July 5, John arrived in late morning and stopped in Arlington to pick up Carl and Charlotte. Then they drove to the Southern Vermont Art Center, so he could try out the piano before the show opened at 2:00 P.M. The main entrance hall served as the auditorium, and the big nine-foot Steinway, rented for the occasion, became the centerpiece. There was also a record player nearby for *Organum.* After John had played awhile, they all went to lunch at the old Equinox Hotel. It was one of the fanciest restaurants around, and John had to retrieve his suit coat from the car before they could enter; Carl announced as they walked in that it was "just like a God damn cafeteria!" Even so, he was dressed in a white suit and looked as dapper as he could be. Charlotte was elegant with her dark hair parted in the middle and braided in buns on each side of her head.

She wore a long dress, dangling earrings and lots of costume jewelry around her neck and on her arms. She was intensely proud of Carl and this was his day; but she knew it was hers, too.

By five o'clock the chairs in the entrance hall and surrounding galleries were filled, and it was time for the music to begin. *Evocations* came first, and at Carl's request, John performed the work twice. Then came the unofficial recording of *Organum*. One of the board members started the machine, but unfortunately started it at the wrong speed, far too slow. The sound came out in low yawps and yaws, and amid much confusion, Carl was heard to cry out: "Oh my God, that isn't my music!" Soon of course, the problem was solved, and *Organum* was much applauded. Afterward there was a great party with Carl in the center of it all, enjoying every minute.[24]

The celebration continued on the following Sunday afternoon, when Robert Frost came down from Breadloaf to read. Before the event, mutual friends got the distinguished photographer, Clara Sipprell, who lived nearby, to photograph Carl and Frost. In the photograph they sit side by side, Carl all in white with his ever-present cigar, and Frost more informally dressed and looking somewhat amused by all the fuss.

Beginning in the fall, Orrea Pernel, a fine violinist on the faculty at Bennington, brought her string quartet, the Estival Quartet, to the schoolhouse every Monday evening for rehearsals. It was an excellent place to rehearse, for the acoustics were very good; and Carl and Charlotte were delighted to have the group, which included: Edwin Sherrard, violin; Anne Bickford, viola; and George Finkel, cello. Carl had real difficulty hearing by this time (deafness had been developing over the years), so he would bring up a chair and sit right beside the players. Charlotte sat off to one side, and when the rehearsals were over, she served tea to everyone. They played mostly the Beethoven quartets, according to Carl, and though he enjoyed the music, he was not interested in quartet writing. "Too much four part stuff and the cello grinding away down there," he wrote to John. As if to support the truth of that statement, the Ruggleses did not attend any of the quartet's concerts, which were given in nearby towns. The rehearsals were enough for them.[25]

On the other hand, Carl was not one to pass up an opportunity to hear some of his music, so he used the quartet to try out some of the things from his new piece. He wrote little snatches for the string quartet and sent them to John (see examples 42, 43, and 44). These are worth noting, for they are some of the few examples from this unfinished late work, and they demonstrate an even richer chromaticism with tone rows consistently of ten notes. They are also the only examples of Carl's writing for string quartet, which, as he himself admitted, he really did not like. And they clearly show how his thinking kept going beyond the four instruments to other instrumental sounds.

In example 42, after the opening solo violin, the aim is to achieve dissonance by holding over a line in one or two voices while the line moves to dissonance in another voice. In measure one of the four

Example 42. From an unfinished late work (letter to Kirkpatrick, Nov. 1952).

parts, for example, there is a nice piling up of sounds: G is held throughout the bar, then A flat is added and held, followed by a G flat also held; and finally on the fourth beat, the F is sounded. So at that moment one hears F, G flat, G, and A flat. Measure two starts with an open fifth, E and B. Then the two upper voices answer with another open fifth, F and C, which descends to E flat and B flat; at which point one hears more dissonance: E and B in the two lower voices against E flat and B flat in the two upper. Then since the E flat and B flat are held, Carl has the bottom voices leap to a D and A, providing still another dissonant sound. But note, the dissonances do not start at the same time; they happen by voices following each other. It is like the children's game of putting one hand on top of the other, over and over again. And it is very characteristic of his style.

Measures four through eight may or may not be a continuation. Carl has called these examples "scattered fragments," so we cannot tell. For these measures he wrote that five parts were needed, and we can see the beginning of imitation in the upper voices against the descending bass line.

Example 43 is another working out of the material from example 42. Here he has called for piano as well as strings. Note that the opening measure, which is for piano here, is the same as measure one for string quartet in the previous example. Then comes the theme, this time for solo viola instead of solo violin, followed by exact imitation in the cello. On beat three of measure three, the second violin begins a line that appears to be an imitation a third above, but which soon turns into a long descending line in octaves with an extension ascending. After this Carl indicated that the piano would then take up the same passage. Now these of course are mere jottings, but they show how his first thoughts were almost always linear.

Example 44 bears this out, for it is essentially two strands of music. Measure one here is the same as measure two of example 42 but one half step higher, and it is another working out of the fifths and fourths. Carl was planning to use variation form in the piece, and this was to be the opening of one of the variations.

It is interesting that even in these fragments the Ruggles characteristics are evident: the undulating line that avoids repetition of notes, the wide melodic leaps that get filled in, the doubling in octaves, and finally the combination of sharp dissonances with sound combinations that hint of the more traditional chords of chromatic harmony. Carl told John that he wanted to score the work for full orchestra and piano, but since performances were difficult to get, he might have to

Example 43. From an unfinished late work (letter to Kirkpatrick, Nov. 1952).

be satisfied with a chamber ensemble. As it turned out, he didn't have to settle for that.

Just after Thanksgiving, he received a letter from Robert Whitney, the musical director of the Louisville Orchestra, offering him a commission for a symphonic work. They would pay him one thousand dollars for a piece of about fifteen minutes in length, and he asked by what date Carl felt that he could complete the work. Carl was thrilled about the commission; but setting a time for the completion of a work was almost impossible for him. He remembered the fights with Varèse

Example 44. From an unfinished late work (letter to Kirkpatrick, Nov. 1952).

over deadlines in the days of the International Composers Guild. On the other hand, he had the beginnings of a new work. First entitled "Experiments" and written for piano and a small group of instruments, it was now called "Variations on Three Subjects," and he did want to make it for orchestra.

So after they arrived at the Chelsea—earlier than usual because of the cold weather—he wrote to Whitney accepting the commission with some reservations. For example, if another orchestra wanted to record the piece before "an opportunity presents itself to your orchestra I should like to reserve the privilege to take advantage of any such occasion." As for the date of completion, he wrote honestly, "It is not possible for me at this time to give you a date of completion for the work," although he did add that "a certain amount of composition has already been done on it."[26]

But Carl never completed the commission. He dabbled at it, he talked about it, and that was all. There was no finished work. Maybe it was age; he was seventy-six years old, and he may not have had the physical stamina or the intense powers of concentration that are required to complete a new composition. It was one thing to work with John on a new edition of *Evocations* and to make small changes here and there, but quite another thing to bring to fruition a new fifteen-minute work for orchestra. Still, he had accepted the commission. Did he know he could not fulfill it? That seems doubtful, for Carl would not have wanted to face failure. Moreover, his pride and prestige were involved. He had to accept. His only comment about it to me, when I questioned him many years later, was that after he had been offered the commission, the orchestra had come to New York, "and I went to hear them and they were terrible. So I never took it."[27] But that is not quite the truth.

Meanwhile, in view of the forthcoming Columbia recording of *Evocations,* Carl and John decided to prepare another edition of the work. John had performed it enough by now to know where the pianistically weak spots were, and he had worked out the proper pedaling and fingering to help sustain the notes as Carl wished. The main issues were the order of the four pieces and the attempt to notate so that the results would look more pianistic and still be close to Carl's conception.

John felt strongly about keeping the order as he played them: the one to Charlotte, the last piece completed, as number three, and as conclusion the piece dedicated to Ives, which was actually the second one finished. Finally Carl agreed. The *Evocation* that Carl had dedicated to John himself came second, and John asked if he could change the heading from "andante, sempre poco rubato" to "andante con fantasia." Carl agreed to that, too. The first piece to Harriette remained at the opening.

Ray Green was now publishing the American Music Editions, and since he had been acting as Carl's agent, he found it only natural to strongly suggest that Carl transfer his published works to him. This meant that Carl would first have to withdraw them from New Music. Cowell was no longer in charge, and, as Ray pointed out, Carl derived no income from them. With American Music Editions, he promised, there would be royalties, however small at first.

It was a very difficult decision for Carl, who was never very decisive on business matters, anyway. Moreover, he could look back on a long and warm association with *New Music,* which, through the major efforts of Henry Cowell and later Lou Harrison, had published all of his works. But Vladimir Ussachevsky was now in charge, and Carl really did not know him. *New Music* had also taken the liberty of getting a copyright on *Organum* without Carl's permission, and he did not like that. So with additional prodding, he finally wrote to Ussachevsky withdrawing the "privilege for use of copyright for my works." And he continued: "It is hereby requested that the copyright certificate for all of my works published in the New Music Edition be returned to me at the address noted below [Arlington, Vermont]."[28]

If severing the connection was hard for Carl, it was shocking to

Henry Cowell. As soon as he heard the news, he wrote to Carl, pleading with him to reconsider his decision, and even offering to handle Carl's affairs personally, if he would only stay with *New Music*. He pointed out that they had just received an Oliver M. Ditson grant that would enable them to get their books in order and to pay royalties, and he urged him to reconsider. But Carl did not change his mind, and Ray Green was now his publisher.

The last weekend in May was a cool rainy one, but that was the time Martha Jackson, director of the art gallery that carried her name, had chosen to visit in Vermont. She had known the Ruggleses for several years and had seen Carl's paintings at the Southern Vermont Art Association exhibitions. This time mutual friends took her to call on them at the schoolhouse, and she fell in love with his paintings. She found the sight of the work there in the schoolhouse overwhelming; and while they visited and sipped tea, she offered Carl a New York show the very next season. Now it was Carl and Charlotte who were overwhelmed, but Jackson was true to her word.

When she returned to New York, she quickly dropped them a note confirming her offer, and she promised to work out a tentative schedule as soon as the current show by Reginald Marsh was hung. It was a wonderful opportunity, but it was also frightening for Carl. What would the New York critics say? Did he want to concentrate on painting for the summer? For that matter, did he want to be known as a painter more than as a composer? What about the Louisville commission? And what about his health? And behind all the questions was the ever-nagging one, "Was he good enough?" Exhibiting in Vermont was one thing; exhibiting in New York was quite another.

He and Charlotte went over and over and round and round the situation. Their indecision continued all summer, while Martha made plans for the show. In late June she sent up the schedule and told them that Carl's show would be offered from December 9 to 26, with the press preview and opening on the evening of December 8. It was all very heady for Carl and Charlotte, and they were torn. But since they still could not come to a decision, they did nothing.

Finally in August, Martha wrote that she needed Carl's consent before mailing the fall schedule, adding that he could do the show with only twelve works if he wished. Carl could not put off his decision much longer. Clearly he had to let her know what he was going to do; and at last he decided to back out. It was simply too much for him to contemplate, and in early September, he finally wrote that he would not be able to have the show, citing his age, his health, and the Louisville commision—all good enough reasons, to be sure. He wrote how grateful he was to her for the honor and for the opportunity that she had offered him, and he assured her that her judgment of his paintings meant a great deal to him. Martha responded graciously and generously, forgiving him the long delay and adding that she hoped to visit them again there in Arlington. Both Carl and Charlotte sighed in relief when that letter arrived.

They planned to spend the winter in New York, and once again Henry made that possible. He and some friends came to see the Ruggleses in mid-August and took them to lunch. He also left a sizable check. Charlotte wrote that the money would "take away their winter worries," and Carl wrote that "by way of thanks" he was going to dedicate to Henry the new composition for Louisville, which was now to be called "Symphonia Dialectica."[29]

In mid-October, a Paris radio orchestra broadcast *Men and Mountains;* but even more exciting for Carl was the Stokowski broadcast of "Portals" over CBS on Sunday afternoon, November 1, 1953. Carl wrote a host of friends, urging them to tune in to the broadcast, and he and Charlotte listened to it at a neighbor's home, finding the reception unfortunately none too clear. Moreover, things were even more difficult for Carl since his hearing loss. None of that, however, dampened his enthusiasm, and he was especially thrilled with Stokowski's introductory remarks about him.

Soon after they arrived in New York, Carl was notified that he was once again a candidate for membership in the National Institute of Arts and Letters. The "proposers" of Carl's nomination were the same as before: Cowell, Ives, and Luening. The election was held on January 22, 1954; this time Carl was admitted. Even before the official announcement arrived, his friends from the institute had telephoned Carl and Charlotte with the good news. They were thrilled. It was an important stamp of status and prestige for Carl, and he was very proud of it. The rosette of the institute, which he wore in the lapel of his best suit jacket, mattered very much to him. Through the years he saw to it that each new acquaintance saw that insignia and fully understood its significance.

He was soon notified by the institute about the official investiture of new members, and copies of his scores were requested for display. Ray Green took care of that. Then he was informed that Pach Brothers, the photographers, would take his picture for the "Gallery of Members." Carl thoroughly enjoyed all the preparations until they returned to Arlington at the end of March. He would make a special trip in May for the investiture.

Finally, after nearly four years of waiting, Columbia Records notified

Carl that the instrumental portion of the record was about to be made. Frederick Prausnitz, the conductor and later assistant dean of the Juilliard School of Music, would conduct "Lilacs" and "Portals." First he would perform both works at Juilliard on April 28, then record them two weeks later. Carl was gratified to learn that he had increased the size of the orchestra and had an extra three hour rehearsal session before making the recording. And Ray Green wrote to assure Carl that he would attend the recording session to be sure everything went according to Carl's wishes.

Schnakenberg, meanwhile, invited Carl to visit him in Connecticut, and promised to drive them both into New York for the ceremonies at the institute. It seemed like a good idea, and Carl was considering it, when Ives died on May 19. The family wired the sad news to Carl and Charlotte, who were both deeply affected. Carl had not been feeling well himself, and when the news came, his grief made him feel even worse.

There was no way they could possibly attend the funeral, nor indeed were they told when or where it would be, but they immediately wired their love and sympathy to Harmony in New York. Carl also wrote to Henry that he could not accept his invitation nor attend the institute festivities and his own investiture on May 26. Ives's death was a great loss for him, and he simply could not make the trip.

The funeral took place in West Redding, and John attended. Afterward he wrote a long detailed letter describing and sharing it with them, for he knew how deep was their grief. Carl responded gratefully: "We have lost a Great Friend, and the world a Great Composer. . . . I shall always regret that I couldn't have been with Harmony and you."[30]

In the process of cleaning out, Harmony came across Ives's notes in support of Carl, dating from 1952, and sent them on to him. "I thought you might care to see this in Charlie's hand writing—" she wrote. "It is his first draft for the Institute voting. He kept proposing you every year and was happy you were elected."[31] Carl was very glad to get the paper. His grief over Ives's death was real, for of all the people in his musical world, Ives was the one he felt closest to. They were both New Englanders; Ives was only two years older. Though there were significant differences between them, and they lived very different lives, they shared much love, respect, and admiration.

Carl frequently said that because neither of them had studied abroad, he and Ives were the first and greatest genuinely American composers, and he was intensely proud of that fact. A measure of the affection between them is that Harmony presented Carl with Charlie's secretary after his death. John had delivered the desk to the schoolhouse, Carl told me.[32] Ives's death darkened their whole summer.

Carl returned to his painting, and that fall, according to John, he completed one of his big flower pictures, "African Daisies," for Charlotte. His work in music consisted in going over *Evocations* one more time. Ray Green was going to bring out a new edition, and Carl wanted to get it just right. Moreover, though he would not admit it, tinkering with *Evocations* kept him busy in music without actually working on a new piece; and he didn't feel up to that.

The winter monetary problems were once again solved by a check from Henry. They took no chances with the weather this year, and moved to the Chelsea on November 26. They were given apartment number 110, and Carl rented a piano from the Baldwin Piano Company on West 23rd Street not far from the hotel.

The Columbia record was at last nearly ready for release, and for the liner notes Carl was asked to write a short statement, which might be printed verbatim, about himself and the music, but because he knew that was too much for him, he sent a list of his works and copies of the flattering reviews by Lawrence Gilman. Columbia took care of the rest. Meanwhile, since John had recorded *Evocations* back in November 1950, Carl wanted him to do another recording with all the minor changes they had incorporated into the work. Columbia agreed, and the second recording was done in early March. Both versions are on the recording, side by side, with the more recent recording first.[33]

The changes between the two versions are slight. Indeed the changes between the earliest versions printed by *New Music* and the later American Music Edition are not changes in musical content; Carl had that set from the beginning. In almost every instance the changes are in the direction of simplicity and clarity, so that the lines of music stand out. Sometimes he has changed the octave range, usually raising it; sometimes he has put the important notes in octaves where previously single notes sufficed. To make the music look simpler for the performer, he has occasionally made enharmonic changes, but the pitches of course remain the same. In a very few instances the rhythm has changed, but this, too, is toward simplicity and a kind of straightening out of the music. That also holds for the few changes in meter; where, for example, there had been two measures, one marked 2/4 and the other 5/8, now the two have been combined into one measure of 9/8. Sometimes Carl had to give up some of his beloved piling up of dissonances, for they simply could not be sustained, even by the pedal and ten fingers. John had performed the pieces enough to know what was possible and what was not, and Carl relied on his judgment. In each case the aim has been to make the music both sound and look as if it fitted the piano.

It was not until June that the record was offically released, and since the Ruggleses, who were back in Arlington, did not own a record player, they had to arrange to go to friends to hear it. They finally took the record down to Bennington to listen with Lionel Nowak and Claude Frank. On the whole Carl liked the recording, but he was not completely satisfied with the piano sound. He told John that all three of them had agreed that recording technology still had not solved that problem.

Slowly other people were taking up his music. Lionel Nowak planned to perform *Evocations* on his forthcoming concert tour, and "Angels" was given a fine performance at the Bennington College Symposium on Art and Music that May. Ingolf Dahl, a composer and conductor from California, was director of the Tanglewood Study Group that summer. In May he had conducted *Men and Mountains* in California, and he planned to do it again at Tanglewood.

It was a busy and interesting summer for them, but not all of it concerned the arts. Charlotte recounted some of the events in a letter to Schnakenberg, thanking him for another gift of money: "The slate roof gave way—a piece of the ceiling fell down in the living room just escaping Carl's head—5 strings on the piano broke—*no tuner* and to cap the climax we have a skunk in the cellar—Of course we haven't a cellar but he is down there and no way of getting under the foundation.—Then we both had a seige of Intestinal flu—."[34] Carl added a note assuring him that "Symphonia Dialectica" was in progress, but in truth not much was being done. However, with Henry's check in hand, they finally did have the piano repaired.

Then suddenly, on August 13, Carl was hit by severe pain in his right side. He dreaded the thought of going to the hospital, and they had no telephone. With neighbors' help Charlotte finally got him to the doctor's office just a few doors away, and the diagnosis was acute appendicitis. He was rushed to the hospital in Bennington, and the doctors operated at once.

"Carl wanted you to know he is in Benn. Hospital an emergency operation Sat. night at 9:30," Charlotte wrote to Schnakenberg five days later. "Acute appendicitis—It came without any warning I am still in a daze No complications so far Of course those 80 years were not in his favor—We have 3 fine Drs—and they are optimistic."[35]

As Charlotte wrote, there were no complications, and Carl, discharged from the hospital on August 31, was soon able to respond to all the messages and gifts that poured in. In addition to taking care of him, Charlotte had her own problem with her leg, which she had hurt some years back when she and Carl had spent Thanksgiving with Micah in Tampa. Fortunately she did not have to go to the hospital, but movement was difficult, and for several weeks she was limping. By the end of October they were both back in good health, and Carl was able to write Micah that he had resumed composing.

What he was doing was writing out single lines of music, notating them on any scraps of paper that happened to be handy. This was especially true as he grew older and seemed less and less concerned about completing a piece. He worked diligently at these single lines, and if he liked them he dated them. Example 45 shows one such line that he wrote on the announcement of the premiere of Varèse's "Deserts."

Example 45. From a manuscript, 1955.

He has omitted a time signature, but with the one bar line, it would appear that he meant 3/4. Also, though he has not marked them, the two penultimate beats would seem to be triplets. We can easily see the wavelike nature of his lines, and the principle of nonrepetition of notes. In this case, the opening is a complete twelve note series from middle C to high C, followed by a ten note series, then a shorter one of five. Note that the high point arrives quickly, followed by a long meandering descent back to middle C. Clearly Carl was experimenting with fifths, both perfect and diminished, and with half steps. Of all the intervals used (note that an interval is the distance between any two notes) only four are not some kind of fifth or a half step.

The ascending line is an interlocking combination of perfect fifth and half step to B natural; then after two descending half steps, there is the largest interval used, a major sixth up to the high point, F sharp. The line briefly slows down with two sets of eighth notes, half steps going in opposite directions with a major third between them. The real descent begins on the high C, where Carl again experiments with fifths. Here the order is half step first, then a skip with first a descending perfect fifth, then a half step and a diminished fifth. At that point the direction of the skips alternate, each preceded by a descending half step. There is an ascending diminished fifth, then a perfect fifth descending, an ascending diminished fifth, and finally an ascending half step before the descending major sixth from C to E flat to match the one at the top; then one last set of fifths: a perfect fifth ascending, D to A, and an augmented fifth descending, A to D flat, followed by the final half step to C. Carl thought he had done a fine job when he finished this. He dated it, "55." Perhaps he planned to incorporate it into the Louisville piece, but we cannot know, for there is no further evidence; and he does not indicate which instrument, or instruments, would perform it.

When they went to New York for the winter, that year of 1956, Carl did not rent a piano. Instead he walked over to a nearby piano sales and rental warehouse and worked there. He was supposed to be working on the Louisville commission, but accomplished little. He was more concerned with the new edition of *Evocations,* on which he and John and Ray Green had been involved with for well over a year. John read the proofs, and it took three sets before the music was ready for final printing.

At last, early in 1956, the new edition came out. It was published as "Revision of 1954," but he still was not completely satisfied with the work. According to John, shortly after it came out, Carl wanted to change and simplify the climax of the first piece, but Charlotte put her foot down: "'Now Carl, Ray has gone to all that trouble to make that edition exactly the way you wanted it, and you just can't do that, at least not just now.'"[36] The changes were to be in measures eleven and twelve, and it is instructive to compare the American Music Edition version of those measures with the changes that Carl wanted (see example 46). The basic musical content remains the same, but the new version is clearly simpler and more straightforward in rhythm, harmony, and pianistic technique. As a result it is also easier to perform.

Note, too, that the new version contains fewer dissonances, though there are still plenty left. For example, the left hand in beat one has been altered from diminished octaves to perfect octaves, and the middle voice at the end of measure eleven moving to measure twelve has been omitted. This not only makes the passage simpler, but it also reduces the number of discordant sounds. Carl insisted on showing it to Green; and in the later printings, Green included this as an alternative, putting it as an "Editors Note" on the blank page preceding the first *Evocation.*

March 11, 1956, was Carl's eightieth birthday, and to celebrate it Julian DeGray invited Carl to choose a program of piano works that he would privately perform for him and Charlotte in the DeGrays' New York apartment. It was a generous and loving offer, and Carl was excited at the prospect. After some thought he wrote out his ideal

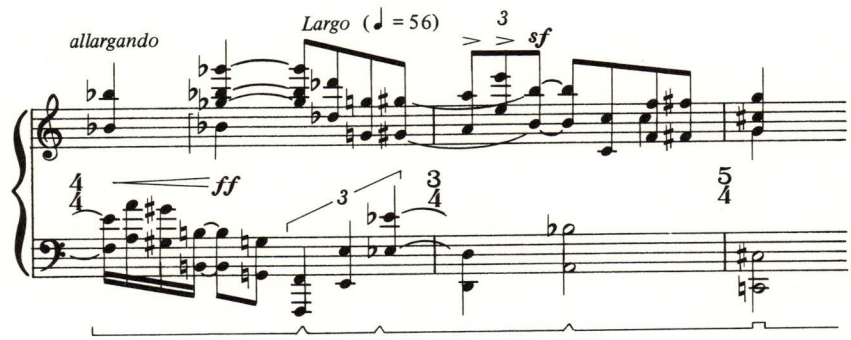

Example 46. Climax from American Music Edition 1954 version of *Evocations No. 1* (top) and the final revisions that were never made (© 1945 and 1956 by Theodore Presser Co. Used by permission of the publisher).

program, which included music by Bach, Beethoven, Schumann, Chopin, Brahms, and Debussy.

It was quite a celebration, and they never did get around to all the works on the program, though of course, *Evocations* was performed. Afterward, while they ate some of Margaret's homemade pie, which Carl dearly loved, there was much shouting and laughter. No evening was complete for the Ruggleses and DeGrays until Carl and Julian had traded stories, ever more obscene as the hour grew later.[37]

Sometime in late summer or early fall Lional Nowak brought a young couple to Arlington to meet the Ruggleses. They were Jim Tenney, the composer, who had come to Bennington to study with Lionel, and his wife at the time, Carolee Schneemann, the media artist. Lionel thought that both Carl and Jim would benefit from the meeting, and he was absolutely right. Carl and Charlotte liked the young couple right away, and they liked the Ruggleses.

Soon Jim was happily going over Carl's music with him. In a small way, Tenney came to replace John as Carl's musical advocate, and it worked to benefit both men. Jim's interest and admiration fed Carl's ego; and his knowledge of music meant that Carl and he could argue and discuss musical points as equals, regardless of the disparity in their ages. Most important, Jim was there, living nearby, so they could see each other often. Not surprisingly, since Jim was an excellent pianist, Carl insisted on going over *Evocations* again, as well as the other works. In the meantime Carolee, an artist herself, was much interested in Carl's paintings. Often after sessions with Jim, Carl would show his artwork to her, and they would spend time going over the details. Then Charlotte would bring out refreshments, mostly graham crackers and milk or tea.

They kept up with the Ruggleses over the years, and when it came time for Jim to perform *Evocations,* Carl had him make yet another manuscript copy of the work that incorporated still more changes, especially in the first *Evocation.* There were variations in meter, or slurs, or the notation of some of the rhythms, Jim remembered. He sent those changes to Ray Green for incorporation into the score in future printings, but they were never used.[38]

As the weather became cooler, both Charlotte and Carl felt unwell. Carl's stomach gave him trouble, and the cold made Charlotte's joints and fingers stiff and painful. They were ready to move to New York, but they had to wait until the Chelsea notified them that an apartment was available. They hoped to get to New York early enough to see May O'Donnell dance to "Lilacs" and "Portals," and to see Henry Schnakenberg's show, which included a portrait of Micah, but they missed both events. When the hotel did notify them in mid-November, they left as quickly as they could, grateful to be out of the cold. That winter both of them needed to slow down. Once during their stay at the Chelsea they had to call a doctor. It was the first time that had happened, and though it was not serious, it made them aware of their age.

Early in 1957 Carl was invited to have an exhibition of his paintings in Washington, D.C., at "Gallery 313," but as with Martha Jackson, he turned it down, more quickly this time. There was one honor accorded Carl in February that he enjoyed very much. John Edmunds, director of the Americana Collection of the Music Division of the New York Public Library, wrote to Carl early in the month that they wanted to arrange an exhibit of his manuscripts. Carl liked the idea very much, and notified Edmunds that he would be happy to cooperate. Almost immediately Edmunds arranged to visit them at the Chelsea to discuss the exhibit, and when they met, Edmunds was completely won over. He returned to the Chelsea in March with a photographer, Wm. Sloan, who took pictures of Carl for the exhibit, and Carl was so pleased with the results that he requested extra copies.

The exhibition was not due to open until October, and that gave them plenty of time to send the necessary materials from Arlington. During the summer they gathered together all the items for the library exhibit. There were twelve dealing with his scores, plus additional sketches and photographs of Carl by John Atherton and others. Taken together, it would make a fine exhibit, and Edmunds was pleased.

Carl and Charlotte had not taken the train back to Vermont that spring. Instead Margaret DeGray arranged to drive them in her Plymouth convertible. When she arrived at the Chelsea to pick them up, they were already standing outside the hotel, waiting beside their suitcases and shopping bags. Bigger items, fortunately, had already been shipped. Carl sat in the back seat with some of the luggage, Charlotte in the roomier front seat where she could be warmer and more comfortable. Margaret had packed a little lunch for them, which they ate in the car as they went along. When they arrived at the schoolhouse, there was a little welcome sign tacked to the door, from Carolee and Jim, who had been told they would be arriving that day.[39]

Carl tried to work each morning as usual. He had not given up on the Louisville piece, though very little was getting written down on paper. Instead he had begun making tiny snatches of music for more piano pieces. Still, on July 1 he wrote with great excitement to Schnakenberg that he had exactly the right title for "our new work." It was now to be called "Affirmations for Orchestra," and in the mock title page that he sent to Henry, he even dated it "1957."[40] Henry acknowledged the title with much pleasure and a check. Carl returned the compliment by sending him a copy of the photograph taken for the Library exhibit, duly inscribed with a snippet from "Affirmations." Early in July, Carl received his first royalty statement from Columbia Records for the first six months of the year. Seventy-five records had been sold, and his check was for $2.79.

Then in early August, while Charlotte was walking in the schoolhouse, one knee gave way, and she fell. At least that is how she remembered it, though it could have been a momentary blackout. Carl rushed to the neighbors and then to the doctor's office. By the time he returned with the doctor, Charlotte was sitting up, protesting that she was all right except for her knee, which pained her. After examining her, the doctor admitted that she did seem all right and agreed that she could stay at home. But he cautioned her to be very careful and take extra rests every day. Then he strongly suggested that they get a telephone. It had been a scary experience for both of them, so in mid-August a telephone was installed.

Charlotte was indeed careful, and gradually she felt stronger. It wasn't long before they began to go out a bit and even to do some entertaining. But it was true that no matter how young at heart they might feel, Charlotte was seventy-seven years old, and Carl was eighty-one.

NOTES

1. Carl Ruggles to Edgard Varèse, [Aug. 1948]; Carl Ruggles to Joe Tarpley, 3 Sept. 1948.

2. Interview with Stanley Bard, New York City, 23 and 24 May 1975.

3. Carl Ruggles to John Kirkpatrick, 30 Nov. 1948.

4. Carl Ruggles to John Kirkpatrick, 29 Jan. 1949.

5. *New York Herald Tribune,* 28 Feb. 1949.

6. Carl Ruggles to John Kirkpatrick, 8 Mar. 1949.

7. Interview with Lou Harrison, Aptos, California, 21 Mar. 1975.

8. John Kirkpatrick to Carl Ruggles, 27 June 1949.

9. Interview with author, 22 June 1967.

10. *New York Herald Tribune,* 26 Nov. 1949; *New York Times,* 25 Nov. 1949.

11. See John Kirkpatrick, "The Evolution of Carl Ruggles: A Chronicle Largely in His Own Words," *Perspectives of New Music* 6:2 (Spring-Summer 1968): 162.

12. Carl Ruggles to John Kirkpatrick, 29 Nov. and 9 Dec. 1949.

13. Charlotte Ruggles to Henry Schnakenberg, 22 Dec. 1949.

14. Carl Ruggles to Charles Ives, 20 Mar. 1950.

15. Carl Ruggles to Virgil Thomson, 29 June 1950.

16. Carl Ruggles to Tom Johnson, 7 Sept. 1950.

17. Carl Ruggles to Charles Ives, 10 Nov. 1950.

18. Carl Ruggles to John Kirkpatrick, 14 Feb. 1951.

19. See Oliver Daniel, *Stokowski* (New York: Dodd Mead & Co., 1982).

20. Carl Ruggles to John Kirkpatrick, 25 Sept. 1951.

21. Interview with Eileen and Joseph Barber, Biddeford, Maine, 27 Aug. 1975.

22. Interview with author, 23 Jan. and 16 Mar. 1967.

23. Carl Ruggles to Henry Schnakenberg, 27 June 1952.

24. Interview with Dean Fausett, Manchester, Vermont, 10 June 1975.

25. Carl Ruggles to John Kirkpatrick, 15 Nov. 1952; interview with Edwin Sherrard, Hanover, New Hampshire, 13 Sept. 1973.

26. Carl Ruggles to Robert Whitney, 12 Dec. 1952.

27. Interview with author, 10 Apr. 1967.

28. Carl Ruggles to Vladimir Ussachevsky, 31 Mar. 1953.

29. Charlotte and Carl Ruggles to Henry Schnakenberg, 18 Aug. 1953.

30. Carl Ruggles to John Kirkpatrick, 1 June 1954.

31. Harmony Ives to Carl Ruggles, [July 1954].

32. Interview with author, 21 Nov. 1966.

33. This information is not on the dust jacket, which fails to state that *Evocations* is played twice.

34. Charlotte and Carl Ruggles to Henry Schnakenberg, 18 July 1955.

35. Charlotte Ruggles to Henry Schnakenberg, 18 Aug. 1955.

36. Kirkpatrick, "Evolution of Carl Ruggles," 165.

37. Interview with Julian and Margaret DeGray, Warren, Connecticut, 20 Apr. 1975.

38. Interview with James Tenney, Valencia, California, 18 Mar. 1975.

39. Interview with Julian and Margaret DeGray.

40. Carl Ruggles to Henry Schnakenberg, 1 July 1957.

13

Life without Charlotte
1957–66

On Wednesday, October 2, 1957, Charlotte was lying down when she called to Carl, who was in the studio room, and asked him to bring her a glass of water (one account says she asked him to open the window). When he got to her room, she was dead.

In disbelief, Carl raced to the neighbors and the doctor, and they all helped him as much as they could. Micah was called in Florida, and then Margaret DeGray, who remembered that it was around 5:00 P.M. when the phone rang, and that she went to Carl immediately. After all the details were taken care of, and the others had left, Margaret remained. She sat up with Carl throughout the night, and in between the tears of grief and Carl's lament that he was "never good enough for her," there was laughter, as they remembered the jokes that were Charlotte's favorites, and recited them to each other, adding others as each joke reminded them of another. By morning Carl had come to a slow acceptance of her death.

Once the news was announced in the papers, scores of calls and notes poured in. A rough list made by John numbers over sixty, for Charlotte touched many lives, and while a good portion of the notes were from musicians and artists who knew her mainly as Carl's wife, there were others—those who simply loved her and knew her as a warm, vibrant woman, rich in feeling and caring. All of them tell of her strength and unquestioning support for Carl.

A former Arlingtonian wrote in part: "I don't think anyone had a nicer childhood than we on the School St. block. I have so many nice memories of you and Mrs. Ruggles. I often used to sit in your yard with her while you were busy at the piano, and she was a little girl's idea of a great lady."

Micah flew up to Arlington as soon as he heard the news, and Eileen Barber came from New York to be with Carl, too. A few days after the funeral they closed the schoolhouse door, and Carl moved to the old Arlington Inn, now known as Flanders Inn, on Main Street. He had two furnished rooms on the second floor in the northwest corner overlooking Main Street; one room for his work, and the other a bedroom. Micah also insisted, and Carl agreed, that he immediately get his own private telephone, which was installed within a few days. The inn had a fine restaurant where Carl and Charlotte had eaten often, and he knew Mr. and Mrs. Flanders, who owned and operated it. Carl had, in fact, stood up far better than anyone could have anticipated. He himself called many of their friends in Manchester and Dorset to tell them of Charlotte's death, and he took part in decisions about the burial as well as about his own living arrangements.

Meanwhile the New York Public Library exhibit opened on October 15, in honor of Carl's eightieth birthday, although by the time of the opening, he was already well over eighty-one. Notes of congratulations on the show came from old friends in all parts of the country. A sad note arrived, too, from Elizabeth Schoen, for along with her congratulations on the exhibit was the news that Eugene had died on August 16. That saddened him, but he was still suffering too much from the loss of Charlotte to grieve too deeply.

Julian and other friends insisted that he rent a piano, and he finally agreed, selecting a baby grand piano from a company in Troy, New York. Once that was put in his living room, he hoped to be able to work again. He found the sketches for piano, which he called "Flower Pieces," still interesting, even though the orchestra piece was clearly beyond him. "Wake-Robin" came the closest to being completed, or so he said, and John, encouraging him at every opportunity, asked about it in every letter. In November Carl wrote to him that he was working three hours every day, and that he would send a copy of the new piece soon. He was working mornings, he wrote, and "it's my salvation, but the nights are lonely."[1]

He surprised all his friends by his acceptance of Charlotte's death. They had been "so married" as one of their friends wrote, that everyone expected him to be quite helpless and in total despair at her loss. Instead "magnificent" was the way several described his behavior, and it does appear that, insofar as anyone can, he had tried to prepare himself for her death. There had been warnings that he had had to notice. Furthermore, if they were as close as everyone believed, one suspects that he and Charlotte had discussed just such an eventuality. Nothing could assuage the grief or loneliness, but he seemed to have been ready for the actuality.

From the time of Charlotte's death through 1958, May O'Donnell tried to write to Carl at least once a week, generally postcards with an occasional long letter. This was just one more example of the loyalty and affection of his friends. He was alone and lonely, it is true, but he was certainly not without those who cared deeply and who watched over him in myriad ways.

In mid-February John wrote that he would be giving a concert in Washington, D.C., on May 18, and he wondered if he could include "Wake-Robin" or any other new piece on the program. Carl's reply was enigmatic. He was working on a new piece, he wrote, and he hoped to send it soon with "Wake-Robin."

Two things were, in fact, occupying him at the time. One was a letter from Jacques Barzun for the Committee on Music and Musicology of the American Council of Learned Societies. The committee was seeking opinions from a variety of people in the musical world on the question of whether musical scholarship helped the work of composers, musical performers, and teachers of music theory. Carl's first reaction was to snort in disgust and ignore it; he probably threw it on the floor as he did with anything that displeased him. Barzun persisted, however, and a month later sent another letter that left Carl slightly irritated, and almost immediately after its receipt, he wrote a reply on a sheet of white drawing paper: "Now in regard to your two questions. Why, of a sudden, all this stressing of musicologhy [sic], and Musicologists? It seems to me that the reserch [sic] boys are having a field-day. Picasso's sumation [sic], is I think, beautifully pertinent, 'When you are in love with a woman, you don't measure her legs.' "[2] Having gotten that off his chest, Carl then turned to Julian, and together the two worked out a longer and more academic answer. Then they sent along both letters, which must have afforded the members of the committee a good laugh, if nothing else.

The other thing that occupied Carl during the spring was an entirely new piece that he quickly completed, to the complete surprise and delight of all his friends. It was a sixteen measure, nearly foursquare, wordless G major hymn to Charlotte, which he entitled "Exaltation." At the end of February he had written to John that he was working on a new flower piece, but in early April he wrote tantalizingly: "Just wrote a hymn for Charlotte — more later."[3]

It would seem that as he sat at the piano trying desperately to work out the flower pieces, which were tied to Charlotte's love of flowers, the happy inspiration came to him that Charlotte had always wanted him to compose a hymn. Why not now compose one for her? It was a comparatively easy task for him, since he could keep the whole work in his mind. Sixteen measures was a small enough segment for him to concentrate on, and he decided on the traditional hymn structure of four phrases with the melody of the first, second, and fourth beginning alike.

The first version (example 47) was written for piano, and not strictly in four-part hymn writing. It also avoids the Ruggles dissonances in the main, except for measures six and seven, where there is first a C natural against a C sharp, and in the next measure an E natural against

Example 47. *Exaltation,* version 1 (© 1977 by Theodore Presser Co. Used by permission of the publisher).

an E flat. A more forceful dissonance comes in measure fifteen on beats two and three, especially on the strong third beat with a simultaneous C, D, E flat, and F sharp, but it is soon resolved to the traditional dominant seventh chord in beat four on its way to the final tonic, G major chord. What is perhaps more remarkable is the chord at the climax in measure fourteen on the fermata. It is a dominant seventh chord in first inversion in the closely related key of D major—all very conservative and academic. But of course Carl did not consider this the final version.

The next rendition (example 48), completed by July 12, has changes in nine of the sixteen measures: numbers three, four, six, ten, eleven, twelve, thirteen, fourteen, and fifteen. The change in measure three provides a dissonance: C sharp against a C natural, by having the tenor move by half steps to D. The alterations in measures four, six, ten, eleven, thirteen, and fifteen are in voicing, for now the work is written in strict four-part harmony. However, the changes at measures twelve and fourteen are substantive. In twelve what had been the dominant seventh chord with the suspension of B resolving to the chord note A, now becomes a real dissonance with the chord on beats one and two comprised of B, C, D, and E flat. Only when the melody note B drops to A is the old dominant chord partially restored—minus the quality note of F sharp and with the minor ninth, E flat held. This is more in keeping with his own style.

In measure fourteen the change is also pronounced. For one thing, the meter is altered. The fermata is written out, and the measure becomes a 3/2 one, the only one not in straight 4/4. In addition, the A dominant seventh chord now becomes a dissonance with C and C sharp heard simultaneously (so the chord is at once a C major and a C sharp diminished, neither of which would have interested Carl, who was concerned only with the clash of half-steps). This climactic dissonant chord then moves to an A sharp diminished triad in first position on the C sharp bass note at the end of the measure. It continues on to measure fifteen with its own dissonances, though all of these are solidly based on D, the dominant of G major, the key of the hymn, to which it finally returns.

One note change in measure fifteen that has a telling effect is the alto change from G, beat one in the first version, to A in this second one. By shifting the G to A, Carl alters the chord from the traditional tonic six-four to an uncertainty with a dissonant A in the alto against a B in the tenor. It does outline a weak seventh chord on the third note of the scale (B), but Carl would not have thought of that. He wanted that lovely dissonance between the A and the B.

Example 48. *Exaltation*, version 2 (© 1977 by Theodore Presser Co. Used by permission of the publisher).

Measure seven continued to plague him, and in late July or early August he changed the tenor and bass parts to B flat on beat one (see example 49). Here again, the former diminished triad, A-C-E flat, becomes a dissonance, B flat-E flat-A natural. Then on August 7 he sent a postcard with this message: "John dear: The bass at 7 should be A sharp, a new note, and it's golden" (see example 50).[4]

Example 49. *Exaltation,* mm. 5–8 (© 1977 by Theodore Presser Co. Used by permission of the publisher).

Example 50. *Exaltation,* m. 7 (© 1977 by Theodore Presser Co. Used by permission of the publisher).

Changing the B flat to an A sharp would not matter on the piano, but it would be important to string players and singers, and we might recall that Carl had been a violinist. Also it made better sense for the voice leading, since A sharp leads to B, and that is the tenor note of beat one of the next measure. This is one of those rare instances — perhaps the only one — when the spelling of a note mattered to Carl. But then since he was writing the hymn in traditional four-part harmony, the voice leading mattered to him. By using the A sharp and then the C natural on beats three and four, Carl surrounds the B, and it becomes the logical note to which the voice part must go.

Even though the hymn was written in four-part style, it certainly was not meant to be sung. Not only did Carl abstain from putting words to it, the occasional large leaps in the tenor and bass parts would make using voices difficult, though the two upper parts could be sung. But Carl really did not want a text put to the work. John made a setting for organ with the bass line in octaves, and that was fine with him.

While he was still tinkering with "Exaltation," his old and much loved friend, Charles Seeger, paid him a visit in June. They had not seen each other in years. Seeger had been visiting in Rutland, Vermont, and drove on down to Arlington. Once there, and knowing nothing of Charlotte's death, he went to the schoolhouse. When there was no reply to his knocking, he went up to the store and inquired after Carl. They told him that Carl was at the inn, and when he inquired at the desk for the "Ruggles apartment," he was finally told of her death. Seeger remembered the shock he felt, and as he walked slowly up the steps to Carl's rooms, he decided to pretend that he had already known, to avoid discussing it with Carl.

Even though the two had not seen each other for a long time, they were immediately comfortable together, and soon Carl told him about the hymn for Charlotte. Just as in earlier times, they began to go over it, line by line, and note by note. Shortly it became clear that "it was a question of one note" that needed revising (probably that bass note at measure seven), and, as Seeger remembered, they worked at it for "quite a long time." Then suddenly the emotion of the reunion and the shock of Charlotte's death welled up in Seeger. "These two old men in that little hotel room, both thinking of their dead wives"— for Ruth Crawford Seeger had died in 1953—it was too much for him. He felt that he had to leave, that he could not stay with Carl any longer. As soon as they had settled on a note, he quickly bid Carl goodbye and hastened to his car.

As he drove on to Albany to a motel, on his way to Indiana, his mind went back to a simple popular tune that had come to him on his way down from Rutland. He remembered that it had formed itself almost unconsciously, and on the way to Albany he suddenly realized that words had attached themselves to the tune, words that concerned the death of Charlotte, with a refrain that began, "Never more. . . ."[5]

In the spring of 1958 Leonard Bernstein, the new music director of the New York Philharmonic, announced that for his first season, 1958–59, he would do a survey of American music, and in July the Philharmonic announced that a work by Ruggles would be included in the survey. Carl wrote Schnakenberg about it with great delight, though at that time exactly which work was not specified. Soon, however, Ray Green wrote to him that Bernstein had decided to do both *Sun-Treader* and *Men and Mountains* on the programs for October 17, 18, and 19, along with the preview concert on the sixteenth. In addition, the concert would be broadcast, and Ray promised to get tapes of the performances.

Carl fairly shouted the good news. Before long all of Arlington, Bennington, Manchester, and Dorset were aware of it, and he wrote to everyone, from Seeger in Santa Barbara to the old friends in New York. He wrote twice to Schnakenberg about the event, and told him that he had begun another flower piece, entitled "White Violets," adding that he hoped Bernstein would do "Affirmations" the following year. Clearly he was carried away.

Carl began to wonder aloud to friends about the possibility of his attending the concerts. Schnakenberg's niece, Betty Madden, sent him a check and encouraged him to make the trip. John, too, wrote that he certainly should attend, and Wallingford Riegger urged him to come to New York and stay with him. At the same time Riegger inadvertently gave Carl the bad news that only *Men and Mountains* would be performed. This was confirmed a few days later by an announcement in the *Times,* with no further explanation beyond a terse sentence stating that the entire program had been changed by Bernstein. It was a major disappointment to Carl. He had lost the one great opportunity to hear his masterpiece, and he knew in his heart that now he probably would never hear it—especially since his hearing loss was becoming greater as he grew older.

Now Carl was not sure that he wanted to go to New York for the performance. Much of the excitement was gone, and he felt deeply disappointed. May wrote and tried to make him feel better, urging him to come to New York. Other friends were encouraging him, too, especially Eileen and Joe Barber, who suggested that he stay with them. That was almost like home to Carl, for he had known Eileen since Micah's school days at Burr and Burton. Furthermore, Eileen knew that Charlotte had always tied Carl's tie for him on special occasions, and she promised to do that for him in Charlotte's place if he would come to New York.

Carl could not put off a decision indefinitely, and finally he agreed to attend the performances, but apparently he did not go to the rehearsals. He did stay with the Barbers, and Eileen accompanied him to all the performances. John Becker and Riegger also attended, and at the end of each program the three old men came out on the stage to make their bows with Bernstein.

After Thursday's concert Bernstein gave a party at his home for the composers, and Carl and Eileen attended. She remembered that Carl behaved like a grand old man on his best behavior. By contrast, the next day following the Friday afternoon concert, the Varèses came back to the Barber apartment for a lovely raucous get together with much shouting, laughter, and storytelling. Carl loved to bait Louise with a story, which she would try to top, to the great enjoyment of the others, who kept asking for more. That party went on until late in the evening, for these good old friends were reluctant to leave each other.[6]

But for Carl the performances brought another disappointment, which may explain why he did not attend rehearsals. Among his papers

there is the following note to Bernstein about the last movement of
Men and Mountains:

> I hope you will play this whole movement through; and not make
> the Climax 43 [the end], which was the original version.
>
> Long, long ago, I felt the climax at 43 was too abrupt, so I made
> a Retrograde Passage, with a new Ending, which rounds out the
> movement, and sounds—to my ears—quite beautiful.[7]

But Bernstein apparently decided to end the work with the original
big ending and to omit the final nine and a half measures with the
retrograde of the opening that winds down through three octaves to
a quiet ending. That explains Carl's note, but the question remains
regarding Bernstein's decision. There are at least two possible expla-
nations, neither of which can be confirmed or denied.

For one thing, Bernstein may have had to use the score and parts
that Hans Lange used when he conducted the work with the Philharmonic in 1936 before the new ending was written. Or it is possible
that the conductor simply felt that the original ending was stronger,
and decided to use it without regard to the composer's wishes. In
either case the ending was not as Carl hoped it would be, and he felt
unhappy about it. When I came to know him, he told me the story,
but no matter how I questioned him, I never heard an explanation.
Once when we were going over the full score together, at the big
Maestoso before the quiet ending, he pointed and said, "And that's
where Lenny ended it. But it's such a grand ending really."[8]

The first performance of "Exaltation" was given by John as part of
a lecture he delivered at Cornell, entitled "Religion and Music," on
December 11, 1958. Six days later he sent Carl a copy of his speech,
which included these prefatory remarks:

> One of the best American composers is Carl Ruggles, one of the
> old guard of the radical modernists, now 82. He had always
> wondered how Ives could stand those stupid hymn tunes. But
> last year, his wife passed on. She was one of the most wonderful
> people I have ever known, a fine church soloist who was still
> singing pretty well around 80. He remembered that she had always
> wanted him to try to compose a hymn, so last spring he did—
> a voice part in old style, to be sung in unison—the accompaniment
> extending the old style to include a few modernist touches.[9]

If his friends did not write to him as often as he liked, Carl would
send them several blank self-addressed postcards. They got the hint.

He liked getting mail, but he wasn't, in truth, that good a correspondent. His eyes were slowly failing him, and he never had proper glasses at any point in his life. He was having increasing difficulty in writing letters even to old friends, like the Varèses. There are half written notes and several versions of the same thing that show his difficulties with memory and the act of writing. He could not fail to recognize these failings, and very soon he stopped even attempting to write letters except brief notes to Micah and his family. When he felt it necessary to correspond, he asked his friends, Lionel Nowak or Tom Brockway from Bennington College, to write for him.

His source for supplies and reading material was Corey's store, which also supplied the only taxi service in town that Carl sometimes used. He was still reading the newspapers and occasionally the *Saturday Evening Post* and *Official Detective* magazines. He smoked about two boxes of cigars a month, and thoroughly enjoyed every single one.

As spring and then summer arrived, the pace of Carl's life quickened. The natives returned from their winter quarters, and old friends came to visit. Harriette often stopped in to see Carl, and Lady Gosford, another old friend, came to the inn for lunch with him with her little dog, which she would leave in the lounge, while they went into the dining room. To everyone, Carl insisted that he was working, and he did have some finished paintings to prove it—but not so in music. There were only separate snatches of two and three measures. Nonetheless his financial support continued. In addition to the stipend and occasional extra checks from Harriette, Henry continued to send substantial sums. And Betty Madden, his niece, sent her contributions, too, "love tokens," she called them.

One important visit that summer was from Jim Tenney and Carolee Schneemann, for they brought him news of the musical world. Tenney played some of his own music for Carl; and then, there in the privacy of his rooms, Tenney played the complete "Concord" Sonata of Ives for him. He remembered that Carl sat very close to the piano, and with no audience distractions, seemed to be hearing it as if for the very first time. Carl showed them his new hymn and some of the snippets from the flower pieces. And once more Tenney played *Evocations* for him. Later Carl brought out a bottle of brandy, and as they sipped, he told them stories—some of which they had already heard many times, but it didn't matter.[10]

Both John and Lionel included *Evocations* on their concerts that season, and Lionel played the work at a Bennington College faculty concert at the end of October. Carl attended the concert and basked in the attention he received. One friend, often selected to be his chauffeur on such occasions, reported that Carl always entered the auditorium as if he were someone very important, marching immediately to the front row to take his seat. This may have been partly because of his hearing, but the rest was Ruggles bravado.

When Harriette's husband, Harlan, had an eye operation in the fall before their departure for Europe, Carl sent him one of his infrequent notes, congratulating him on his recovery. He tried several versions before he got it right, and Harlan sent a thank you note in return a month later. The two men were never friends; they were too unlike each other. It is also possible that Harlan never quite approved of the financial support that Harriette gave to Carl, which began before their marriage. While she lived, he had to put up with it, but he stopped it immediately after she died.

John visited in mid-December, and once again urged him to complete one or two of the flower pieces, but to no avail. "Wake-Robin" was the most nearly finished, but even that remained incomplete. For Carl the decade of the sixties was one of garnering honors and dealing with ill health. By 1960 he was eighty-four years old. He could still paint, even though he often complained of flickering eyesight. But try as he might, composing was really too much for him by now.

Life at Flanders Inn suited him. He had his piano, and he could work whenever he wished. The restaurant downstairs was a good one, and he could afford to entertain his friends, though more often it was they who entertained him. His living expenses were well within his means, even when the rent was raised to $225 a month. But there were lonely times, too.

One evening some members of the board of the Book of the Month Club had dinner at the inn. Although Carl knew many of them, he was not invited to join them, and he felt snubbed and hurt. He sat alone at his table and spoke loudly and raucously to anyone who passed by. The board might ignore him, but they certainly heard him. Later, back in his room, he wrote on a slip of paper, "Manners, courtesy and *Respect* Due a World Figure."[11]

He did not stay hurt for long, however, for performances and honors were growing in number. In early January the San Francisco Symphony notified him that *Men and Mountains* would be done in April. Then he was invited to be a visiting guest at the University of California, Los Angeles, in either spring or fall. Carl did not even bother to respond to that, nor did he reply to an invitation for a residency at the MacDowell Colony. Jim Tenney, meanwhile, was working on *Evocations* in preparation for a performance that incorporated those changes that he and Carl had made during the summer visit.

In a letter to Jim and Carolee at about this time, he complained of the flu and of neuritis in his left wrist. Then he added: "I had to stop composing on account of my wrist and arm, but prior to that I think I've made a contribution."[12] It was a good excuse, and one that allowed him to make his first public admission that he was no longer composing. Still, for a little while longer, he would write out a few snatches now and then.

On April 25, 1960, he received word that the University of Vermont wished to award him an honorary doctor's degree at the June graduation ceremonies. He was elated, and quickly broadcast the news. Interestingly, once again he owed this honor to Schnakenberg, who had written to the head of the music department, Howard Bennett, nearly two years before this, in September 1958, suggesting the honor for Carl.

By mid-May Carl had written his acceptance, and he was asked to send his measurements in order for them to furnish cap and gown. On May 23, he wrote to "Dear Miss Secretary" and told her that his cap size was $7\frac{1}{8}$, his height 5 feet 5 inches, and his weight 150 pounds.[13]

A few days before the ceremonies, John Whalen, Carl's lawyer and friend, suggested that he try on the regalia that had only recently arrived. The two men went up to Carl's rooms for the fitting, and amid much muttering and swearing and "How do I get this damn thing on?" he finally succeeded. Drowning in the gown, he appeared with the cap teetering on his bald head, and standing very straight and proud, he asked John, "Well, how do I look?"[14]

When June 12, commencement day, arrived, a whole caravan of cars from Arlington went up to Burlington for the ceremonies, and Schnakenberg drove from Connecticut. No one was more solemn or proud than Carl when President Fey placed the academic hood on his shoulders and pronounced him a Doctor of Humane Letters. Of course at the festivities following the ceremonies, Carl entertained everyone with the stories he had boned up on for the occasion. It was a very special day for him, and only Charlotte was missing; she would have been so proud.

That summer the Japan Philharmonic Symphony, under the direction of Akeo Watanabe, recorded *Organum* for Composers Recording, Inc., and Carl once again received congratulations from friends around the country. He was glad it had been recorded, but sorry Stokowski had not done it.

Old friends watched over him, and often visited. Once, Lady Gosford drove up to the inn when Carl was sitting on the porch. He jumped up and quickly came to her car to open the door with a grand expansive flourish. They were both amused, and when she protested that such chivalrous treatment was not necessary, he laughingly assured her that it was, "because you are a Lady!" Then he laughed even louder at his pun.[15]

On September 12, 1960, Hurricane Donna struck the East Coast, and Arlington felt its full force. There were torrential rains and winds up to seventy miles per hour. Primary power lines were broken, the Central Vermont Public Service Corporation substation was put out of action, and all the telephone lines were down. The storm was so fierce that Bill Safford, the ex-fire chief of Arlington, went up to spend the night at the inn because he did not want to be alone in his own house.

That night there were only seven guests, including Carl, at the inn, and by 9:00 they had all gone upstairs to their rooms, including the innkeepers, Mr. and Mrs. Flanders, who had their own apartment in the back with their three small children. Everyone was apparently asleep except for Mrs. Flanders, who decided around 9:30 to make one final check before she, too, went to bed. She remembered that it was raining heavily, and she could hear the noise of the wind and the rain as she walked through the halls.

Suddenly she smelled smoke, and as she followed the odor came to a back storage room. Opening the door just slightly, she could feel the heat and see the smoke. She quickly closed the door and rushed back to their apartment to awaken Mr. Flanders. One of the red phones used to notify the Arlington volunteer fire department was right there at the inn, but on this night it, too, was out of order. So Mr. Flanders dressed as quickly as he could, ran to his car, and drove up the hill through the storm to East Arlington to get the fire truck himself.

Meanwhile Mrs. Flanders, awakening the children, had them dress quickly, take their raincoats and hats and go down to the front lobby. Then she went around to awaken the guests, telling them to assemble, too, as rapidly as possible in the lobby. Mrs. Flanders remembered that she had trouble arousing Carl, partly because he was a deep sleeper and partly because of his hearing loss. She pounded and pounded on the door and kept shouting until he finally awakened and opened the door so she could explain the situation to him. He reacted calmly, she recalled, and soon all the guests and some of their belongings were gathered downstairs.

By this time Mr. Flanders had reached the fire station and was on his way back to the inn, driving the fire engine at full speed, and using all the sirens and bells and lights that he could find to awaken the village. A host of townspeople gathered at the inn, along with the volunteer firemen and Lee Marsh, the fire chief, who raced for his car to follow the fire engine, though he had no idea where the fire was. The inn guests, including Carl, were now out on the porch, where Carl paced up and down worrying about his scores and paintings that had been left behind. However, he had taken his big paintings and carried them under his arm.

While the fire fighters went to the back of the building, Mrs. Flanders made arrangements for the guests to be taken in for the night by neighbors. Just as she was about to see to Carl, there was a loud explosion from the back of the building. No one was hurt, but the force of the blast blew the north wall about eighteen inches away from the rest of the building. Assured that everyone was safe, Mrs. Flanders walked Carl across the street to the rectory of the St. James Episcopal Church, where Mrs. Agnes Belcher, the wife of the rector who was out of town, gladly took him in. Mrs. Belcher remembered clearly that he carried a suitcase in one hand and some paintings under his other arm and seemed quite all right. He stayed in the upstairs guest room and announced to her the next morning that he had slept very well.

Clearly he could not return to the inn, nor could anyone else, for that matter, but electricity and telephone service had been restored. So after breakfast Mrs. Belcher telephoned the Cut Leaf Maples Motel on the south side of town, owned and operated by Carl's old friend, Dorothy Cullinan, whose husband, Orlando, ran the Cullinan store. Happily she had room for him, and in a little while she came to drive Carl back to the motel, where he would remain until he entered the nursing home.

The damage to the inn was severe. When Mr. and Mrs. Flanders returned the next morning, a thick smell of smoke enveloped everything. The drapes and bedspreads disintegrated at a touch, so intense had been the heat. All remaining belongings were put into boxes and delivered to their owners. Then the piano company in Troy, New York, was notified to come and pick up Carl's piano, for it still stood in Carl's big room near the bulging north wall.[16]

News of the hurricane and fire was carried nationwide, and many of Carl's friends wrote to offer help, among them Leonard Bernstein, who sent a wire offering his aid. A few months later Carl wrote about the fire to Carolee, adding: "After the fire was put out, they managed to save all of my music, thank God. They saved also most of my belongings."[17]

As the years went by, the experience became more harrowing and dramatic in Carl's mind, and the story, as he told it, was ominous and filled with danger. To some he said that the entire floor had collapsed, and his piano had fallen through to the floor below. I heard a slightly different version: he said that when he opened the door to his room to go downstairs, the hall was completely filled with smoke, and he wondered if he was going to be able to get out: "Then I remembered that someone had told me that when there was a lot of smoke, the best way to get through it was to get down on your hands and knees and crawl. So that is exactly what I did. I crawled through the hall and right down those steps. And I made it!"

After that there was a long silence, as he put his hands together in front of him and looked out the window. At last he drew a deep breath and continued: "Well, the really bad part of that whole affair was that I lost some valuable manuscripts. Some of the flower pieces for piano. That was tragic. Of course I wrote them over again, but this time they were different."[18]

Of course that was not the truth, but nevertheless it had been an upsetting experience. Luckily for him the move to the Cut Leaf Maples was a very good one. The Cullinans were old friends. Carl and Charlotte had traded at their store for years, and Carl had watched Orlando grow up. He was sure to be treated like one of the family. He had two rooms and a private bath, the larger room facing the front, and there he worked and slept. The smaller room to the right was used to store his paintings.

When Carl arrived at the motel, he and Dorothy made an agreement. He would tell her if he did not like what she did, and she would tell him if she did not like what he did. By and large the agreement worked, though on occasion they certainly had words. One time she stored a turkey in the little room because it was cool there, and Carl fiercely objected, roaring at her: "I pay for that room, God damn it!"

At first his rent was $160 a month, which included room and board. Over the years it was gradually raised to two hundred dollars. Dorothy usually served only breakfast and dinner to the guests, but Carl got his lunch, too. Sometimes she even shopped for him, buying shirts and other things that she felt he needed.[19]

There was no piano, however. The move effectively brought to a complete halt Carl's composing career, though, except for "Exaltation," he had done very little since Charlotte's death. "Wake-Robin" was the most nearly complete of the flower pieces, but that was by no means finished to his satisfaction. All the rest were short sketches and snippets.

Carl was finished with traveling as well. He never returned to New York, and the trip to the University of Vermont in Burlington, though not all that far, was the last trip he would make. More and more he turned to his local friends for company and support, especially to

Lionel Nowak, Tom Brockway, and Julian DeGray and their wives, all from Bennington College, and old friends right there in Arlington.

There were bad days, of course, and lonely times, but Carl always tried to look on the bright side. Orlando remembered that when Carl felt low and miserable, he would try to make a list of the nice things he used to get at home. These almost always included crab meat and lobster, for he dearly loved to eat. On nasty days when it rained or snowed or was gray, he would think up reasons to go up and down the steps to get his exercise, since he could not go outdoors. One of his favorite remarks at such times was: "I think I'll go revise my shit list. It's a good day to do it."[20]

Shortly before Christmas he received a letter from Charles Schwartz of the Composers Showcase in New York. They were planning a concert to take place at the Museum of Modern Art in March 1961 in honor of Carl's eighty-fifth birthday. "Portals," "Lilacs," "Angels," and *Evocations* would be performed, with additional music by Ives. That was the best Christmas gift that Carl received, though cards and presents flowed in from all over the country. The Varèses and others in New York urged him to come to the city for the March 2 program, but Carl knew he could not.

There was more excitement in store for Carl. The Vermont Legislature issued a Joint Resolution proclaiming March 11, 1961, Carl Ruggles Day throughout the state. When Carl received the proclamation, he immediately had copies made and sent them out. It was the fulfillment of one of his dreams—to be famous and recognized, as it were, in his own backyard.

Once, some years before, because he wanted to find out how well known he was, he had asked Micah to send a letter to him addressed simply "Carl Ruggles, Vermont." It worked; he had received the letter, much to his delight and satisfaction. Now he no longer had to wonder about his renown, and he loved it. But he was also forcibly reminded that fame was one thing and pecuniary reward quite another. In July his six month royalty check from Columbia Records for the recording of "Lilacs" and "Portals" came to exactly $5.94.

During the years at the motel, Carl painted several works, including, "Tempo Rubato," considered by many to be his finest. Some years later he talked about how he painted two of his favorites. For "Sunflower," done in 1948, he had first put white or orange shellac on the regular watercolor paper. Then after it dried, he had applied the watercolor tubes, using the end of the tubes rather than a brush. "I don't use a brush very much," he explained. He used only Windsor and Newton watercolors, and the key, he said, was knowing when to stop the application.

For "Tempo Rubato," also a watercolor, he had worked differently. According to Carl, it was his last painting, and "All those other paintings are working up to Tempo Rubato." For this work he had made preliminary sketches before starting on the larger sheet. It was different because "there is not one line that repeats itself. That's a piece of music. That's like the Sun-Treader. Let the thing follow of its own accord. That's the way you write music, too. Now you've got the answer," he nodded emphatically. He was very proud of "Tempo Rubato." He knew it was a good work.[21]

When spring training for baseball began in Florida, Micah, who wrote to his father once a week, reminded him how the two of them had loved to watch the teams in St. Petersburg. He also wrote of the days when Carl was umpire for the Arlington team and how excited he would get if Micah was playing. He remembered Carl once became incontinent in his excitement, and after the game, had to ride home in the rumble seat all by himself in his wet and dirty trousers.[22]

One of Carl's major concerns was the disposition of his papers — letters, scores, manuscripts, and paintings. He had hoped that the state of Vermont would take over the schoolhouse and turn it into a Ruggles Museum, so that everything could remain there, cataloged and put in order. But while the state honored him as a living composer, it was increasingly evident that they did not intend to do more.

Matters came to a head in the fall, when Carl received several letters from Sidney and Henry Cowell discussing the disposition of the correspondence between him and Henry that had taken place over the many years of their friendship. Sidney wrote that Henry was uncomfortable with the thought that their letters might be read while they both were still alive. She, therefore, enclosed a note for Carl's signature, which stipulated that the correspondence remain sealed until both men died. She also suggested various locations as repositories of Carl's papers.[23]

When Carl considered his own situation, he realized that someone else would have to take care of these matters for him, and he kept returning to John, to whom he owed so much and whom he trusted so completely. On his next three day visit in October 1962, Carl asked him to be his music executor. It was not a light decision for either man, and they talked about it a great deal. Finally John agreed, adding the proviso that Micah also put into writing his agreement to John's appointment.

A few weeks later John wrote to Micah, telling him of his appointment as music executor. He and Carl, he noted, had already begun the attempt to put his father's papers in order, and he hoped Micah would let him see whatever correspondence and papers from Carl he had saved. He added that he hoped to learn about Carl's life and activities while he was still alive, so, John assumed, it could be confirmed. Micah readily agreed to cooperate, and Carl was relieved that the problem was solved.

But John had set himself a difficult task. In the first place, Carl's hearing was steadily deteriorating, and one had to be sure he understood what was being said. In addition, while Carl was grateful and glad that John was doing this research, he was also reticent about admitting or revealing too much of his past. So he cooperated only up to a point, then suddenly at some unexpected moment, he would simply stop with a flat, "I don't remember." At times that was doubtless true; at other times he did not want to admit to certain things, and not remembering was an easy solution.

Winters were hard for him. He could rarely go out and he depended on visits from old friends and the guests at the motel for company. And this winter, one of the coldest on record, was especially hard on him. He was not feeling well. He had a bladder infection, and his eyes continued to bother him. Stubbornly he refused to get new glasses, perhaps because he felt that at his age glasses could not help him. The telephone, which he and Charlotte had once eschewed, now became his connection to the world. He frequently phoned old friends, sometimes just to remind them of a joke they had once shared. His calls to Micah became more frequent, too.

In May Betty Madden wrote that she had finally completed a project she had begun several years earlier—that of donating paintings to West Point, each one to represent a different state. When she began the undertaking, she asked to purchase one of Carl's works, "one of your Florida ones on paper (that you poked a hole in when you were playing with it in the bath tub)." He was delighted to have her purchase it, and now having completed the entire collection for West Point, she made the presentation. She wrote that Carl's painting, "Storm over Coconut Grove," was "second as you enter the Hall and got much comment. And I worked you into my very brief speech."[24] He was thrilled.

In February 1964 Brandeis University notified him that he was to be the recipient of one of their prestigious Creative Arts Awards. He would receive a medal and a grant of one thousand dollars. The presentation ceremony would take place at a dinner at the Waldorf-Astoria Hotel in New York on May 26, 1964, and Carl was to invite any friends he might wish to include. In addition he was to supply a brief biography and a photograph.

Carl knew he could not attend, and his first choice for someone to represent him was his son, Micah, who was deeply touched by Carl's suggestion. But since he could not get away, Carl turned to Tom Brockway, the old friend who at the time was acting president of Bennington College. Tom agreed, and with his help they sent the necessary publicity and a list of Carl's friends who were to receive invitations.

Meanwhile in mid-April Carl finally received his Christmas present from Harriette. She had purchased a television set for his room, but the Cullinans had kept it downstairs, hidden from Carl, until they could get the service man to install it. When the snows melted and he could do the outside wiring, they brought the set to Carl's room. He was so pleased that he managed to write a thank-you letter to Harriette and Harlan by himself, and in it he added that he would have two new paintings to show her when she returned from Paris.[25]

Just as the tourist season was winding down and Carl was getting ready for the long winter, he was notified that he had been selected for the Naumberg Recording Award for 1964. There was to be a new recording to include *Men and Mountains, Sun-Treader,* and, if space permitted, "Angels." Shortly after Thanksgiving John McClure, the director of Columbia Masterworks, sent more information on the recording. At the most there could be only twenty-five minutes of music, and therefore it would not be possible to record all three of Carl's works. McClure suggested using either *Men and Mountains* or *Sun-Treader,* and possibly "Angels" if there was sufficient time. He added that "Angels" was the only score he had been able to obtain from American Music Editions, and Green had told him that Carl would provide the other scores. (This was interesting, since Green had been handling all of Carl's scores, though Carl had ambivalent feelings about his ability to do so.) Zoltan Rozsnyai was to conduct the music with the Vienna Symphony, and they hoped to make the recording in January.

Carl never kept his scores in any order, but fortunately John had started to arrange some of the papers, and with help, he was able to find the *New Music* edition of *Sun-Treader* and the later score to *Men and Mountains.* Rozsnyai visited Carl before returning to Europe, and they went over the scores as carefully as possible, given Carl's poor eyesight. They agreed to record *Sun-Treader* first, and if possible, *Men and Mountains.* "Angels" was no longer considered.

He didn't feel well during the cold winter, and Dorothy suggested that he take his meals in his room. There were few motel guests at that period, and that meant that she would not have to open the dining room. Also, Carl was becoming less neat in his eating habits, and she thought it would be easier for him in his room. He agreed.

But there was more good music news. Copland began conducting "Portals" on his programs that year, and in early April he did the work with the Boston Symphony Orchestra, arranging for a private recording from the Friday afternoon broadcast to be sent to Carl. Then he was told that *Men and Mountains* would be done at Tanglewood the following summer with the student orchestra under the direction of Gunther Schuller. And in June Tenney performed *Evocations* at the New School, while Ingolf Dahl conducted *Men and Mountains* in Ojai, California.

Nineteen sixty-five was turning out to be a fine year for him, if only he could stay well, but at eighty-nine that was becoming more and more difficult. Even little chores like washing and dressing were harder to do. Still, each additional performance gave him a boost, and he so wanted to go down in history as an important and famous composer.

During the summer Carl received his visitors, and at the end of August 1964, on a hot sunny day, I, too, had come to Arlington to meet him for the first time. We talked only briefly in the motel, so I did not see the schoolhouse. Then in the summer of 1965, I returned. At first he said he was too busy to see me. But when I started to leave, he called me back. "Well, as long as you're here," he said, and took me up to his rooms.

His work table was placed near two windows in between his unmade bed and the two chairs in the big room. It was covered with scores, papers, and dust. Pinned to the wall was a list of telephone numbers, and next to that was the dedication page to Charlotte for the unfinished "Flowers" composition. He admitted that the pieces were not finished, but that page was ready. On the table and also pinned to the wall, in Carl's large handwriting, were various mottoes that he instructed me to copy:

Warning, never argue about art except with artists.

If you're going to last — the *test of time* is the thing.

I'm a lone eagle — a herald — proclaiming the shapes of communication.

Dissonant chords should have talismanic ecstasy.

The minute you're satisfied you're through.

After he had shown me some of his concert programs, he suggested we visit the schoolhouse; I accepted the invitation immediately. We drove the short distance, and on this summer day I could still see where Charlotte had planted flowers lining the walks to the doors.

When we arrived, Carl took out a set of keys and started to fumble with them. When finally he tried one, it did not work. He tried a second, which did not work either. He said he hoped he'd brought the right set of keys, though I was sure he knew very well that he had. Then he gave me the third key to try. It fitted smoothly into the lock, and I opened the door.

We walked right into the kitchen, which still had dishes in the sink, and on through to the large studio room with its high ceiling, huge stove, and grand piano. Along the walls were paintings, mostly by Carl, with a few by old friends like Boardman Robinson and Rockwell Kent, and a copy of his portrait by Thomas Hart Benton. There was also a model of the head of Stokowski, a kind of bas-relief. The electricity had not been turned off, so he lighted the lamp by the piano, and we walked around the room, stopping at each picture and momento.

He showed me the manuscript score to *Sun-Treader,* with its dedication to Harriette, and I saw other Ruggles scores on the piano, including the beginning of the piece that was to be dedicated to Schnakenberg, "Symphonia Dialectia." When I asked him why he had not completed it, he replied that after he had started on it, he didn't like it. So he dropped it.

Then we took a quick tour of the rest of the house, and I noticed that one of the bedrooms was full of more of his scores and papers. Carl explained that this was the material John was working on. When we left the schoolhouse, Carl suggested that I go to see John, the Varèses, and other old friends, who could tell me more about him.[26]

Carl received his copy of the Naumberg recording of *Sun-Treader* in early September. Since he did not own a record player, he took it to Nowak's, where several friends gathered to listen. They had to turn up the volume for Carl, and he sat very near the speakers. When it was finished, Carl remembered, there was a long silence with everyone caught up in that tremendous sound. "Oh, it was wonderful! I knew then that it had great *impact!*" he told me.[27]

That was the very first time he had ever heard *Sun-Treader,* and while it was indeed wonderful, it was also sad, for Charlotte was not there to listen with him, and the truth was that he himself could not hear all the inner details. He shook his head slowly and looked out the window as he admitted this to me. But the piece was now on record, and this gave him enormous satisfaction.

Soon there was more good news. His music and art would be featured at the Bowdoin College Biennial Institute for 1966 in Brunswick, Maine, on January 22 and 23, 1966. And in conjunction with the institute, Jean Martinon, then conductor of the Chicago Symphony Orchestra, and the Boston Symphony Orchestra, would give the American premiere of *Sun-Treader* on January 24 at the Portland City Hall Auditorium. Henry Brant may have set it all in motion two months earlier, when he wrote to Bertram Turetzky (who forwarded his letter to Elliot Schwartz at Bowdoin) urging a concert of all of Carl's orchestral music.

So the planning began, with Bowdoin depending on Carl's friends, especially John, to help produce the paintings and the hard-to-find scores that Ray Green's American Music Editions did not have. Everything swirled around Carl, whose permission had always to be obtained. They hoped to be able to perform "A Clear Midnight" from *Vox Clamans in Deserto,* but Carl had never been satisfied with that whole work and would not permit it to be done, nor would he give permission for a performance of one of his earlier songs that John had found.

Even the excitement over the festival did not completely make up for the sense of loss that Carl felt when he learned of the deaths of two of his best friends. Edgard Varèse died on November 6, and Henry Cowell on December 10. He knew his world had grown much smaller with their loss.

Carl was finally to have his time of national recognition with the Bowdoin Festival. The advance publicity was sent to all the major newspapers, and hundreds of flyers went to music schools and universities. Many of the major newspapers and magazines picked up the story, and suddenly there were stories about Carl, often with his picture, in such magazines as *Time* and *Newsweek.* He was having a marvelous time. Reporters telephoned or drove through snow and winter weather to interview him, and there were congratulatory notes and cards from friends and acquaintances all around the country.

Robert K. Beckwith, chairman of the Music Department, wrote asking if they could perform "Exaltation." He felt that any number of hymn texts would fit the piece, and if Carl did not like that suggestion, perhaps, he wrote, Carl would allow the poet, Louis Coxe, in residence at Bowdoin, to set words directly to the tune. But Carl did object. He simply did not want them to use "Exaltation."

Beckwith tried again. In the letter acknowledging receipt of paintings, he pleaded with Carl to reconsider. The Chapel Choir could sing it in unison to Coxe's words with accompaniment for brass choir arranged by Elliot Schwartz. Still Carl remained adamant. No "Exaltation."

So the big event took place. Musicians from all parts of the country attended, including critics from all the major newspapers. Carl's music was performed and his paintings exhibited. There were lectures and discussions about his works, and then on Monday, the final day, everyone drove down to Portland through a severe snowstorm for the evening performance of *Sun-Treader*. The concert was a stunning triumph for Carl.

Sitting through that weekend back at the motel was probably one of the hardest things Carl ever had to do. Fortunately John and Lionel and Tom kept him closely informed by frequent telephone calls. Monday evening was the most difficult time for him until Jim Tenney telephoned immediately following the performance with the news of its superb success.

Carl had his ninetieth birthday on March 11, and everyone, it seemed, wanted to help celebrate. *Newsweek* interviewed him, and there were articles about him in many music magazines, including *Hi-Fi/Stereo Review* and *The American Record Guide*. Carl himself had a cold on March 11, but he didn't let it dampen his enthusiasm.

Meanwhile the Southern Vermont Artists Association planned to honor him with a show during the summer, and as the final part of the Bowdoin Festival, he was to receive an honorary degree at the June commencement ceremonies. Once more the issue of performing "Exaltation" came up. The Bowdoin people wanted to perform it at the graduation exercises, and as Beckwith had previously suggested, they wanted Louis Coxe to write an appropriate text for it. Carl tried hard to remain firm, but he vacillated, torn by the pull of a performance versus the intimate nature of the work. Finally in a weak moment, he said yes to John, who had been pushing for it, and that settled matters. A score was quickly sent to Bowdoin, and it was put on the commencement program to be sung by the Bowdoin College Chapel Choir, directed by Beckwith, and accompanied by the Brass Choir.

In Carl's mind the issue was unfortunately not at all settled, for on June 5, barely a week before the event, he dictated this letter to Louis Coxe: "Dear Mr. Coxe: I would like you to know that, if I ask that my Hymn not be performed at the Bowdoin College commencement exercises after all, this is not because of any lack of appreciation for your poem, or for your generous effort in adapting your own creative ideas to a pre-existent form such as is represented by the music. My decision is based rather on the highly personal nature of the Hymn itself."[28] However, Carl did not sign the letter; and it was never sent, for once again he was persuaded to allow the performance, which took place on June 11 at the graduation ceremonies in the college gymnasium. Carl never again allowed a text to be put to the hymn. The piece remained his highly personal tribute to his beloved wife—a deeply felt outpouring, and he half-regretted that it had been performed at all.

When summer arrived, the plans for Carl's show at the Southern Vermont Art Center moved forward quickly. But Carl was not feeling well. He had complained to Micah all through April and May, though there seemed not to be any specific symptoms that he' talked about. Micah kept urging him to see a doctor, something that Carl would not do, and he attributed much of his discomfort to all the excitement.

Then on Thursday, July 14, just two days before the opening of his exhibition, Carl fell at the motel. It may have been a blackout, but in any event he began severe hemorrhaging. He was rushed to the hospital in Bennington. At age ninety, it seemed unlikely that he would survive. Micah was called, and everyone was prepared for the worst. But Carl was not yet ready to die. He rallied, and by mid-August it was clear that he would soon be able to leave the hospital. It was also clear, however, that he would not be able to return to the motel. He needed more care and closer supervision than Dorothy could provide. So after consultation with Micah, and with Carl's acquiescence, if not agreement, friends found a room for him at the Crescent Manor Nursing Home in Bennington. He moved in on August 30, 1966.

NOTES

1. Carl Ruggles to John Kirkpatrick, [late Nov. 1957].
2. Carl Ruggles to Jacques Barzun, 23 Mar. 1958.
3. Carl Ruggles to John Kirkpatrick, 9 Apr. 1958.
4. Carl Ruggles to John Kirkpatrick, 7 Aug. 1958.
5. Interview with Charles Seeger, Bridgewater, Connecticut, 20 Nov. 1974.
6. Interview with Eileen and Joseph Barber, Biddeford, Maine, 27 Aug. 1975.
7. Carl Ruggles to Leonard Bernstein, n.d., note handwritten by Carl.
8. Interview with author, 11 Jan. 1967.
9. John Kirkpatrick to Carl Ruggles, 17 Dec. 1958.
10. Interview with James Tenney, Valencia, California, 18 Mar. 1975.
11. Interview with Mr. and Mrs. Charles Flanders, Ossipee, New Hampshire, 1 July 1974.
12. Carl Ruggles to Carolee Schneemann, 25 Mar. 1960.
13. Carl Ruggles to the Secretary to the President, University of Vermont, 23 May 1960.
14. Interview with Mrs. Margaret Whalen, Arlington, Vermont, 19 Dec. 1973.
15. Interview with author, 3 Mar. 1967.
16. Interview with Mr. and Mrs. Charles Flanders.

17. Carl Ruggles to Carolee Schneemann, 12 Dec. 1960.
18. Interview with author, 25 Nov. 1966.
19. Interview with Dorothy Cullinan, Arlington, Vermont, 3 Oct. 1974.
20. Interview with Orlando Cullinan, Arlington, Vermont, 4 Oct. 1974.
21. Interviews with author, 20 Mar. 1967 and 11 July 1967.
22. Micah Ruggles to Carl Ruggles, 9 Mar. 1962.
23. Sidney Cowell to Carl Ruggles, 17 Sept. 1962.
24. Betty Madden to Carl Ruggles, 19 May 1959 and 31 May 1963.
25. Carl Ruggles to Harriette and Harlan Miller, 24 Apr. 1964.
26. Interview with author, 21 June 1965.
27. Ibid.
28. Carl Ruggles to Louis Coxe, 5 June 1966.

14

The Final Years
1966–71

In 1966 the Crescent Manor Nursing Home was a relatively new structure, low and rambling like a motel, and not far from the hospital. It is situated at the top of a steep hill with broad vistas of the mountains beyond. Carl had a private room, number twenty-three, about five doors down the hall from the main desk and lobby on the left-hand side, and the staff was soon aware that one of their clients was a distinguished personage.

Carl moved in with just a suitcase full of clothes, but within a week or two John and the Cullinans brought over the rest of his things, including his favorite painting, "Tempo Rubato," which they hung in his room. Later John also brought "Forest Interlude" and "Sunflower." Some of his favorite reviews were pasted onto the wall, and he had a sketch pad and pencils to use if he wanted to jot down anything or perhaps to do a sketch. He also had his own private telephone.

In mid-September, at the beginning of my sabbatical term, I moved to North Bennington to spend the year visiting with him and gathering information for this book. I telephoned him a few days after I arrived, and we made an appointment for the following day, the first of many visits and numerous telephone conversations. At 2:00 P.M. on September 19, I drove up the hill to the Crescent Manor Nursing Home. When I asked at the desk for Carl Ruggles, the girl said, "Oh yes, he's waiting for you."

When I walked into his room, he was sitting, almost hidden, in an armchair, looking out the window; he had lost thirty pounds during his hospital stay, but his voice was strong, and so was his handshake. I told him he looked fine, and he said he had gotten dressed for me. His mind was still active and alert, even if his body was more frail. He was quite hard of hearing, but if you made yourself heard, he could still carry on a conversation. We quickly settled into a routine; I would sit on the bed or on the second chair, and he in the armchair facing the window. That way I could shout or talk loudly into his right ear.

Sometimes he would tell me with some indignation, "You don't have to shout, you know. I can hear just fine."

We talked of many things, but mostly about Carl and the events of his long life. Several times during the year he suggested that I look up old friends of his to hear their stories. He would send regards to them and wait eagerly to hear what information they had given me. I was not his only visitor by any means. Lionel Nowak visited, and often he would take Carl out to lunch. Tom Brockway came, too, and John drove up to see him as often as he could.

He was still smoking cigars and thoroughly enjoying them. He took deep puffs and seemed to cherish each act of inhaling and exhaling. I had never seen anyone enjoy smoking so much, but after several months the doctors insisted that he give it up. At first he switched to mentholated cigarettes; then he stopped altogether. Periodically he would put a cigar in his mouth without lighting it, just to feel it again.

One day I came into his room, and on the bed, very neatly laid out in a row, I found five of his pencil sketches done there at the nursing home. He got up and came around, and we stood looking at each one, a composition of lines and shadows. He said he always started with "the line," adding that there were no straight lines in nature, so he didn't use any either.[1]

Then we talked about his way of writing music, for painting and composing were closely related in his mind. Everything in his music stemmed from the line, too, he said. When he stopped using traditional chords, he did not substitute others; he simply stopped thinking in terms of chords and harmony altogether. Instead he started with a line, the line of music, and then put other lines against it. Of course, looked at vertically, chords would result, but he did not consider that, he explained. His concern, rather, was nearly always to see that there were dissonances between the notes. Thus, if one line ended on a high A flat, say, then he would hold that note and begin another line below it on an A natural.

The other consideration was the way each note was approached. That is, he tried to have a jagged line with different intervals between each pair of notes; and in the main melody at least, he tried not to repeat a note until seven or eight others had been used. He always wanted contrary motion between the lines, and if that could not be, then he avoided exact parallel motion by holding some notes while others moved. Further, by this procedure, the "chord forms itself," he concluded. This entire method of working—it was hardly a system— had developed over the years by trial and error at the piano in a conscious attempt to break away from traditional harmony and to compose truly modern music.[2]

When I read to him my notes from Virgil Thomson's lecture at Bowdoin, he grinned and admitted that he wasn't too sure what was meant by "non differentiated secundal counterpoint," Thomson's phrase to describe Carl's musical style. "Dissonant counterpoint," Seeger's phrase, was more to his liking.

He tried to keep as physically active as he could, and sometimes he would walk down the hall with me. When I took his arm, he felt very fragile. He looked comical, too, for his clothes were far too big for him now, and he kept his trousers up by buckling his belt very tightly and letting the trousers bag and bulge underneath. Sometimes he didn't lace his shoes or even have laces in them, and then he would shuffle to keep them on. But other times he would wear his good clothes, especially if he was going out for lunch, and he would point proudly to the insignia from the National Institute of Arts and Letters that he wore in the lapel of his jacket. "Now that means something," he would say.

One day he took me across the hall to meet his new friend, Mr. Barry, a retired lawyer from a nearby town, who had suffered a stroke and also had emphysema, though he continued to smoke his cigars. Since Mr. Barry had a television set and Carl did not, Carl would watch the ball games with him. That was fine, except that even if Carl sat very close to the set, they had to turn up the volume so he could hear. Mr. Barry remarked about this to me, but he continued to put up with it. Both men left their doors open, and sometimes when Carl was holding forth about how famous he was, Mr. Barry would shout across the hall to me, "Don't listen to that old man!"

Martinon was scheduled to perform *Sun-Treader* with the Chicago Symphony Orchestra, and Carl was so pleased with the news that we wrote a note to thank him. Martinon responded by inviting Carl to attend, if it were possible, which, of course, it was not. So Carl asked Tom Brockway to send his regrets.

Carl's eyesight was so poor that it was not possible for him to write checks to pay his bills or, for that matter, to read his mail. Very soon after I arrived on the scene, these became my duties. It was a routine. Each time I saw him, after our initial greeting, I would go over the mail, which was generally lying on top of his dresser. Any envelopes that were unopened we would look into. I would tell him what they contained, and read aloud each letter. Once finished with the mail, he would get out his checkbook and the bills, which might be in the top drawer of his dresser, and we would decide which ones to pay. Then

I would put his hand on the signature line, and he would write his name. I would make out the rest of the check and the entry in the check register.

We had started the other way around. When he asked me, "Can you write a check?" I said yes, and he explained that he had a bill for his medicine that he wanted to pay, so if I would write the check, he would sign it. I made it out, and he tried to sign it, but his signature was so large and uneven that it ran over my writing. We had to tear it up and start again. This time he signed his name first, and I wrote out the rest of the check around it. That worked fine. Carl was very proud of his signature and, even then, wrote it with a flourish.

He was also very proud of his knowledge of the English language. And Carl did love words. He wrote little poems or epigrams in big letters with dark lead. Then he would recite them for me with great dramatic flourishes, letting the words roll out. And this was no mean feat, since he no longer had any teeth.

One poem was:

> Stormy petrels
>> Wheeling, circling, diving,
>>> Lighting, and walking with web feet upon the
>
> water.
>> Rembrandt's wondrous painting comes to mind
>
> and
>> Ryder.

Another began: "A darkling night / And sounding sea / And waves like purple horses."[3]

Part of Carl's fame was his storytelling, and before long he told me how he used to entertain everyone with his tales. He was hesitant about telling me some of his jokes, and he could no longer remember many of them. But as we came to know one another, he did tell me a few, including this favorite limerick:

> There was a young man from Eau Claire
> Who tried to make love in a chair.
> On the twenty-ninth stroke
> His Chippendale broke
> And he shot off his gun in the air.

"You know limericks are just wonderful," he laughed, but of course, you had to be careful who you told them to. Nice young girls might pretend to be offended, he added, but usually they knew more than they let on. Charlotte had liked good jokes, and so had Louise Varèse, and he laughed again, remembering.

Sometimes someone would come to shave him or check on his bowel movements while I was there. At first he was slightly embarrassed, but not for long. He would send them away either with a laugh or a snarl, depending on his mood. "They haven't come to give me a bath yet," he said on one occasion. "You know they do everything for me. But you don't have to have a bath everyday. I have that on good authority—just so you don't stink—that's all. And what does that have to do with writing music!" he exclaimed.[4]

All through the fall he railed at his old age and longed for a piano so he could continue with his work. Never mind that he had not done much work before he got sick. Now, perhaps because he felt that he was living on borrowed time, he wanted to finish the *Flower Pieces* that were to be dedicated to Charlotte. "They are really a continuation of the *Evocations,*" he said. There were to be five: Delphinium, Verbena, White Violet, Hollyhock, and Catalpa, the last named after the big tree in front of the schoolhouse. The first two were nearly sketched out, he said. If only he had a piano. "If only my eyes," and he threw up his arms and leaned back in the chair. "I could weep," he said.[5] But the truth was that he was simply too frail to put down more than a few notes. A piano would not have helped. Still, when he felt well, he continued to fight his declining years.

Even in advanced age, Carl remained a difficult man, full of prejudices. He did not like African Americans, calling them "niggers," and said he didn't think they would be allowed to stay at the motel in Arlington. Nor did he like Jews any better. One time, while reminiscing about his home town, Marion, Massachusetts, he said: "I haven't been there for twenty-five years, but they tell me it hasn't changed a bit. It's very restricted. Not like Provincetown and other parts of the Cape—all messed up, where a lot of cheap Jews go."

I interrupted, "Mr. Ruggles, not all Jews are cheap."

"I didn't say they were, did I?"

"No, but I think you should know that I am Jewish."

"You are not!" he flashed back.

"Yes, I am."

"Well, so what—I didn't say all Jews were cheap. In the South there are a lot of terrible people and they aren't Jews. And Brandeis University is Jewish, and they gave me an award and a thousand dollars." We cleared the air, then and there; and to me at least, he never again made another anti-Semitic remark.[6]

As winter came on, he grew more frail. There were skin problems and stomach problems. None too serious, but all signs of decline. Sometimes he needed an enema, and he began to keep track of his bowel movements. Once he timidly admitted, "I'm a little scared, don't you know." Still, that mood didn't last long, and soon he was talking about his music. But he knew life was slowly draining away.

Just before Christmas he fell in his room, apparently slipping on a grape skin. Mr. Barry had yelled and shouted and banged on the walls until the nurses came to help. Miraculously Carl was not hurt, but it frightened him, and he became more cautious. When he walked around his room, he carefully avoided the spot where he had fallen.

Each time I visited him, he would talk about some aspect of his music and paintings. He wanted me to understand, but at the same time he seemed to need to explain it for himself, too. He continued to compose snippets and sometimes he drew and made little designs.

Carl loved to talk about the music he knew, and often he would sing sections for me. One day we were talking about art songs, and he asked, "What is the German for the Schubert song, 'Impatience'?" ("Ungeduld" from *Die Schöne Müllerin*). He sang it. Then another Schubert song, only this time he tried to sing both the melody and the accompaniment. "Jesus, isn't that wonderful!" he cried, for, of course, he'd heard it all in his inner ear.

For Carl the most exciting news was that *Sun-Treader* would be performed under the direction of his favorite conductor, Leopold Stokowski, with the American Symphony Orchestra during the following season on December 3 and 4, 1967. It was a dream come true for him, and he could hardly stop talking about it. "Stokey" was a great musician, Carl announced to everyone. In July Stokowski himself sent a personal letter to Carl from Switzerland, and Carl's joy and pleasure was beyond measure. He was on top of the world. In the letter Stokowski told Carl of the December concerts and wrote that he was pleased to be able to conduct his music again, which he greatly admired.

What Carl never knew was that when his old friend, Mimi Salzedo, read the announcement of the concerts in the *Times,* she wrote to Stokowski and suggested that it would be wonderful if he would write a personal note to Carl about the program, as he did. He also sent a copy to Mimi, who in turn sent a postcard to me, asking me to let her know when Carl received Stokowski's letter. I did, of course, and we kept the secret.

Our routine continued with each visit: first the mail, then the bills, then talk. In March Carl's bill at the nursing home for custodial care was $560 a month, but he could afford it, thanks to Harriette's continued support and the help of his other wealthy friends, as well as his own savings. Sometimes when the piles of paper got too much even for Carl, we would have a great cleanup time, putting the wastepaper basket nearby and going through every single sheet of paper. I'd read each item to him, and he would decide whether to throw it away or save it by putting it in his top dresser drawer. Anything that was complimentary to him was saved, even if he no longer remembered the sender, as when someone who had met him casually at the motel sent a card expressing pride in having met such a "great genius." Carl admitted he hadn't any idea who wrote it, but he thought it ought not to be thrown away.

If he felt well, he would tell me another joke for which he was famous. "There was a man," he would begin, "who was deeply in love with this woman. He loved her passionately and told her that nothing would do but that they must get married. But first, he said he hoped she wouldn't mind, but he would have to ask her some very personal questions. She said all right. So he asked, 'Are you a virgin?' And she answered, 'I was, until my cross-eyed sister gave me an enema.' "[7]

Carl loved his stories as much as his listeners. The first time he told me one of his jokes, he was so pleased with it, that he slapped his knee and cackled with joy. Here it is: It seems that this wealthy woman decided to have her home redecorated. So the painter came and painted some of the rooms, including the bedroom. When her husband came home from work that day, he touched some of the wet walls in that room and marred them badly, much to the disgust of his wife. The next day when the painter returned to continue working, the woman met him and somewhat frantically said, "Come into the bedroom and look at what my husband did last night!" To which the painter replied, "Lady, I'm too old for that sort of thing, but I'll split a bottle of beer with you."

Occasionally Carl would refer to "the dark places" in the past. "It was always a question of money, and we didn't have any." There was a long silence, then he added, "It was Charlotte who saw us through. She took care of everything, teaching, and earning money. I was always fooling around with music."[8]

They had had a good marriage. Charlotte had truly been his mainstay. Virgil Thomson said Carl had treated Charlotte so well that one would think she was his mistress instead of his wife. But there were bad times, occasionally, for Carl was difficult, and now and then Charlotte felt she had to resist. Even Carl admitted this, and remembered once when she exploded and told him to leave the schoolhouse—and he did. Then he came back shortly with a bouquet of flowers in his hand, and they made up.

Micah remembered that on one occasion when they quarreled while Charlotte was fixing breakfast, in desperation she took the frying pan, hit Carl over the head with it, and ran out of the house. Carl followed and caught up with her, Micah said, and they walked around the nearby cemetery for a while. When they returned to the house, everything was peaceful again.

Neither of them was a shrinking violet, but Charlotte always put Carl's career and desires ahead of hers, even to the telling of jokes. As they got older, they realized that they were forgetting some of the stories, so they began making a file on them. Then before they went out or entertained at home, they would consult the file and refresh their memories—Charlotte, too, for when Carl would hesitate, often she would say, "Now, Carl, do you remember?" and give him a line or a cue.

Charles Seeger visited Carl that summer of 1967, and they had a "grand" visit. But, Carl added, Seeger couldn't hear a thing without his hearing aid. At that, Mr. Barry, who had been listening to our conversation, as he nearly always did, shouted across the hall, "I wish that old man would use one!" Barry kept up a sort of running commentary throughout our visit, which I could hear, but Carl could not. Nor could I tell Carl what I was hearing from the other room.

Perhaps Barry felt he had some right to make his comments. Carl had fallen again just that day, and Barry had struggled across the hall to help him, to little avail. Barry could hardly walk himself, and he had no strength to get Carl to his feet. So the two men had shouted and banged on the floor until one of the staff finally took notice and came to the rescue. Miraculously, once again Carl had not hurt himself. When I was ready to leave, Carl and I walked carefully over to Barry's room, where he sat deep in his chair. Carl wanted to thank him once more. Barry replied that he would help Carl off the floor anytime, and when I repeated this for Carl to hear, both men laughed loudly.

One time I asked Mr. Barry if he had heard any of Carl's music. "Yes," he replied, "once they brought up a tape and I heard it. Awful stuff," he said, shaking his head. "Awful!" I told him that I thought Carl was a pretty important composer, and he said, "Is that so? Well, I like classical music, but I didn't like that!"[9]

The entire staff did their best to care for all their residents, but there was such a great disparity in health among them that sometimes when I went to see Carl and Mr. Barry, it seemed an unreal world that I entered. Though the building was designed to allow bright sunlight inside, it always seemed dark and slightly dreary. Occasionally one of the staff would be mopping the halls when I arrived. I shall never forget the musty, soiled odor of the place that never changed over the years, or the pitiful shouts of some of the residents who had to be strapped into their chairs or beds: "Help me!" or "Take me home!" I could hear them as I sat talking to Carl about his life and music, and the music of Bach, Beethoven, and Brahms. Like Mr. Barry's comments, these sounds and odors formed a counterpoint to our conversations, though, luckily for Carl, he could not hear any of it.

When autumn came, I began teaching at a small liberal arts college in a nearby state, so my visits to Carl were curtailed. I did, however, continue to see him every six weeks or so and kept to this pattern for the rest of his life. He always knew me.

Finally December came and the performances of *Sun-Treader*, with Stokowski conducting the American Symphony Orchestra at Carnegie Hall. The first performance was on Sunday afternoon, December 3, and the hall was filled with regular subscribers and many of Carl's friends. *Sun-Treader* opened the program. It was a stunning performance that would have thrilled Carl; and not only did his friends assure him that such was the case, but so did the critics.

Meanwhile the music faculty and administration at Bennington College decided to honor Carl with a Carl Ruggles Festival planned for early fall in 1968. The aim was to perform *all* of Carl's music that was available. In addition the organizers also planned a Ruggles painting exhibit from private collections to coincide with the concert. Amazingly it all gradually fell into place, thanks to indefatigable organizers like Henry Brant, Louis Calabro, Lional Nowak, and others. The date was set for September 29. Guest speakers were announced: George Hughes, artist; Eric Salzman and Peter Yates, critics; and John Kirkpatrick. To top it all, Governor Philip Hoff announced that Carl would be given the 1968 Vermont Governor's Award for Excellence in the Arts, and that it would be presented to him that evening at the concert. John would accept for him. The organizers even arranged for a special telephone hookup to a loudspeaker at the nursing home, so he could follow the proceedings.

The entire event was held at the recently constructed Mount Anthony Union High School. The paintings were hung in the lobby so one could view them before and after the concert and at intermission. It was truly a festive occasion, and the auditorium was filled with Carl's friends and neighbors, as well as music lovers and critics from New York and Boston. It was clearly a major event and the last one in Carl's life that he tried to listen to. Although his hearing was too impaired for him to get anything more than the broad outlines, it was a great triumph for his music, and he relished that, as well as all the attendant publicity.

Day by day Carl was failing and shrinking, and oftentimes he would sleep sitting in his chair through the long hours. Sometimes they would have to strap him in to prevent his sliding to the floor. Shortly after Christmas 1969, he was so weak and ill that they had to take him to the hospital. He required several blood transfusions, and then once again he rallied. Two weeks later he was strong enough to return to the nursing home.

I saw him the day after he came back, and he said he didn't like it very much "up there," meaning the hospital. There wasn't anyone to talk to, he said. Unfortunately, there were fewer people to talk to at the nursing home, too, for as Carl's deafness increased, it became harder to communicate with him. One simply had to take the time to shout loudly, and then wait patiently while he slowly absorbed the sounds and returned to the outside world. Fewer and fewer people took the time.

By the summer of 1970 he was incontinent, and a green pitcher was left beside him that he could use whenever necessary. But he could still discuss the Beethoven symphonies and, of course, his own music. He even took an interest in my activities and asked about the music I had heard and the concerts I had attended.

Mr. Barry was still there, too, sitting in his chair in dirty pajamas and bathrobe, watching television, alert and bright, however bitter and alone. When I stopped by, before going in to see Carl, he asked me how "the old man" was.

Money was on Carl's mind, and not without reason. Harriette Miller had died, and almost immediately his stipend was stopped. Henry Schnakenberg was gone, too. With both of his major donors lost, Carl couldn't help but worry about his finances. Fortunately he had a fair amount to start with, and the nursing home had helped him to obtain some Social Security, but the monthly bill for his care steadily cut into his resources. As it turned out, his money ran out almost at the same time as his life. One bill was left over, and friends took care of that.[10]

On December 7, 1970, he had grown so weak that once more he had to be taken to the hospital. Again he rallied, returning to the nursing home in four days. By now he required complete nursing care, and everyone wondered whether he would live to his ninety-fifth birthday on March 11, 1971. He did, but Mr. Barry died in early March.

I drove over to see Carl on a cold snowy day just eight days before his birthday and found him dozing in his chair, looking like a cadaver with his head sunk down on his chest. He was wearing a new royal blue shirt and was strapped into the chair. He wore socks but no shoes, and over the bottom part of his body was a heavy cotton blanket, for he was not wearing any trousers. Beside him on the chair was the green plastic pitcher. I touched him on the shoulder, and he looked up immediately. We greeted each other, and he said, "Well, for goodness sakes, it's good to see you!" His blue eyes seemed even more blue, and they blazed with life in his sunken face.

We talked of his music, then about Beethoven and Rossini. He told me about his being included in the new edition of the *Riemann Musiklexicon,* a German music dictionary. He was proud of that. By May he had gotten even weaker. "I wish I could get well," he said, "but I can't." Not even the summer performance of *Sun-Treader* by the Boston Symphony Orchestra at Tanglewood could stop the decline.

By the end of the summer he had shrunk even more, except for his hands, which seemed large and bony with their long fingernails. Now the room was slightly messy and smelled of a mixture of body odors, urine, and cleaning solutions. At the beginning of each visit, he would slowly mouth the words he wanted to speak, regaining the thought processes, then we would be back on our old footing. I read his unopened mail to him, and we talked about music.

But his strength was going, and shortly he was even too weak to get out of bed. They moved him to a room closer to the nurses' station and put up barriers on both sides of his bed to prevent his falling. He developed pneumonia on October 21, and on Sunday, October 24, 1971, he went into a coma around 1:00 P.M. About five hours later his long life ended.

The funeral was held on Wednesday, October 27, at the St. James Episcopal Church in Arlington. It was a beautiful fall day. The church was not very full. There were only a few old friends from Arlington and Bennington, Micah, John, and me. It was a brief ceremony, and Carl was not mentioned once. And I kept remembering our last visit, just two weeks before, on October 10.

I had driven over to see not only him, but also a man from California who had come East to find what help he could be in furthering the music of Ives and Ruggles. We had briefly corresponded and had agreed to meet at the nursing home, since he wanted to meet Carl. It was a bad time to be encountering Carl for the first time. He seemed only partly alive, lying there in that bed with the sides up, looking tiny and fragile like a very old doll. Only his eyes showed the blue flame of life.

While we were in the room with Carl, the man from California began to talk about him as if he were already dead, and I protested that we could not do that. He replied, looking down at him, "He doesn't even know what's going on. It doesn't matter." But I insisted, and he agreed to talk further out in the lobby. After he left, I went back into Carl's room. When I touched his shoulder, he opened his eyes and greeted me. Then he said, "There's some guy here from California. Did I behave all right with him?" I assured him that he had done just fine.

We sat in silence for awhile until it was time for me to leave. Then I leaned over the railing of his bed and kissed his forehead. He opened his eyes again and looked at me, and shaking his finger at me, he said, "Don't you forget the book."

NOTES

1. Interview with author, 27 Sept. 1966.

2. These discussions took place over several visits: 27 Sept., 3 Oct., and 17 Oct. 1966.

3. Interview with author, 27 Oct. 1966.

4. Interview with author, 22 Dec. 1966.

5. Interview with author, 17 Nov. 1966.

6. Interview with author, 8 Dec. 1966.

7. Interview with author, 3 Mar. 1967.

8. Interview with author, 9 Mar. 1967.

9. Interview with author, 7 Apr. 1967.

10. Interview with Mr. Guy Alexander, former director, Crescent Manor Nursing Home, Bennington Vermont, 28 Sept. 1978.

Epilogue

There were obituaries for Carl in most of the major newspapers and magazines. Donal Henahan called him "one of the great characters of American music," and Martin Bernheimer, on the other side of the country, called Carl "a stubborn Yankee iconoclast, an original thinker and a wholesome wholesale damner of most accepted conventions."[1] He wrote that fame and fashion did not interest Carl, but he was partly wrong. Fame did matter. Carl would have been glad to read the numerous articles on his death and sorry there were not more. But what of Carl's place in history? He wanted so much to be important, this little blue-eyed, bald-headed man.

Consider his paintings. He painted well over three hundred works, the vast majority of which are in private collections, with a few sprinkled among various museums: the Detroit Institute of Art, Brooklyn Museum, Whitney, Andover, and the Southern Vermont Art Association. He looked on his paintings as extensions of his musical compositions. "I paint music," was his cry. But the paintings were expendable. He would change them, toss them off in an afternooon, and sell them to anyone willing to pay for them.

At the annual shows in Vermont, the critics often singled out his paintings for commendation. Twice Carl turned down opportunites to have one-man shows outside of Vermont: once in New York, and once in Washington, D.C. I think the wisest judgment of his work was made by Alfred Frankenstein, when he wrote, "But at his best his pictures have an inspired, mystical, radiant, jewel-like quality which is by no means unlike the spirit of his tonal creations."[2]

Perhaps Carl could have made his fame as a painter, but he chose composition instead. He wanted to be an important and famous composer, in part, because he wanted to move listeners as deeply as he had been moved when he first heard such composers as Beethoven, Brahms, Wagner, and Strauss. It was no small ambition. He wanted to write soul-stirring and sublime music, nothing less.

It is true that he was drawn to music as a child through his mother's influence. Composition began later, in his late teens and early twenties. Not until he began studying privately with Paine, Spaulding, and Winternitz, was he given any systematic education in theory and composition, though he learned much by playing in theater orchestras and local groups.

The opera was never finished, but working on it all those years enabled him to forge his own modern style. It was a wrenching trial and error method of work that continued throughout all the years of his creativity. Seeger first named it "dissonant counterpoint." Others analyzed it and continue to do so. Not Carl. He couldn't, and he admitted it.

That is worth remembering. All the analytical articles about Carl's music may be correct in explaining the music, but they do not explain Carl's own thinking about the music, or the way he himself put the sounds together. He worked in a totally intuitive way, by trial and error—trying out everything at the piano over and over again, then over again some more. He did not and could not analyze his own music on a consciously intellectual level. Furthermore, he admitted to me several times that he could not understand theoretical articles, even those about his own music. He snorted that such analysis was "intellectual stuff!" Leave it to the theorists and musicologists! Because he was not able to analyze his work and did not have that intellectual training, ability, or interest, he was condemned to work slowly, always experimenting, trying each musical idea over and over incessantly, and trusting at last to his gut reaction. Surely this lack in his musical knowledge kept him from moving ahead very much in his style, and certainly it contributed to his insecurity as a composer.

On nearly every composition he wrote, he sought help from someone more schooled in the field than he was. From Seeger and Henry Cowell, to Franz Lorenz, to Julian DeGray, to John Kirkpatrick, there was always another person to observe, to criticize, and even to alter what he composed. He always needed that extra help. Even then, he was never sure when a work was finished. Each piece continued to go through many revisions. When he was in the nursing home, he even wanted to go back over "Angels" and change the final chord. For Carl, there was always a gnawing sense that maybe something further needed to be done.

His life was hard in many ways, so completely dependent as it was on patronage. Carl may have felt that as an artist he deserved support, but he surely must have had some qualms when he saw his wife and son wearing cast-off hand-me-down clothes, and especially when his son was taunted in school. He made life hard for those who loved him. Some say Charlotte died out of sheer fatigue from caring for him, and his son, while dutiful, admitted that he often felt very distant from his father. Love of sports was their one shared interest. Carl was prejudiced and selfish, he was demanding, and he never swerved from his goal.

Did he succeed? I think he did, at least in part. The music stands, and if it is not all sublime, as he would have had it, there are wonderful moments. Lou Harrison may have expressed it best, when he wrote in 1946:

> he is surely one of the most astonishing among the composers of his time. None other that I know of has pursued to quite so great a degree the constant clarification, and, still further, the ultimate, right form for work which already, at the drawing of the double bar has been the mercilessly investigated subject of over a hundred intent listenings by its creator. That works made in such a manner should have survived in his mind in gently altered ways the swift violence of the fashions of our time is not a wonder, for they are not the constructions of an opportune moment, either inside or out, but sharp, revealed drawings of a burning personal unity. And they will survive geometrically longer in the minds of others for the confidence and faith Ruggles has put into their makeup.[3]

NOTES

1. *New York Times,* 26 Oct. 1971; *Los Angeles Times,* 21 Nov. 1971.
2. *San Francisco Sunday Examiner and Chronicle,* 30 Jan. 1966, "This World" section.
3. Lou Harrison, *About Carl Ruggles* (Yonkers, N.Y.: Oscar Baradinsky, the Alicat Bookshop, 1946). Reprinted in *Soundings: Ives, Ruggles, Varèse* (Spring 1974): 60.

Selected Bibliography

Since there has been no full-length book on Carl Ruggles, the following is a highly selective list of articles dealing with his life and work for those who wish to do further reading.

Archibal, Nina Machetti. "Carl Ruggles: An Ultramodern Composer as Painter," Ph.D. diss., University of Minnesota, 1979.

Babcock, David. "Carl Ruggles: Two Early Works and *Sun-Treader*." *Tempo* 135 (Dec. 1980): 3–12.

Booth, Earl Walter. "New England Quartet: E. A. Robinson, Robert Frost, Charles Ives and Carl Ruggles." Ph.D. diss., University of Utah, 1974.

Devore, Richard O. "Stylistic Diversity within the Music of Five Avant-garde American Composers, 1929–1945." Ph.D. diss., University of Iowa, 1985.

Dombek, Stephen. "A Study of Harmonic Interrelationship and Sonority Types in Carl Ruggles's '*Angels*.'" *Indiana Theory Review* 4:1 (Fall 1980): 29–35.

Faulkner, Susan. "Carl Ruggles and His *Evocations* for Piano." Master's thesis, American University, 1973.

Gilbert, Steven. "Carl Ruggles (1876–1971): An Appreciation." *Perspectives of New Music* 11 (1972): 224–32.

————. "Carl Ruggles and Total Chromaticism." *Yearbook for Inter-American Musical Research* 7 (1971): 43–50.

————. "The 'Twelve-Tone System' of Carl Ruggles: A Study of the *Evocations for Piano*." *Journal of Music Theory* 14:1 (1970): 68–91.

Harrison, Lou. *About Carl Ruggles*. Yonkers, N.Y.: Oscar Baradinsky, 1946. Reprint. *Soundings: Ives, Ruggles, Varèse* (Spring 1974): 47–60.

Kirkpatrick, John. "The Evolution of Carl Ruggles: A Chronicle Largely in His Own Words." *Perspectives of New Music* 6:2 (Spring–Summer 1968): 146–66.

————. Liner notes to *The Complete Music of Carl Ruggles*. CBS Masterworks Records M2 34591. 1980.

Klemm, E. "Carl Ruggles (1876–1971) ein anderer amerikanischer Aussenseiter." *Musik und Gesellschaft* 37 (July 1987): 370–72.

McMahan, Robert Young. "A Brief History of *The Sunken Bell*, Carl Ruggles's Unfinished Opera." *American Music* 11:2 (Summer 1993): 131–57.

——. "The *Sunken Bell* by Carl Ruggles." D.M.A. diss., Peabody Conservatory, 1990.

Miller, Bruce Edward. "Intervallic and Structural Cohesion in the *Sun-Treader* of Carl Ruggles." Ph.D. diss., University of California, Los Angeles, 1989.

Nicholls, David. "On Dissonant Counterpoint: The Development of a New Polyphony, Primarily by Charles Seeger, Carl Ruggles and Ruth Crawford." In *American Experimental Music: 1890-1940*, 89–133. Cambridge: Cambridge University Press, 1990.

Orkiszewski, Paul Thomas. "An Analytic Overview of the Music of Carl Ruggles." Master's thesis, Rice University, 1988.

Peterson, Thomas Elliot. "The Music of Carl Ruggles." Ph.D. diss., University of Washington, 1967.

Richardson, E. P. "Three Contemporary Americans." *Bulletin of the Detroit Institute of Art* 20:3 (Dec. 1940): 25.

Robison, Robert Tucker. "Carl Ruggles' *Sun-Treader*." D.M.A. diss., University of Illinois, 1991.

Rosenfeld, Paul. "The New American Music." *Scribner's Magazine* (June 1931): 624–32.

Saecker, Jan. "Carl Ruggles in Winona." Master's thesis, Winona State College, 1967.

Seeger, Charles. "Carl Ruggles." *Musical Quarterly* 18:4 (1932): 578–92. Reprint. *American Composers on American Music,* ed. Henry Cowell. New York: Frederick Ungar Publishing Co. 1962.

——. "On Dissonant Counterpoint." *Modern Music* 7:4 (June–July 1930): 25–31.

Thomson, Virgil. "Carl Ruggles." In *American Music since 1910*, 31–39. New York: Holt, Rinehart & Winston, 1972.

Ziffrin, Marilyn J. " 'Angels'—Two Views." *The Music Review* 29:3 (Aug. 1968): 184–96.

——. "Carl Ruggles and the University of Miami." *ex tempore* 4:2 (Spring-Summer 1987): 115–35.

——. "Carl Ruggles, Music Critic." *American Music Teacher* (Feb.-Mar. 1983): 42–46.

——. "Interesting Lies and Curious Truths about Carl Ruggles." *College Music Symposium* 19:2 (Fall 1979): 7–18.

Discography

All of the recordings of Carl Ruggles's music on long playing records are out of print, including the complete works brought out by Columbia Records. Here is a current list of the available recordings on compact disc.

"Angels"
London Brass, "Modern Times with the London Brass," Teldec CD 2292-4644-2.
London Gabrieli Brass Ensemble, Hyperion CDA 66517. Alexander Weisberg, Ensemble 21, Summit DCD, 122.

Evocations: Four Chants for Piano
A. Stokman, piano, Centaur CRC 2082.
M. Boriskin, piano, New World, 80402-2.

Sun-Treader
Boston Symphony Orchestra, Michael Tilson Thomas, conductor, "Twentieth Century Classics," Deutsche Grammophon 429860-2GC.

Index

MARILYN J. ZIFFRIN, now retired, was an associate professor of music at New England College in Henniker, New Hampshire. She has written numerous articles on Carl Ruggles and was a co-contributor to the Ruggles entry in *Grove's Dictionary of Music and Musicians* (6th ed.) and *New Grove Dictionary of American Music*. She is also a composer.

Books in the Series Music in American Life

Sing a Sad Song: The Life of Hank Williams
Roger M. Williams

Long Steel Rail: The Railroad in American Folksong
Norm Cohen

Resources of American Music History: A Directory of Source Materials
from Colonial Times to World War II
D. W. Krummel, Jean Geil, Doris J. Dyen, and Deane L. Root

Tenement Songs: The Popular Music of the Jewish Immigrants
Mark Slobin

Ozark Folksongs
Vance Randolph; edited and abridged by Norm Cohen

Oscar Sonneck and American Music
Edited by William Lichtenwanger

Bluegrass Breakdown: The Making of the Old Southern Sound
Robert Cantwell

Bluegrass: A History
Neil V. Rosenberg

Music at the White House: A History of the American Spirit
Elise K. Kirk

Red River Blues: The Blues Tradition in the Southeast
Bruce Bastin

Good Friends and Bad Enemies: Robert Winslow Gordon
and the Study of American Folksong
Debora Kodish

Fiddlin' Georgia Crazy: Fiddlin' John Carson, His Real World,
and the World of His Songs
Gene Wiggins

America's Music: From the Pilgrims to the Present
Revised Third Edition
Gilbert Chase

Secular Music in Colonial Annapolis: The Tuesday Club, 1745–56
John Barry Talley

Bibliographical Handbook of American Music
D. W. Krummel

Goin' to Kansas City
Nathan W. Pearson, Jr.

"Susanna," "Jeanie," and "The Old Folks at Home": The Songs of
Stephen C. Foster from His Time to Ours
Second Edition
William W. Austin

Hot Man: The Life of Art Hodes
Art Hodes and Chadwick Hansen

The Erotic Muse: American Bawdy Songs
Second Edition
Ed Cray

Barrio Rhythm: Mexican American Music in Los Angeles
Steven Loza

The Creation of Jazz: Music, Race, and Culture in Urban America
Burton W. Peretti

Charles Martin Loeffler: A Life Apart in Music
Ellen Knight

Club Date Musicians: Playing the New York Party Circuit
Bruce A. MacLeod

Opera on the Road: Traveling Opera Troupes in the United States,
1825–60
Katherine K. Preston

The Stonemans: An Appalachian Family and the Music That Shaped
Their Lives
Ivan M. Tribe

Transforming Tradition: Folk Music Revivals Examined
Edited by Neil V. Rosenberg

The Crooked Stovepipe: Athapaskan Fiddle Music and Square Dancing in
Northeast Alaska and Northwest Canada
Craig Mishler

Traveling the High Way Home: Ralph Stanley and the World of
Traditional Bluegrass Music
John Wright

Carl Ruggles: Composer, Painter, and Storyteller
Marilyn J. Ziffrin